A is a Critic

A is a Critic

ANDREW LAMBIRTH

Edited by Sarah Drury

Foreword by T G Rosenthal

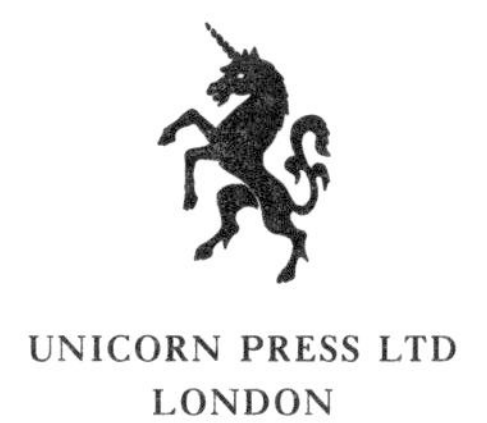

UNICORN PRESS LTD
LONDON

These writings by Andrew Lambirth, selected and edited by Sarah Drury, first appeared in the pages of *The Spectator* whose editor's permission to publish them in this book is gratefully acknowledged by the author, editor and publisher.

First published in 2013 as a collection by

Unicorn Press Ltd
66 Charlotte Street
London W1T 4QE

ISBN 978 1 906509 20 0

978 1 906509 25 5 (e-book Mobi)

978 1 906509 31 6 (e-book Epub)

Cover drawing by Sarah Drury

Designed by Camilla Fellas

Printed and bound in Great Britain by CPI Group (UK) Ltd, CR0 4YY

ACKNOWLEDGEMENTS

My grateful thanks to *The Spectator* for allowing me to reprint these pieces, and especially to the Arts Editor, Elisabeth Anderson for her understanding, appreciation and encouragement. I owe a particular debt of gratitude to Sarah Drury, who fearlessly undertook to arrange these articles in some sort of order and designed a cover image both witty and eye-catching. And finally my heartfelt thanks to all at Unicorn Press who have contributed to the successful publication of this book.

A.L.

Monographs by Andrew Lambirth

The Life and Work of Ivor Abrahams: Eden and Other Suburbs

John Hoyland: Scatter the Devils

David Inshaw: Between Fantasy and Reality

Margaret Mellis

John Armstrong: The Complete Paintings

Trevor Felcey: Nature's Instantaneous Text

Rose Hilton: Something to Keep the Balance

Stephen Chambers

Nigel Hall: Sculpture and Works on Paper

Roger Hilton: The Figured Language of Thought

Maggi Hambling: The Works

Allen Jones: Works

Kitaj

Craigie Aitchison: Out of the Ordinary

L S Lowry: Conversation Pieces

Ken Kiff

Cooking the Books: Ron King and Circle Press

Kitty North: Love and Landscape

Part 1 GETTING TO KNOW YOU: INTERVIEWS AND REFLECTIONS

INTERVIEWS:

REFLECTIONS:

Part 2 HIGHS AND LOWS: EXHIBITION REVIEWS

POSTSCRIPT

Andrew Lambirth is that rare beast, a critic with a regular weekly output as art critic of *The Spectator*, who also writes introductions for exhibition catalogues, articles of considerable value because they usually avoid the restrictions of length imposed upon the weekly *Spectator* slot. On top of all that, he writes books, to date some seventeen volumes, mostly full-length monographs on artists who thoroughly deserve such accolades but, until Lambirth's book comes along, have escaped that necessary degree of recognition.

For the current book, Sarah Drury has had the unenviable task of choosing from Lambirth's vast output which of his shorter pieces should comprise this, his eighteenth full-length volume. With all due respect to the Disraelian view of statistics, this book contains a judicious balance and utterly non-mendacious selection.

Perhaps surprisingly, of the three groupings, the largest section, the 39 straight reviews, possibly on the grounds that even the best newspaper and periodical reviews have a nasty habit of turning into tomorrow's fish and chips wrapping, are the last section. They are preceded by an opening section entitled '*Getting to know you: Interviews and Reflections*' with 15 interviews, and 22 reflections which, perhaps because they are more timeless than the others, are the most interesting.

Overall this is a finely judged compilation made from a massive œuvre which I, as a worker in the same field but a generation older—Lambirth is 54—find positively awesome. Here is a writer who combines the snap, topical review with the more subtle and analytical qualities of the timeless practitioner and I would, as it were, back for posterity some of his monographs. His books on Roger Hilton and Rose Hilton are classics and models of how to *construct* a definitive monograph. They are like some of his best articles but made large. The very first interview in this collection, with George Rowlett, done in 2005, involved a difficult journey to the wilder parts of Wales and, apart from the standard encounter between artist and critic, Lambirth delves in a scholarly, but always lively style into an account of the locus and how that locus and particular background affect both the interview subject and we, the literate public which Lambirth is seeking so elegantly to educate:

> Rowlett had read David Jones's strange masterpiece *In Parenthesis* in 1961 whilst a student at Grimsby Art School and knew a little about the Gill household at Capel-y-Ffin. Seeing the Twmp painted by Jones and the Monastery where the community had once lived, made history come alive. In fact Rowlett stayed at The Grange, now owned by Mary Griffiths, Gill's granddaughter, and run as a trekking stable, and painted there in an outhouse where the stable-hands usually made tea. In some of his Twmp pictures, Rowlett painted from very nearly the same sites as Jones did. He even began to recognize similarities between the surface rhythms of Jones's work and the compositional organisation of his own paintings.

This is typical of Lambirth: an apparent digression, yet full of cultural history and never losing sight of the focal point of the paragraph, namely the artist George Rowlett.

Having myself written a vast tome devoted to Paula Rego's graphic work, I might be excused for feeling faintly proprietorial about someone else's writing about her while also interviewing her. Having now read Lambirth's piece twice, I can relax. He has caught her exactly and I can tell from his quotations that he has appreciated her combativeness, her swiftness of repartee and her serious dedication to the graphic nature of art. And while she is still, aged 77, executing large – even huge – paintings requiring a fork-lift in her studio to raise her to the upper regions of the canvas, as Lambirth reports she still sees the art of fine drawing as her, occasionally elusive, objective.

Lambirth points out that 'Rego makes figures for ... tableaux which are a cross between rag dolls and plaster models. Is she becoming a sculptor? "No," she says, "A prop-maker!"' Talking of her model-making she tells him, 'You find out what it is you want to do through the process of doing it. You have an idea beforehand and then it changes, sometimes quite a lot. Then, when you've come to the end of the paper, you realise, "Ah, that's what it was all along."'

Lambirth can move easily from the particular to the general and he touches, even if tangentially, on the contemporary major issues of the relationship of the Church to Art in 'Church Patronage' when he is sound and, where necessary, acute on the Church's relationship to art in the last 100 years. He relates the absurdity of Lincoln Cathedral's showing of (the wholly admirable) Leonard McComb's statue of a naked gilded youth. Inevitably it was removed after the idiocies of 'public opinion' and one cannot but root for Lambirth in his riposte: 'You would have thought that nothing would be more acceptable in the eyes of God than the unclothed human form, free from all vain encumbrance. Yet our traditions are such that the loincloth must at all times remain in place.'

Lambirth also mounts a spirited defence of Bill Viola in his clash with the Dean and Chapter of Durham Cathedral. This great architectural masterpiece is not, in artistic terms, wholly villainous since it commissioned and permanently exhibits a portrait painting (by Paula Rego) of St Margaret of Scotland. The Cathedral did not fare so well with Viola who supplied a video entitled 'The Messenger' doing no more than showing a naked man 'rising and sinking through great depths of water.'

'What could be more expressive of the trials and tribulations of a particular soul? It is a deeply moving piece and it is also remarkable for its essential purity.'

While I follow Lambirth on 'The Messenger' and on the rest of Viola's œuvre, I find Viola interesting as a video artist, i.e. a maker of short, cheap and beautiful filmstrips. Whether it's art or not is not unimportant. When it comes to many videos of a prize-winning nature I find it impossible to be interested, let alone moved, by the majority of the short-listed Turner Prize videos. What on earth is the point of an apparently endless photograph of a bunch of stationary policemen? It's like watching paint dry and for the sake of the general health of art a separate category should be set up for these things. Perhaps the category should be called Cinema Video so that we know where we are and can, while watching these excruciatingly boring non-events, think of real films, such as *Nanook of the North* or *Battleship Potemkin* or *The Third Man* or *The Searchers*.

As this is an introduction to specific prose writings on art, it would be wrong to quote from works not included here. Thus I must not select an extract from Lambirth's book on Lowry's relationship with the late Andras Kalman. This saddens me, not for the obvious reason that it's such an interesting book, full of insights into both Lowry's paintings and the wholly original mind and character of one of Lowry's most effective dealers, but because Lowry is just one – but perhaps the most significant – example of our shared artistic tastes. Most important now that we know that Lowry is to have, at last, a retrospective at Tate Britain in the course of 2013. For obvious reasons, I wish to record that there are only three practising current art critics in this country who are enthusiastic about Lowry, if only to anticipate the flood of hindsight when the Tate show opens. One, Edwin Mullins wrote luminously in steadfast praise of Lowry but, sadly, no longer writes on art and gives us admirable history books instead. The other two are Lambirth and myself and we met for the first time, bonding immediately, at the launch party for his own Lowry book at a time when I was just beginning work on my own study of the artist. Inevitably, in writing this accolade of Lambirth's work, I have to cross-examine myself and ask whether it's because we share so many enthusiasms apart from Lowry, or am I writing this merely as an act of friendship. Yet the truth of the matter is that both these factors are relevant but they are far from the be-all and end-all of the purpose. Writing *merely* out of friendship M'lud, is a mug's game because it is patently dishonest. Writing because of such closely shared critical tastes is, in isolation, merely boring and does a disservice to both writer and subject. In any case, there are several, indeed many, artists represented in this book whom I regard as over-rated by Lambirth, such as Cy Twombly, or admittedly not in the book but in vigorous conversation his inexplicable enthusiasm for Alex Katz, in my view a classic case of the one-trick pony.

But then how feeble it would be in writing this to state that this is a wonderful book because Lambirth and I agree on everything. I would also like to stress the fact that Lambirth is also a poet, a matter to which our attention is not specifically drawn in this volume. Yet any attentive and alert reader will, or at least, should notice that his writing, unlike that of so many current practitioners of the art critic's trade, has a distinct lyrical bent. Just look at the opening of his article on curating an exhibition devoted to Euan Uglow and landscape:

> Euan Uglow is dead. It has to be said that a light in English painting has gone out. Not everyone, thank God, liked his painting – that would probably indicate ineptitude or worse - but there are few who didn't admire his rigour and dedication. Let alone the sheer beauty of his work. I find it hard to write about him: I was not a great friend of his, but I loved him. I used to go to his studio once in a while, and shared with him the finest wines I have ever drunk. At the time he reminded me that we probably weren't worthy of drinking them. I wasn't but he was.

The rest of the piece operates at a more prosaic and instructive level but, in its unfolding of a list of distinctly out-of-the-way landscapes by Uglow and other hands, Lambirth shows that he is also a curator of exquisite taste, one who has an eye for a good picture, who sees no need – or, indeed, capacity – to write incomprehensible and pretentious labels in 'artspeak'.

In all ways Lambirth, especially as a topical reviewer of exhibitions, is perhaps the most user-friendly of current art critics. If it's a small one-man show he tells you all you need to know as a background for that man or woman. If it's a large mixed show or a major exhibition of either an old master or a contemporary flavour-of-the-month artist, he adopts the tools and value systems of the curator. He produces for the interested reader a guide to the various and several rooms which the reader does not yet know he needs but which will be invaluable when and if he visits the exhibition.

For those whose time is limited or precious or both, he presents in effect a mini-guide, a concise Baedeker with frank and direct advice: skip the first room, it's boring; whatever you do, concentrate on rooms three and four where the best work is displayed; don't spend too much time on the last which, sadly, shows a marked falling-off of both interest and talent. In other words, Lambirth is nearly always reliable and never other than interesting.

Perhaps what binds Lambirth to me most firmly in critical terms is a deep suspicion of nearly all conceptual art. Neither of us can stand the adulation and coronation of Martin Creed's on/off light switch, nor the unreadable artspeak of the wall captions attached to such works. It's all a rather horrendous contemporary version of the Emperor's New Clothes, garments which Lambirth neither wears nor needs. In my book he is, as an art critic and historian, quite simply an Emperor *tout court*.

T G Rosenthal
October, 2012

FRANCIS BACON INTERVIEWED BY DAVID SYLVESTER
10 October 1998

Over the years I have learnt more from interviewing artists about the practice of their art than from any book of theory or criticism. Besides visiting artists' studios socially or to view new work, I also conduct interviews for the National Sound Archive. This involves talking to an artist about their life and work from the very beginning. What colour were the walls at home where you grew up? What toys did you have? That sort of thing, modulating into questions about first attempts at art and other seminal experiences. The Artists' Lives section of the National Life Story Collection is located in the British Library, and is available, with certain restrictions, to any member of the public with a Reader Pass from the BL. This is oral history at its best, replete with riveting digressions and scabrous anecdotes.

Listening to tapes of an artist talking – the more informally the better – is a little like eavesdropping. As you respond to phrasing and inflection, you feel more closely tuned to the character of the speaker than in most written dialogue. Written interviews often seem deliberately constructed, edited or angled in a particular way. At the opposite pole is the unexpurgated transcript: the worthy but rambling record of every 'um' and 'er', the kind of document that earnest historians claim to be more authentic than any edited interview. In fact, there's nothing more tedious than most pure transcription: it's guaranteed to stifle the most ardent enthusiasm after very few minutes. That's why the Bacon/Sylvester interviews constitute such a glittering artefact.

One of their peculiar uses is as a benchmark for readers, who can test Bacon's remarks against their own experience, or try to imagine themselves in his place, or use him as a role model. Good interviews are more rewarding and more revealing in these ways than any biography – they have the immediacy of (largely) unmediated response. Suzi Gablik in her remarkable book

Conversations Before the End of Time (Thames & Hudson, 1995) demonstrates that dialogue is one of the most potent forms of cultural exchange currently available to us. In society in general, the art of conversation has decayed somewhat; it needs now to be practised, renewed and reinvented. It's a great civilising force, and we need as many of those as we can get.

Recently rereading David Sylvester's endlessly fascinating book *Interviews with Francis Bacon* (Thames & Hudson, first published in 1975, reprinted 1995), I was struck anew by how easy it is to assume that its effortless flow is due to the brilliance of Francis Bacon's talk. However marvellous a conversationalist Bacon was, people do not talk ordinarily in perfectly structured sentences filled with polished clauses. The success of the Bacon interviews lies first of all in Sylvester's skill in asking questions, and then in his subtlety as an editor. However much he may have adapted the text, he manages to preserve the artist's voice, by identifying his speech rhythms and distinctive verbal habits. Thus the text, carefully edited into coherence, still has enough rough edges to sound convincingly like someone talking.

Compare another book of Bacon interviews – *Francis Bacon in conversation with Michel Archimbaud* (Phaidon, 1993). This was published posthumously (would Bacon have happily authorised it, I wonder?) and was originally written in French, the language in which the interviews were conducted. Bacon liked to speak French, but self-deprecatingly referred to his 'patchy and inadequate grasp' of the language. He even went so far as to state, in one of these Archimbaud interviews that 'because I think you can only talk about your work in your own language, or at least in a language you have totally mastered, I've always felt that the conversations I have in French would be limited'. Remarkable, then, that Archimbaud should have persevered with a project so obviously doomed. The end result is a distressingly trivial book in comparison with Sylvester's, rather journalistic in tone, and crass through ignorance.

Archimbaud covers a lot of the same territory as Sylvester though less sensitively. His text is both less penetrating and less revealing, but then Archimbaud quite evidently did not enjoy the same unique relationship with Bacon as Sylvester did. On page after page of Sylvester's book, trust, respect and genuine affection shine through; and they're mutual. With Archimbaud, Bacon could be mischievous. At one point this famously articulate artist comments airily (in translation, of course): 'Most of the time when one talks about painting, one says nothing interesting. It's always rather superficial. What can one say? Basically, I believe that you simply cannot talk about painting, it just isn't possible.' Well, you can see his point – he'd said it all already to Sylvester.

If David Sylvester's book has the true ring of authority, its 'narrative' is still susceptible to new discoveries. Bacon, like most artists and indeed most people, recounted the version of his life which most suited him. Since his death in 1992 it has come to light that Bacon, contrary to popular belief, made drawings at different times (and very regularly, if we accept all that have been brought forward as genuine) throughout his career. Yet the Bacon legend admits of no drawings. There is a marvellous story recounted against himself by the rather academic draughtsman, painter and writer, and sometime Spectator art critic, Michael Ayrton. Ayrton had once asserted that Bacon could not draw, and, encountering Bacon in a bar, he rashly maintained his view. 'Is drawing what you do?' Bacon silkily enquired, pausing before the kill: 'I wouldn't want to do that.'

A wickedly witty response on Bacon's behalf, and fuel for the myth. In the Sylvester interviews, towards the end of the book, Sylvester says: 'I suppose it's because you improvise so much that you're exceptional in doing figurative paintings as big as yours without any kind of preliminary drawing or oil sketch.' Bacon replies: 'Well, I sketch out very roughly on the canvas with a brush, just a vague outline of something, and then I go to work...' No mention, you see, of any other kind of drawing, which we now know Bacon frequently made. Does this evasiveness in any way invalidate or cast doubt upon the veracity of the interviews? What is the truth? In the end, it's always partial; it's always a matter of interpretation. The sheer weight of comment and elucidation – of, dare I say it, wisdom – in the Bacon/Sylvester dialogues, will continue to compensate for any lapses. As Bacon said, 'all art has now become completely a game by which man distracts himself.' No doubt by modifying his own truth, Bacon was only deepening the game.

GEORGE ROWLETT At full throttle

3 September 2005

On a warm but dampish day a month ago, I set off for the wilds of south Wales to explore the Llanthony valley in the black mountains. The train takes the visitor as far as Abergavenny, after which you're somewhat reliant on a car, unless you favour pony-trekking or have the leisure for hill walking. The darker green on the hillsides in July was bracken, the distinctive red earth slipping here and there into red mud after the cloudbursts of the day before. The narrow, twisty lanes climbed hills and traversed vales embowered with dank herbage, but the views when the hedges opened up were glorious. This article is as much about a place, a tract of country, as it is about art. It is also by way of being a preview of an exhibition *George Rowlett in Wales: Capel-y-ffin paintings 2005* (The Art Shop, Abergavenny, 1-29 October) rather than the usual review, for although I saw the paintings which make up the show, I also went to Wales specifically to see the dramatic landscape which is their subject. I was not disappointed.

The Llanthony Valley is already famous in art circles for being the one-time home of the sculptor Eric Gill (1882-1940). Gill lived and worked at Capel-y-ffin in the mid-1920s, having moved there from Ditchling in Sussex purportedly to escape the publicity surrounding the unorthodox craft-and-religion community he'd set up. David Jones (1895-1974), who had been an apprentice of Gill and an on-off member of the community, found his own artistic voice at Capel in depictions of the countryside, picking up especially on the strong rhythms of the hills and the bright counter-rhythms of the little brooks. As Gill's biographer, Fiona MacCarthy, writes of Jones: 'His days at Capel gave him that perception of his Welshness which emerges after that time in his painting and poetry.'

George Rowlett (born 1941) is one of our leading landscape painters, whose chosen territory is London River and the coastal plains of east Kent. He paints the river at Rotherhithe or the Thames Barrier, registering the play of weather on water, the river traffic and bankside activity, the changing face of London. In Kent he paints the corn and rape fields, the cows at pasture, a sunlit beach, breakers in winter. Rowlett is a thick painter, of the fraternity of Auerbach and Kossoff, employing great tongues and spreads of pigment, laying it on with energy and brio. He also applies paint with impressive delicacy and due attention to detail. He is an artist at the height of his powers, whose subtle understanding of landscape seems only to deepen with each new group of paintings. Brought up in Scotland, what would he make of the Welsh landscape?

I had visited him several years ago when he was on a similar painting jaunt in Northern Ireland, and the results had been impressive. Would the Black Mountains exert a similar charm? Rowlett is represented by Michael Richardson of Art Space Gallery in London, and it was through his good offices that this exhibition was arranged. The idea for the artist to stay for a short period in the Llanthony Valley, on a sort of working residency, was put forward by Pauline Griffiths of The Art Shop, and a reconnaissance trip was booked.

Rowlett responds well to a commission or a new project, and although initially unsure whether he could get to grips with the landscape on short acquaintance ('I was very wary, not believing in holiday painting, any landscape demands more'), he was soon convinced that he had no choice but to try to paint its beauty. The moment of truth occurred in the Gospel Pass, so named because in rough weather you needed to call on all the strength and belief of the Gospels to survive your passage through it. (Even tough all-weather Rowlett was later blown off his bicycle there in a gale and had to be rescued by horse-box.) There came a moment when the snow and sleet of February were transformed by the chance appearance of the sun 'gilding the distant tops of the Malverns and Brecon Beacons like golden lace [that] was the clincher and I had to try to paint here, hopefully informed by history, my childhood and my engagement with this landscape'.

The reference in this letter to his childhood is obviously of deep relevance to the artist. 'The sights, sounds and particularly smells, damp and mossy, took me back to my childhood at Kilmun in Argyll and life with my grandparents in what had been the dowager house for the Campbells of Argyll, probably the most formative of my years.' This reconnection with his first experiences of landscape, and with early memories of observing nature on the hill at the back of his grandparents' house, directly informed his Welsh paintings and brought to them a depth of empathy quite remarkable for an incomer. Vanessa Horne, a local hill-dweller and my spirited guide through Rowlett Country, had been astonished by his immediate grasp not only of the basic structure of the landscape, but also of its distinctive colouring and moods. It was as if he managed to distil a whole year's observation of the area and its changing seasons into a few short days.

It's a major expedition each time Rowlett goes out into the landscape – apart from taking the boards on which he will paint, there are the tins of paint. He always takes five litres of Titanium White, and two-and-a-half of Bright Red, Lemon Yellow and Ultramarine Blue. The paint is applied with a whole range of spatulas and palette knives, and directly with the fingers. His first visit was for a fortnight in March. He painted the ruined arches of Llanthony Abbey in the rain, the Gospel Pass in mist after drizzle, the distinctive hill (or Twmp) above Capel-y-ffin in bright sunlight. Rowlett returned for a further foray in June, when he painted several views of Patricio Church (where there's a tremendous mediaeval Doom mural) surrounded by summer verdure.

Rowlett had read David Jones's strange masterpiece *In Parenthesis* in 1961 whilst a student at Grimsby art school, and knew a little about the Gill household at Capel-y-ffin. Seeing the Twmp painted by Jones and the monastery where the community had once lived, made history come alive. In fact, Rowlett stayed in the Grange, now owned by Mary Griffiths, Gill's granddaughter, and run as a trekking stable, and painted there in an outhouse where the stable-hands usually made tea. In some of his Twmp pictures, Rowlett painted from very nearly the same sites as Jones did. He even began to recognise similarities between the surface rhythms of Jones's work and the compositional organisation of his own paintings.

The paintings are splendid – Rowlett at full throttle. Somehow he has reached to the heart of this country with his luscious slabs and tender flicks of paint. His palette transforms the red earth with its cloak of greens, the moving skies and enduring hills, into images of extraordinary beauty. With a memorable lunch at The Angel in Abergavenny, and a visit to the magnificent Jesse Tree in St Mary's Church thrown in, it was a thoroughly enjoyable expedition, and much to be recommended.

JAMES TURRELL Lighten Our Darkness
20 May 2006

Lately I have adopted *Word from Wormingford* by Ronald Blythe as a bedside book. Composed of weekly bulletins from a Suffolk village, it combines observations on the countryside with reports on the spiritual welfare of Blythe's parish. In its gentleness and generosity, it is the perfect antidote to the strain of London life, and cools the mind after anxiety-ridden days. (In this, it has the same welcome effect as the glorious novels of Alexander McCall Smith.) Cools the mind but doesn't dim it, for Blythe mixes in comments from his wide reading with a deft hand, and leavens the brew with the wisdom garnered from a long life devoted to looking and pondering. Here he is, writing about light: 'there has never been so much light in the world as we have now, such instant dismissals of darkness. As for half-light, gloaming, we are not allowed to know what it is. This was when we used to do our thinking.' Someone who has thought long and intently about the psychological significance of light is the leading contemporary artist James Turrell (born 1943), who makes sculptures and installations which engage directly with our perceptions of light.

Turrell is an American and a Quaker who has been making light-works since 1962, and who has the distinction of having worked on the light effects of such films as *2001: A Space Odyssey* and *Star Wars*. He is also a keen aviator, and much of his work is informed by his experiences of flying. (He gained his pilot's licence at the age of 16 and has flown for the CIA taking high-level photographs above China and Russia. The wonder of his descent through the northern lights continues to delight and inspire him.) Turrell studied perceptual psychology as well as mathematics and art history before graduating in fine arts from the University of California; he subsequently became part of the California Light and Space movement of the 1960s and 70s. His work with light employs both artificial and natural sources: his rooms of ambient coloured light have been likened to American colour-field painters such as Rothko. His natural light pieces make us look anew at the sky.

The Yorkshire Sculpture Park is currently hosting a temporary Turrell exhibition (until 3 September) of three remarkable but unsettling light installations in their elegant new galleries (shortlisted for this year's Gulbenkian prize for museums and galleries), and has just unveiled a permanent 'Skyspace' designed by Turrell elsewhere in the grounds. Commissioned by the Art Fund (the NACF as was) to celebrate its centenary in 2003, the James Turrell Deer Shelter is a magnificent gift to the nation, the most significant Art Fund project since Rodin's 'Burghers of Calais' was handed over in 1911. It is a hypaethral building, a shelter open to the sky (think of the Pantheon), from which to survey the passing parade of cloud. Its purpose is to change our perception of the sky, to help us re-shape our visual experience. I last interviewed Turrell in 1993 when he was staying in a lodge at the Yorkshire Sculpture Park, at the time of his exhibition at the Henry Moore Sculpture Trust in Halifax. He had then been commissioned to produce a piece called 'The Gasworks', a domed perceptual cell into which you were slid lying on a couch, shut in like the drawer of a filing cabinet. I thought it would be terrifyingly claustrophobic, but the infinity of light which opened up above your head was mesmerizing: the small space was forgotten, transformed by lambent colour. Talking afterwards to Turrell in the grounds of YSP we ranged over projects past, present and future, and he told me of his plans for a disused deer shelter nearby, a 19th century brick building with sandstone pillars built onto the face of an old quarry. Thirteen years later, those plans have finally come to fruition.

It has taken YSP that long to find the money to make Turrell's vision a reality. The original plans for transforming the deer shelter have been modified slightly, but the overall design remains unchanged. Originally, Turrell had wanted to access the square inner chamber, which had to be dug out of the hill behind, from a single central entrance. This however would have meant doing too much violence to the Grade ll listed structure, so two side entrances were substituted. And Turrell's first thought had been to make a circular aperture to the sky; this was later changed to a square one. The construction has been carried out immaculately: the chamber is lined with concrete seating (warmed from within during the winter months), against which the viewer can recline and contemplate the frame of sky cut into the ceiling. The walls are painted white, Turrell's usual white which has just a trace of yellow in it. A constant artificial light glows softly from behind the top of the concrete seating slabs, but appears to change as the daylight alters. The resulting Skyspace is a viewing station of considerable presence, an underground vault from which we may watch the celestial activity with new attentiveness.

As Turrell says: ' basically I'm very interested in direct experience

– as with the pieces in the other part of the exhibition, that you actually *feel* the light, *feel* its physical presence – and here I'm interested in this work about the sky and different skies, and also the relationship of inside to outside.' This is perfectly suited to YSP which displays sculpture in a combination of open terrain and dedicated galleries. Turrell, who lives in the dry atmosphere of Arizona where he's busy transforming Roden crater, an extinct volcano, into a vast earthwork and observatory, relishes Yorkshire's 'maritime skies'. The Skyspace is less invasive or threatening than the gallery pieces, which may cloak you in exquisite lavender light but make you doubt the space you're standing in. Seeing, constantly taken for granted, is too often considered a passive activity; not by children or poets or naturalists, but by most people. Turrell makes it active.

Ronald Blythe, definitely a man who knows how to use his eyes, writes tellingly of the little-acknowledged beauty of the skies, and their power to get the spirit moving: 'Chinese businessmen used to invite a few friends back to clouds and a drink after a hard day in the counting-house. Freshly robed, they would sit on the terrace in silence and allow cloud patterns to fill their heads for an hour or so. No one was permitted to comment, as we did as children, "There's a giant! There's an elephant!" One must eventually make a grown-up response to clouds.' James Turrell's Skyspace helps us to do just that.

MAGGI HAMBLING 'Time is eating away at one's life'
10 February 2007

I'm talking to Maggi Hambling in the downstairs studio of her South London home, because her beautifully light upstairs painting space is being given a new coat of white paint, the first for years. She always says that if she ever comes to sell this house the agents can market it as having 'four reception rooms, two bathrooms and a ballroom. No bedrooms.' It's a misleading description of the Hambling lifestyle: work is the order of the day, not partying, and the ballroom is of course the main studio. Hambling is not out on the tiles every night, but is more likely to retire to bed early in order to rise before dawn. She got into the habit when she was obsessively painting the sunrise in the 1980s; these days, her subject is primarily the North Sea, where it meets that bit of the Suffolk coastline Hambling has known all her life, around Aldeburgh and Thorpeness.

She owns a cottage near Saxmundham set in a large expanse of water meadow. Whenever she's there, she gets up early to draw the sea, before anyone else is about. 'When I began the sea pictures in November 2003, I would just look at what was there in front of me. Empty myself and try to take the subject in, and then go back and work from memory. But for the last couple of years I've taken a sketchbook with me, to get myself tuned in, like a pianist doing the scales.'

We are talking about drawing because this is the theme of a small but well-chosen touring exhibition of her work, called *No Straight Lines*, which has just opened at the Fitzwilliam Museum. (It's there until 29 April, then moves on to the Victoria Art Gallery Bath, 9 May - 10 June, before travelling to Abbot Hall in Kendal, 6 November – 21 December. A show of her new wave drawings will be at Marlborough Fine Art, London, 15 March - 5 April.) The selection brings together work from five decades. The subjects, until we get to the waves, are all animals and people, and it rapidly becomes clear that Hambling identifies a marked kinship between them.

She loves animals and birds, depicting them with passionate empathy, and has several times painted herself as an animal. She is accompanied everywhere by Lux, her devoted year-old Tibetan terrier. 'I became a temple overnight when Lux came into my life, because Tibetan terriers were bred to guard the temples and the monks.' She pauses and looks at me intently; a faintly alarming experience even though I've known her for 20 years. 'A perceptive friend of mine has noticed a similarity between Lux and my sea drawings,' she eventually intones. 'I suppose it's something to do with her black-and-whiteness and energy. I do see the sea as an animal - very particularly as a great mouth, eating the coast. In a very corny way I associate myself with the land and the sea with time, so the older I get – though I don't feel it – time is eating away at one's life. Meanwhile the sea is eating away at the land. You can actually watch erosion happening. The sea's like a hungry monster. Frightening, sexy, beautiful, very mysterious.' She pauses, for thought and for effect. Hambling is a seasoned performer: good value on stage and off.

She continues: 'The drawings are specifically of that very moment of a wave breaking, crashing on the shore and bouncing up again in a million bits. I think it's quite interesting the way the shape of the moon is echoed in the particular curve of the underside of a wave. But I wouldn't say that I followed the drawing of a particular morning when I paint on that particular day. It's more to do with getting into the feel, the rhythm, getting the subject inside me. Drawing is very much a *taking in* of the subject.'

Does she always make preliminary studies before painting? There is no rule. She does tend to make a charcoal study before beginning a portrait in oils, in order to investigate the landscape of the face. She calls this research. 'That makes it sound deadly dull and boring, but it's the opposite: drawing is actually very exciting, the most intimate thing. That first beginning to look, trying to get at the essence of the person. When I make a drawing the charcoal is with any luck re-living the life of the subject on the paper. Take the argument between drawing and photography. A photograph has happened, it's history, it's gone. If a drawing has any life to it, it hasn't happened, *it is happening in front of you as you look at it.*' We look at the modest but handsome exhibition catalogue, and examine a couple of drawings of Oscar Wilde made with her eyes shut, at the time when she was working on her memorial sculpture of him. 'Oscar as a subject was so inside me they just drew themselves. I shut my eyes with a sketchbook in my lap and a piece of graphite in my hand and it just happened. The drawing of my mother from memory was done at Christmas which was her favourite time of the year - quite traumatic for the rest of us but my mother wanted to feel surrounded by family and laughter and charades. She really lived for Wimbledon and Christmas. That drawing suddenly came – I can't predict when something is going to happen. If I dream something, or if something suddenly obsesses me, then probably the first thing I would do would be to put it down in the sketchbook.'

Hambling uses both hands when drawing. 'Recently I had to work with my left hand because I pulled a tendon in my right arm using the painting knife for most of the summer. It was quite a good thing as the right hand had become full of tricks over the years. I don't feel in charge of my left: it does unexpected things, which is exciting. And quite often I'm using both hands – having the black (the dark) in the right hand and the white (the light) in the left.' This quite literal hands-on approach she sees as crucial. 'As we're completely surrounded by everything technical – the web and computers – that human, frail, physical act of making a mark on a piece of paper becomes even more important.' It's hard to disagree.

Two years ago, to get in training for her approaching 60th birthday, Hambling gave up smoking. (Despite vicious rumours, she hasn't stopped using mascara.) She says she's coping 'with difficulty' without cigarettes, though only in moments of extreme stress does she seriously miss them. She sticks firmly to her resolve, except when we go upstairs to her studio and she naughtily steals a drag from the builder who is busy repainting the walls and ceiling. Has she discovered any alternatives? 'I'm more interested in food than I used to be, which has made its mark where one least requires it', she admits ruefully. Aside from that very slight addition to the

Hambling avoirdupois, she looks her usual energetic self: hawk-eyed and direct, curling locks a distinguished grey, never happier than when trying to do a dozen things at once. A busy life becomes her.

SIR PETER BLAKE Knight vision

19 May 2007

Sir Peter Blake is much in demand. A popular figure since he rose to fame with his unforgettable design for The Beatles' Sgt. Pepper album (1967), he has long been a spokesman for his generation and for the arts. His knighthood in 2002 brought a whole host of new requests and obligations, much of it figurehead stuff: his name on lists of patrons, or as the chairman of selection committees. To take these things seriously is time-consuming, and Blake has to be rigorous about preserving his hours in the studio, where typically he is busy on a number of projects at once. On the eve of a retrospective of his paintings at Tate Liverpool (29 June - 23 September) I visited him in his West London studio, which is a treasure house of objects and art. Blake is an inveterate collector, and the studio is partly a museum or cabinet of curiosities, as well as being the place where he paints, draws, makes collages and assembles his box constructions and sculptures.

I asked him if he has a strong sense of public responsibility. 'I've always felt that I wanted to give things back to art because it gave to me.' Blake is known for his readiness to espouse a good cause or give freely of his time. In private life, he is equally generous, a loyal friend and supporter. The public figure and the private dovetail in terms of promoting a particular ethos: not quite Pop Art, though it encompasses some of Pop's characteristics and coincidentally includes a number of celebrated Pop musicians including Paul McCartney and Eric Clapton, and not quite a simple cult of celebrity, though Blake has always enjoyed the company of the show-biz famous. His world is unique: part archaising, with an obsessive interest in past art and artefacts, and part utterly contemporary. 'I'm friendly as you know with most of the so-called YBAs, simply because when I was a young artist, people were nice to me. They don't need encouragement or me to like them.' But he does, and he not only drinks with Tracey and Damien, but he puts them into the cast of characters which populate his paintings, along with Duchamp, Picasso and Cheetah the chimp. The forthcoming retrospective was initially planned as a show of what Blake calls 'large-ish key paintings', but it soon outstripped those modest beginnings, and became more wide-ranging, providing a detailed survey of Blake's career as a painter. When he was the third associate artist of the National Gallery (1994-6), and given a show there at the end of his residency, Blake chose to regard this as an impossible act to follow, and announced his retirement in 1996 at the age of 64. (Spot The Beatles' reference.) Since then, his exhibitions have been what he terms a succession of 'encores', though the Liverpool show is a pretty substantial one. And there's a new twist. 'The new concept is that I'm into my Late Period as well', says Blake. 'I'm having a stencil made saying 'Late Period' and I'm taking advantage of the fact that I'm aware I'm in my Late Period.' As he points out, artists usually have to be dead before a late period is recognized. 'I'm hoping not to be too infirm but to take advantage of the fact that I'm 75 in June. Use it to finish things, perhaps, but also to do things that might not be characteristic. The first group of Late Period pictures are called 'Costume Life' and they'll be six of those, of nude young women but wearing costume clothes. They're also a direct homage to Klimt – I like to copy directly some of his backgrounds, as though I'm painting my girls in his studio.' What are the characteristics of this new period? 'I hope stylistically looser and faster and maybe thicker, but whenever I try that it ends up pretty much the same. It always seems to tighten up, but it may well be different. I may be prepared to put something in that isn't in the category of Unfinished or Work in Progress, but is lighter and slighter than some of the earlier work, but finished.' Do the same themes still engage him? 'Most of the themes do ebb away and come back. I might paint a group of wrestlers and then not paint any for five years, but it doesn't mean I won't forever. Elvis is on hold at the moment. I'm still collecting Elvis material and some of the Elvis pictures are half-way through. At this very moment he isn't a major subject.'

Does he still collect? 'I'm not collecting in a covetous way anymore. Collecting used to be about getting to the Caledonian Market at 5 o'clock to get something before a fellow-collector might get it. It's not like that anymore. Part of my statement about retirement was that I'd given up competitiveness. The main collecting now is to do with work. I'm doing a lot of work at the moment around the subject of the alphabet so I'm collecting existing alphabets and making new ones. Also I'm doing a series called 'Museums of Black and White'. There was a wonderful antique shop just round the corner which has now closed. I would go once a week. I bought quite a lot of Outsider art from them. I'm still doing that series 'Memories of Place', so certainly if I go somewhere like Hastings I'd be collecting for that. I'm also doing a series of prints with Brad Fane of Coriander Studios called 'Found Art' where I take a found object and scan it on the computer and print it out with inkjet.'

Recently Blake has been called a Conceptual artist. How does he feel about that? 'I wouldn't want to be categorized as just one thing - I don't mind categories, but I like lots of categories. My work is usually about diversity.' In his time, he's been identified as a proto-Pop artist, a Pop artist and a Ruralist, and he certainly doesn't disown any of those labels entirely, any more than he would his early work. And looking at him, you can see why he might like the idea of the Brotherhood of Ruralists, a mutually supportive exhibiting society with echoes of the Pre-Raphaelite Brotherhood

–Blake looks a little like a latter day Dante Gabriel Rossetti, with his beard and dark suit.

Is he doing any portraits these days? Certainly there will be none in the Liverpool exhibition, but that's because he's hoping to show them all together elsewhere. 'At the moment I'm painting Chris Frayling for the [Royal] College, and an ongoing pair of pictures of Paul and Pauline Smith. I'm being drawn back to the idea of sitting in front of somebody and painting them. The last time I did that was with Helen Mirren, 20 years ago, and I haven't done it since. I'd love to paint Kate Moss, for her to come and sit quietly for her portrait.'

The last room at Tate Liverpool will show the five pictures in Blake's recent 'Marcel Duchamp's World Tour' series, a cross between a road movie and the art world's House of Horrors. Then, just when you thought it was all over, there'll be a further encore within the show, a postscript, an idea derived from Monty Python which always had something else happening after The End: the really last room. 'That's about the future, so I'm going to put some big pieces in which are really very unfinished. Clearly works in progress.' Quite an achievement for someone who's retired.

JOHN HOYLAND Collaborating with chaos

31 May 2008

John Hoyland dislikes being called 'one of Britain's leading abstract painters'. He thinks it's lazy thinking, and over-reliance on labelling. 'They don't say: "Lucian Freud, leading figurative painter" - he's just a painter. Or "Francis Bacon, leading melodramatist". Mention of Bacon sends him off on a tangent, one of the digressions that make Hoyland's conversation – along with his forthright opinions – so rewarding and enjoyable. 'I look at Bacon's paintings and instead of being moved by them they make me want to laugh. They're supposed to be horrible and moving and frightening, but they're so shrill and so theatrical. I like drama in music or painting, but not melodrama.' And having dismissed one of the most expensive and sought-after of modern British artists, he leans back and grins. Hoyland is not too keen on auction rooms and the prices they generate. His own Sixties work is currently a focus of buyers' attention, generating auction records, and he finds it rather annoying. A true artist, he is really only interested in his latest work or what he is about to do, not the achievements of 40 years ago.

'I think the vultures are circling a bit', he says with a chuckle. 'I suppose artists' early work always fetches more money. It can be irritating when people forget whole swathes of work, like the paintings I did in the Seventies and Eighties.' Of course, what is needed is a full-scale Hoyland retrospective, and the Tate Gallery is the place for such a show, though under the current regime, such an exhibition is unlikely. Has England so many artists of international stature that they can afford to ignore such a figure as Hoyland? Of course not, yet it seems that our museums are more interested in showing foreign artists than the home-grown variety. Meanwhile, Hoyland continues to paint in his London studio just north of Smithfield Market, and to have shows of vibrant new work. One exhibition has just finished at Beaux Arts in Cork Street, while another continues at Lemon Street Gallery in Truro until 7 June.

Although Hoyland's latest work with its effervescent colour combinations and its wild paint-trails seems to some like an arsonist's night out in a firework factory, it's not all madcap celebration. A very recent painting, a dark beauty we look at in the studio, is called 'goodbye'; not exactly exuberant. In fact, he can't stand art that is perpetually euphoric. He himself is more often than not in elegiac mood these days. 'I've been doing these paintings called "letters" to people I admire. There's one to Chaim Soutine and a couple to Van Gogh. I've been re-reading his letters. I've done a number of paintings in the last couple of years that just came over me from the death of friends, Patrick Caulfield, Bryan Robertson, Terry Frost, Piero Dorazio'. Robertson was the inspired critic and director of the Whitechapel Art Gallery who gave Hoyland his first museum show in 1967, Dorazio was a famous Italian painter, all were close friends that Hoyland misses. The grim reaper has been busy.

'I think painting should express all kinds of different things, not be limited. I can't think of anything worse than just taking painting towards refinement, if you don't allow yourself to change. I don't force change on myself, it just happens. I'd probably get bored if I did the same thing all the time. Not so long ago I said I'd like to be able to paint anything in a painting. I think I'm getting there slowly. Robert Motherwell gave me a book on Miro. He's supposed to be the great surrealist with a fantastic imagination but he went on the beach every day picking stuff up – a bit of string, a shell, a bit of wood. If Miro needed outside stimulation then who am I to think that I can keep on developing through a kind of formalist grid? That opened me up to plundering nature.' His work now is as likely to take its impulse from something seen on his travels as it is to be formed from one colour working with or against another. After half-a-century of endeavour, he has won through to a hard-earned freedom of expression.

John Hoyland was born in Sheffield in 1934 and went to art school there before gaining a place at the Royal Academy Schools and coming to London. He first made his name in the 1960s for bold abstract works which entirely rejected the observable world and dealt exclusively in shape and colour. (A selection of these paintings along with some gouaches, all from Hoyland's own collection, is being shown at Nevill Keating Pictures, 5 Pickering Place, St James's Street, W1, 020 7839 8386, 11 June - 4 July.) From 1967 he spent increasing amounts of time in America, associating with such artists as Rothko, Newman and Motherwell, but in the Seventies he returned to settle in England. 'I've managed to make a living out of painting – a precarious one. When I came back from New York in 1972, the big announcement had been made – it hadn't hit America – that the death of painting had already occurred. I'd had a posh job here, principal lecturer at Chelsea [1964-70]. When I gave that up, William Scott said to me "you're mad, that's the best job in London: three days a week and 7 months' holiday a year with pay". But I'd heard this David Sylvester interview with de Kooning. De Kooning said that he thought it was important psychologically to put 'Artist' in your passport not 'Artist/Teacher'. So I decided I was going to do that and get out of teaching. Looking back on it, it was a smart thing to do.'

Why did he come back? 'It was partly private. My girlfriend at the time was a singer. I learnt a lot from her and really enjoyed being around that music scene and meeting all those guys – Thelonius Monk, people like that. But the trouble was that she wanted me to travel with her. The thing is, if you're an artist, you've got to stay in a room on your own and work. You can't be always hanging around late at night for the second show. I'm an early riser. And I missed the richness of Europe and my friends. So it was a combination of things. Also I wasn't a great success in America. Art has to come from inside you. What I really didn't like was that in America, it was all coming at you. Like: "are you in this show? D'you know what he's just sold for? You'd better get on the ball, kid, you'd better get in there." Pressure all the time. I came back and decided I wouldn't paint a lot of pictures, I'd just keep on one until I'd completely resolved it. So I switched working methods.'

Instead of the staining of colour he was known for, he began to use a palette-knife and polyfilla along with the paint. It was a very different approach and typical of his ability to change tack, whatever the cost to his reputation. Since then, he has altered course whenever he had to. He lives and works in London, travels regularly to Spain and the Caribbean, making little diagrams of possible forms for his paintings in sketchbooks. In the studio he tends to put down a dark ground on a canvas with a paintbrush and then add glazes of iridescent paint. On top of that he works mostly with spilled or poured paint, with the canvas on the floor. 'And of course I throw paint which gives it a kind of energy. I can throw four colours in one clump. It's like the blind Zen archer – you gradually get more accurate.

'Pollock used to draw with paint through holes in cans to get the extended line you can't get with a brush. I'm doing something very similar.' Hoyland squeezes liquid acrylic paint from bottles, exploiting the unpredictability of its behaviour, though long years of experimenting have taught him how his materials will react. 'I'll often do a test on the floor, to see how the paint is going to come out.' [Hoyland's studio floor is famous and much photographed. People have even wanted to buy it.] 'But when it comes to the actual act on the painting you just have to grab your balls and charge.' 'I've spent a lot of the last 10 years looking for visual structures that I find satisfying, though at the moment there is less and less structure in my work. Suddenly I find that my paintings seem not to require it. I'm painting oxygen or something. Air. I've always thought that paintings needed to be structured, otherwise all you've got is chaos.' But now he is collaborating with chaos and still somehow managing to ride the wave. 'I like to try and make these pictures paint themselves', he says. 'The less you impose, the fresher it is. Painting is a kind of alchemy. When you're young, you want to show everybody what a tough guy you are, how strong you can paint and how you can knock everybody around. As you get older you want to show how intelligent you are, how you know the game and how subtle and penetrating you can be. Then when you get old, you're just compelled to paint what you don't know. That's what's happened to me.'

(This conversation was recorded in 2008. John Hoyland died in 2011.)

PAULA REGO Power of the pencil

28 March 2009

Paula Rego is an artist working at the height of her powers, internationally celebrated and with a museum dedicated to her about to open in her native Portugal. It's been a long climb to this pinnacle of success, and Rego has worked exceptionally hard to reach it. Born in Lisbon in 1935, she grew up largely in the care of her grandparents while her father, an electrical engineer, took a job in England with Marconi. His anglophilia was responsible for Rego herself going to London to study art. She attended the Slade in a golden period (1952-6), with such contemporaries as Craigie Aitchison, Michael Andrews and Euan Uglow, and it was there that she met Victor Willing, whom she married. To begin with they lived in Portugal (1957-63), then spent increasing amounts of time in England until Willing's death from multiple sclerosis in 1988. Since then she has continued to live and work in London and her reputation has gone from strength to strength.

Although trained as a painter, these days Rego draws rather than paints. Her current popularity rests principally on a remarkable body of graphic work which includes pastels, ink drawings and a huge range of etchings and lithographs. Most recently she has eschewed the succulent textures and sensual layering of pastel and has reduced her art to the bare bones of linearity, using mainly graphite and conte pencil. Her work is essentially narrative in impulse: she is a great storyteller who is unafraid to engage with the darker aspects of the human psyche.

I visited her in her north London studio, and asked her about the Rego museum, which is planned to open this September. 'I didn't know whether to accept or not. It's a big honour to have something like that. It's in Cascais, which is a beautiful place very near where I was brought up, and it has a marvellous architect called Souto de Moura.' Appropriately, the building will be called

House of Stories and Rego is donating to it a complete set of her prints (now numbering well over 300 items), together with her collection of paintings and drawings by Victor Willing. 'We can't really show together – it's very different work – therefore I will have the opening exhibition and then it will be him. My involvement [with the museum] is very little. The whole point is to collaborate with other countries, especially England, to do shows of narrative art, Hogarth and Daumier, for example. The chance to show things that most people don't see.' Apparently it's being funded by the local casino, a sponsorship solution unlikely to occur in England.

When I visited her, Rego was in the process of completing and proofing a suite of five new etchings on the taboo subject of female circumcision. These powerful prints confront the cruelty of ritual mutilation with images of the vagina dentata, stitched up orifices and grimly-watching mothers. Rego comments: 'I can't remember exactly what made me decide to do them. I read several things, and there's a doctor here who treats the women who come over to give birth and have a terrible time because they're ripped open, and she mends them. People say you mustn't criticize the customs of another culture. Maybe not, but if they cause such pain I don't see why you can't say something. Later on I did see a marvellous documentary on BBC4 which showed all those things happening in a country where it is forbidden by law. Yet it happens all over the world. Out of tradition, the mothers insist that their daughters have it done. Apparently it goes back to the Pharaohs.'

Rego was distressed by the injustice and cruelty of the practice and 'the slight kinkiness of the mother wanting this done when she's had it done herself. There's a lot of stuff that's not ever talked about. It's always the fathers – the mothers are never talked about.' What does she hope to achieve – that the practice will stop? Don't underestimate the power of the pencil. Ten years ago Rego's abortion series managed to get the law changed in Portugal. Before her hard-hitting prints and paintings on the subject were shown there, abortion was illegal. 'I feel very pleased that they legalized abortion. Sooner or later they would have done it, but I'm very glad that I did something, that I painted something so much after my own heart. It meant so much to me.'

She maintains that she has always been a political artist, since the days of her early collages attacking the Portuguese dictator Salazar. And the main subject of her work has long been the relationships between people, which is really the politics of power. Rego suffers from depression and insists that it is only art that keeps her sane. She certainly keeps busy. The main room of the studio is dominated by an altarpiece she is making for the Foundling Hospital, to be part of an exhibition of three artists, Rego, Tracey Emin and Matt Collinshaw, scheduled for 2010. 'I went to see the place and I saw the little trinkets that the women left when they left their babies – heartbreaking stories.' What Rego has made is a kind of portable altar that folds up like a cupboard, containing eight large drawings with a group of figures or props in front. Her habit of drawing from life has recently been extended by creating increasingly complex tableaux. Rego makes figures for these tableaux which are a cross between rag dolls and plaster models. Is she becoming a sculptor? 'No,' she says, 'a prop-maker.' Last year she exhibited her props for the first time in a show at the Marlborough Gallery in New York. Before that she felt that the props she'd made to staff her pictures could only work with people, but now she'd made objects capable of standing alone.

She says: 'You find out what it is you want to do through the process of doing it. You have an idea beforehand and then on the way it changes, sometimes quite a lot. Then, when you've come to the end of the paper you realise "ah, that's what it was all along".' She rejects the idea that she may be a conduit for some external force, like a spirit medium, and emphasizes the role of the individual. 'It's you who do it. And when you discover what things look like from drawing them, it's most exciting. You forget everything else because your attention is totally focused on what you're doing. I've always been better at drawing than painting. I just try to get better and better. That is my wish: to be able to draw really well.'

FRANK AUERBACH Living in the moment
24 October 2009

Frank Auerbach (born 1931) is flavour of the month. A museum exhibition of his early paintings has opened at the Courtauld (until 17 January 2010), a substantial monograph by William Feaver has just been published (Rizzoli, £100) and a commercial show of recent paintings at Marlborough Fine Art runs until 24 October. Meanwhile, the notoriously retiring and work-obsessed artist has been seen at Private Views and has even granted one or two interviews. Does this mean that Auerbach is relaxing the habits of a lifetime?

Not really. He still works seven days and five evenings a week, gets up extremely early and puts in long hours in the same smallish studio he has occupied since 1954. The myth that Auerbach never leaves the country, travels by plane or stays in a hotel was dispelled some decades ago when he flew to New York and loved it. For the rest, he does what he needs to do. He says: 'As one gets older one has less energy. It's simply a choice between working and doing something else, and I prefer to work. If I'm not doing that now I watch a bit of television (which I never used to) – Morse or Sherlock Holmes – isn't Morse good?' He reads less than before, but returns to favourites. 'Yeats keeps coming back and Eliot. My generation was energized by *The Waste Land*, and Pound seems to me to be marvellous, the language is totally magical.'

The Courtauld exhibition, which focuses exclusively on the 14 building site paintings (and related studies) Auerbach made between 1952 and 1962, takes us back to the beginning of his career when he began to paint in the radical way which made his name. The paint is thick, the approach realistic rather than abstract, but much of the expected imagery is buried in the churned layers. The paintings are remarkable physical objects, in some ways equivalents to the earthworks of the sites, their heaped and crinkled surfaces trenched with lines of energy.

Auerbach was initially drawn to the bomb-sites which littered London in the post-war years. 'It was when they became building sites that they became formally active', he says. 'I feel that I react formally, not with sentiment. I don't say "isn't this moving?", but there was such implicit drama in those things – destruction, phoenix rising again – it was the most active, the most eloquent landscape you could possibly imagine. This was a raw subject, and I think the whole business of painting is to capture some undiscovered territory for art. And as it turned out, the end results seemed raw and strange to me.'

The paintings conjure up a world of much darkness, rifted through with light. As he moved around the city, Auerbach made drawings of sites in Bruton Street or Earl's Court, Oxford Street or the Embankment. Most dramatic of all was the Shell Building. 'That was gigantic. I must have been stirred by its grandeur and size. The holes were deeper, the buildings were higher. And I have to say that the rebuilding of the Empire Cinema was an absolute gift. I was passing and I looked in and did some drawings. It looked so amazing.' The paintings that grew from these drawings were the labour of many weeks in the studio: the brilliant flaring of 'Shell Building Site: from the Thames', with all the intensity of a religious subject; the Stygian gloom of 'Workmen Under Hungerford Bridge'; and the real beauty of 'Rebuilding the Empire Cinema, Leicester Square', with its crusty but not unsubtle surface, capable of moving from emphatic to fragile and back again.

Auerbach insists that the paintings just emerged in response to the subjects. 'There was no sense of essaying or finishing a series.

I've more or less sleep-walked all my life. I've tried to listen to my instincts rather than make plans. I think there are two sorts of painters: one sort is buoyed up by saying how good they are. They're not to be despised: you've got to remember that Courbet was a provincial braggart and a marvellous painter.' And the other sort, to which clearly Auerbach himself belongs? 'I have felt all my life that my work is inadequate and I try to do better with the next painting, and that's worked for me.'

His aim has always been to achieve a true but not a literal representation of the physical world, an approach which owed something to Existentialism. 'I very much liked the idea that you made your own justification for existence. I don't think I can exaggerate the degree to which consciously or unconsciously the atom bomb hovered over all our heads. Very few of us thought that we had many years to live. So what are you going to do? You live in the moment and you try to construct your own framework to justify this brief and instinctive existence.' Feeling he had nothing to lose, he didn't want to play safe. At the same time he was also painting Primrose Hill. 'It was an antidote. The building sites were angular, Primrose Hill a swelling thing, and of course I painted the people. All my life I've painted people.' The long series of searching portraits for which is he is perhaps best known is the result. He paints landscape but not still-life, and for the last 30 years he hasn't used really thick paint, though there's a common misapprehension that he does. These days, it is the succulent colour that distinguishes his paintings.

'I never visualize a picture before I start', he says. 'I have an impulse and I try to find a form for that impulse. The great benefit of manuring the thing with reality is that reality continually belies one's expectations: where one expects the grand sweep it suddenly starts becoming petty, where one expects it to be hard it becomes soft, the proportions – almost every day one goes out there, one has different sensations about them.' This is reflected in his habit of scraping off and re-working: 'I change the painting every day.' So how does he decide when it is resolved? 'Firstly it's got to look new to me. At the time of finishing it's got to look like nothing I've seen before. Secondly, there's got to be nothing in it that isn't part of a coherent geometrical entity of a new sort. And thirdly it must feel like the subject. One's got to have the most pretentious aims – without pretensions there's nothing to live up to – but in retrospect I've never lived up to them, so I go on with another picture.' Long may he do so.

ROLAND COLLINS In praise of older artists
5 December 2009

One of the least endearing traits of our age is youth worship. I can understand that advertisers might need to target a large and gullible audience suddenly and unaccountably blessed with disposable income (or should that be credit?), but to attribute wisdom or originality to youth is a rash act indeed. The attention paid to young artists in recent decades has grown increasingly disproportionate, for no good reason apart from the follow-my-leader media circus which keeps their antics before an increasingly bored and bewildered (if not downright cynical) public. Meanwhile the invariably more substantial achievements of mature artists are ignored because not considered 'newsworthy'. Thus is the serious and rewarding disparaged, and the immature and meretricious lauded to the telegraph poles, if not quite the rooftops.

This is doubly disturbing because it is rare for a young artist to have much to say, or the ability to say it interestingly. Experience counts for far more, both in terms of content and the acquired skills with which to communicate it, as anyone with direct knowledge of the art world will readily admit. There are scores of mid-career artists out there, working away with very little encouragement or reward, some of whom were once the Bright Young Things of their generation. Fashion takes up and then it discards, and the blight of post-war British art has been the obsessive hunt for the next youthful star, while the richness and diversity of our artistic achievement across all age groups goes largely unrecognized.

However, beside the fascination for youth lies an ingrained public enjoyment of the Grand Old Man. A reverence for age is altogether more understandable: speaking personally, the friendship of older artists has taught me an immeasurable amount about both art and life, and I am deeply grateful for it. John Craxton, who has just died at the age of 87, was a supreme example of an artist full of knowledge and experience, capable of imparting his enthusiasms in the most wonderfully vivid and life-enhancing conversation. I greatly mourn his loss. Craxton's art is well-known and justly celebrated, but amazingly there are artists of his generation still at work whose careers remain a closely-guarded secret to all but the specialist. One such is Roland Collins.

Roland Collins was born in 1918 in Kensal Rise, before moving with his parents to a block of mansion flats in Maida Vale at the age of eleven. His great love there was the canal, and he made many drawings of it, aware from very early on that he wanted to be an artist. (At the tender age of eight he won a competition organized by the *Evening News* to colour in a poster.) At Kilburn Grammar School, where he helped to paint the scenery for the annual Shakespeare play, he was encouraged by the art master, Robert Whitmore, and consequently went to study for two years at St Martin's School of Art. Aged 18, education was at an end and he must find work, which he duly did, his first job being studio assistant for an advertising agency called the London Press Exchange. He prepared layouts and designs for advertising, and worked freelance as a lettering artist. (Collins was responsible for the letter-heading for London University's first notepaper.) Meanwhile, he had begun what was to be the main work of his life: a long series of gouache paintings, mainly of buildings, which link directly to the Romantic topographic tradition so strong in English art. Collins particularly admired the work of three of his older contemporaries, all of them born in 1903 – Edward Bawden, John Piper and Eric Ravilious. They set a high standard to follow, but Collins has been no mere imitator of their stylistic idiosyncrasies. He is his own man, his work given to a mixture of bold delineations and fine detailing, atmospheric washes of colour alternating with crisp pattern-making. He has a particular feeling for all horse-drawn conveyances (for 20 years he rode in Hyde Park), and especially carts, for fishing boats and sea defences, canals, the Thames and for Dieppe.

Although he is a passionate Londoner, for many years a denizen of Fitzrovia, who endured a five-year Cornish exile before settling in south London, his second home (spiritually) is in France. 'You could say I first went to Dieppe in the early 1950s in search of Sickert', admits Collins. He and his wife Connie return there regularly, though these days he finds the town rather too smartened up, with far fewer potential subjects for him to paint. He has nevertheless published a book of his photographs, *Dieppe – le visage d'une ville de province* (1995), one of the earliest of which is of a farrier, taken in the 1950s. Utterly professional, Roland Collins prides himself on turning his hand to many techniques. He has worked successfully as a designer and illustrator (he designed the sleeve for the first British LP record in 1945), a printmaker (he made a superb suite of lithographs to illustrate Noel Carrington's book *Colour and Pattern in the Home* in 1954), a muralist (Greek restaurants a speciality), a photographer and a writer (he wrote the text for a children's book, *The Flying Poodle*, in 1951, and illustrated another poodle book, the novel *Fifi and Antoine* by Charlotte Haldane in 1956), but above all he has been a painter.

He has produced a distinguished body of work which documents a fast-vanishing world. As he says: 'So many of the things I was interested in and attracted by no longer existed after the war.' He explains how he is drawn to the past: 'I think it reflects my search for rural origins. My grandfather on my father's side came from

Cottenham, north of Cambridge, and was described as a farmer. They produced a very well-known blue cheese and lived in Cheese House on the green.' If his work has a nostalgic air, it is partly because his style was firmly established in a realistic idiom through the 1930s, 40s and 50s. He has never been tempted by abstraction, preferring always to stay in close touch with what he sees. His habit is to go out walking, with his canvas painting bag over his shoulder. 'Finding a subject that suits me – that's the tricky bit.' If he succeeds, he will settle down to paint it *en plein air*. A pause for lunch in a nearby pub and then back to work. He'll be happy if he completes a painting in two sessions, but sometimes he'll wander all day in search of a motif and not find one. But the enjoyment he derives from looking at buildings never pales.

In 1937 he showed a painting for the first time in the Royal Academy Summer Exhibition, and has continued to exhibit regularly since, though an innate modesty has kept him from the limelight. As a consequence, his delightful and unaffected paintings are less well-known than they might be, and a talent which has been continuously in use for more than 70 years has largely gone uncelebrated. It is high time for a Roland Collins retrospective: an exhibition which could demonstrate the breadth and depth of his interests, and introduce to an unsuspecting public a very distinct, articulate and highly enjoyable artistic voice.

JEFFERY CAMP A great individualist
15 May 2010

More than 20 years ago when I first interviewed Jeffery Camp, he forbade me to bring a tape-recorder as he would find it off-putting. 'I speak slowly enough for you to write it all down', he drawled in measured tones. Although born in Oulton Broad, Suffolk, and spending his early years in East Anglia, Camp has a place-less accent but a memorable delivery: you can indeed jot down most of his obiter dicta if you're nimble with the stylus. Sitting in his kitchen sipping hot chocolate (he doesn't have coffee) on a balmy spring day, I begin to make notes, but even this it seems is inhibiting to his flow. I shall have to be more surreptitious and scribble his bon mots on my shirt cuff.

Now 87, Jeffery Camp is a Grand Old Man of British painting, but still something of a well-kept secret within the confines of the art world. He studied at Lowestoft and Ipswich Art Schools, and then at Edinburgh College of Art (1941-4), where he was taught by the celebrated landscapist William Gillies. As a young professional artist, Camp gravitated to London, first showing at Helen Lessore's famous Beaux Arts Gallery in 1959. Among his friends and contemporaries are Patrick George and Anthony Fry, the late Craigie Aitchison and Euan Uglow. Between 1963 and 1988 he taught at the Slade School of Fine Art in London, and exercised a benign and sympathetic effect on generations of students who vie to speak well of him. So concerned was he to ensure the continuance of the principles of what he saw as a proper art education, that he undertook the mammoth task of enshrining the essence of his approach in two 'how to do it' manuals. 'Draw' was published in 1981, and 'Paint' followed in 1986.

Camp says now that there is 'very little I would change' in either of what he calls his technical manuals, both of which were international best-sellers, though rather surprisingly they've subsequently been allowed to go out of print. He recalls writing chapters on demand for the publishers Dorling Kindersley, dictating much of it over the telephone. 'The only one I jibbed at was on perspective, because I had to say why it was bad. I couldn't get on with perspective. It goes against the natural touch of the eye. You know as well as I that railway tracks don't go to a point.' Camp has his own take on many received ideas, but still believes in the primacy of drawing in an artist's practice. In his south London home, he has various studios on different floors. He might draw a bird 'behaving badly' on a scrap of envelope while he's in the kitchen, but painting is generally reserved for a ground-floor room at the front of the house, or for his first-floor studio-cum-living room.

This first-floor studio is cluttered with furniture: comfy chairs, two easels, a litter of paint tubes, brushes and palette knives, two plan chests full of drawings, a loudly ticking clock, drawing boards, mirrors, and his father's Windsor chair with wooden stilts to make it higher. On the walls are a number of small oddly-shaped paintings on board, depicting moments in the life of the world observed and interpreted by Camp. The colours glow, and the drawing takes you at once to the heart of the scene. Camp is a superb vignettist, but he also paints on a grand scale, often working on canvases 10 feet wide. His house is currently empty of his latest efforts, which have either been sent to the Royal Academy Summer Exhibition (Camp has been an RA since 1974, and had a major retrospective there in 1988) or to his new show with Art Space Gallery in Islington (until 12 June). The Art Space exhibition will launch his latest book, 'Almanac' (RA Publications, £35).

Both of his earlier books promoted the fundamental disciplines of copying great art and trying to depict what you see. They were copiously illustrated with Camp's own versions of other people's pictures, as well as a richly idiosyncratic choice of original art by other artists. The text was equally unusual, consisting of gnomic instructions and exhortations, compiled in an affectionate and poetic vein. Camp's third book reaches new depths of autobiographical revelation, and is magnificently illustrated with over 500 of his own paintings and drawings. It's even got photos of the youthful artist splashing about at Hayling Island, and then some years later married to the painter Laetitia Yhap. He pays a nice tribute to her in this caption to one of the many portraits of his wife in the book. 'She learned to draw and paint at the Slade at a good time. The tower [which appears in the painting] was for seeing the future. The future was not as beautiful as the hat [she is wearing]. The girl became as beautiful as the hat.' A kind of pictorial memoir, 'Almanac' chronicles a life of dedicated looking and painting in the second half of the 20th century and beyond. It's a great read and a great picture book: I know of nothing like it.

Camp's writing style, always enjoyably brief and pithy, has been further honed to provoke and enlighten. He works by association of ideas, with little clusters of thoughts, offering – almost in passing – some of the best analysis of his own work and that of his friends. He talks of nude models being 'centrally heated', and describes an abstract painting as 'a proudly brushed, peacock-coloured squawk'. He writes of Beachy Head, a favourite subject: 'The drawing tears at the largest spaces in eyefuls of raw suggestion.' His prose is elliptical and evocative, but unexpectedly precise, and frequently carries a didactic charge. 'A rough-touch drawing can help you to shrug chubby paint marks, to make them quiver with life. It means you have to build a special language to carry you from drawing to painting.'

Camp is a master of that special language, what his friend and fellow East Anglian Michael Andrews called 'a sort of sweeping brevity'. His paintings and drawings are remarkably generous statements about the world, full of love and sensuality and a singular appreciation of beauty. He writes: 'In summer I like Green Park to be full of spread eagled bodies, honey golden and pink, half tanned against leafy green, seen from a deckchair. Low as spines.' A typically original touch, that last comment. The imagination stirs as you read Camp. Before I leave I ask him to sign my copy of 'Almanac'. He dedicates it, but neglects to add the important bit – his own name. 'I'm not used to these things', he says, self-deprecatingly. He deserves to be, for Jeffery Camp is one of those great individualists and survivors the British love to treasure.

 Picasso: Angel and Monster
19 June 2010

John Richardson has spent a lifetime in the company of great art
and artists, and is justly celebrated for his ability to evoke, explain
and evaluate their work in beautiful prose. Best-known as the
biographer of Picasso, he has written about many other artists
including Manet and Braque, and has curated a number of seminal
exhibitions since the Picasso retrospective he staged in New York in
1962. For the last 50 years he has lived in New York, though born
in England in 1924. He was in London recently for the installation
of his major new curatorial excursion, 'Picasso: the Mediterranean
years 1945-62' at Gagosian Gallery (6-24 Britannia Street, WC1,
until 28 August). I found him on site, giving a genial but informative
tour to gallery staff.

His command of the minutiae of his subject is enviable, and
it's difficult to believe that this charming and elegant man is 86.
Although he must be exhausted from organizing this extraordinary
exhibition, co-curated with Picasso's grandson Bernard Ruiz
Picasso, Richardson is still apparently full of energy and enthusiasm.
To start us off, I ask him the inevitable question - why choose
the Mediterranean period? 'Because it had never been covered
before as a totality. It's a very complex period because so many
different things are going on. Picasso revolutionizes ceramics and
engraving techniques – linocuts for instance, in which he gets these
extraordinary delicate effects – and the endless printing processes
he works on with the Crommelynck brothers and the lithographer
Mourlot in Paris. And then he tries a completely new way of
sculpture, putting it together out of bits and pieces. The surrealists
had done that a bit, but Picasso does it in the interests of reality.'
Here Richardson digresses into a passionate diatribe about Picasso
and surrealism. It's this passion which fired his determination to be
a writer on art, although to begin with he wanted to paint. 'I didn't

enjoy school at all, but when I went to Stowe (1937-9) I was very lucky that there was a lively art teacher and his wife there. This Canadian couple took 'Cahiers d'Art', 'Verve', 'Minotaure', 'Vingtieme Siècle' [the cream of avant-garde art magazines], which I should think was unique in school art departments, and I got obsessed by Picasso. I didn't particularly understand it then but it blew me over and I found it enormously exciting.' Subsequently Richardson studied painting at the Slade. 'Fairly early on I realized that if I wanted to become a good painter I was going to have to sacrifice everything and become completely absorbed into it. I was detached enough to realize that I wasn't capable of doing that. And I'm glad I didn't because I love writing about painters.'

He made his living for a time as an industrial designer before moving into journalism. From there he graduated to writing monographs and organizing exhibitions, worked on the other side of the fence in the commercial world, first for Christie's in New York and then as vice president of Knoedler's. Since 1980 he has devoted his time to writing. Besides the monumental Picasso biography, Richardson has been a regular contributor to 'The New York Review of Books', 'The New Yorker' and 'Vanity Fair'. A volume of his articles was collected under the title of *Sacred Monsters, Sacred Masters* in 2001, and in 1999 he published an enthralling memoir entitled *The Sorcerer's Apprentice*. Richardson not only marshals and deploys his facts to unusually telling effect, but writes in a lucid and beguiling style that draws the reader effortlessly on. How did he come to write so well?

'It's not false modesty, I still think I'm a beginner, but I did have one enormous advantage. The first remotely serious writing I did was for 'The New Statesman'. V S Pritchett was the literary editor and his right hand was somebody called T C (Cuthbert) Worsley. Cuthbert would give me 200 word unsigned pieces to do. I'd do them and he'd throw them back to me saying: "you write like a train shunting. Have another go." Still the train was shunting. He was tough as they come, but it worked. I ended up reviewing art and fiction under my own name, and as the ballet critic under another name, Richard Johnson.' Then at the beginning of the 1950s he went to live in a chateau in the south of France with the great collector and art historian Douglas Cooper, and a new era opened in his life. He became friends with Picasso and Braque and laid the real foundations for a life of connoisseurship.

Cooper was a monstrous egotist but a superb teacher with an unparalleled collection of cubist art. Richardson learnt an enormous amount and through him came to know Picasso well from 1953 onwards. 'Virtually every time there was a bullfight in Arles or Nimes, we'd have lunch, go to the bullfight then he'd come and have dinner with Douglas and me and we'd get in some gypsies from the Camargue.' It is this personal knowledge which underpins and makes sense of the meticulous research of Richardson's books.

Was Picasso really as monstrous as his detractors claim? Richardson is emphatic: 'whatever you say about Picasso, the reverse is equally true. When we say Picasso was an angel, it was perfectly true – he was angelic in certain circumstances – but he was also a monster. The sweetness wasn't sentimental. For instance, after the Spanish Civil War, there was a huge amount of Spanish refugees. Any Spaniard who said he was a painter, Picasso would help with brushes or paint. He was enormously generous to people, but never drew attention to it. He was a wonderful friend. He was very physical and would give you huge hugs or stroke the side of your head. And then he was incredibly funny – anything obscene or sexually outrageous he enjoyed.'

The fourth and final volume of Richardson's biography of Picasso will cover an extended period, from 1932 until the artist's death in 1973. Richardson is remarkably sanguine about the future of his masterwork. 'I've got Gijs van Hensbergen who is my collaborator and a brilliant Spanish scholar. If I drop dead tomorrow, Gijs will take over.' Let's hope John Richardson stays around to enjoy the well-earned plaudits of a huge project successfully completed. In the meantime, there's the magnificent exhibition at Gagosian to enjoy.

LEON KOSSOFF Silent witness

30 October 2010

A new exhibition of paintings and drawings by Leon Kossoff (born 1926) is an event in the art world. Kossoff is an intensely private man and keeps such a low profile that many people react with surprise to the information that he is still very much alive and working. Not for him the carefully calculated public appearance or widely-disseminated views; he is reluctant to give interviews and finds it increasingly difficult to say anything at all about his pictures. In fact, he is so reticent about his art, and so much wants it to speak for itself, that he has discouraged several people from writing books about him. To date, there are a number of Kossoff exhibition catalogues, with more or less revealing texts, but no heavyweight monograph. For an artist of his international stature, this is remarkable.

Kossoff's work is increasingly celebrated in America, and his current exhibition, after its London run, will travel first to New York (Mitchell Innes & Nash, 534 West 26th Street, NY 10001, 5 May – 18 June 2011) and then to California (LA Louver, 45 North Venice Boulevard, Venice, CA 90291, 8 September – 8 October 2011). In recent years he has had museum shows in America, Australia and Switzerland, and in 2007 there was an exhibition of his drawings from the old masters at the National Gallery in London. His paintings are achieving higher and higher prices at auction, and after years of relative obscurity, Kossoff's work is finally beginning to receive the attention it deserves.

In order to write about this exhibition before it opened, a special preview was arranged for me at Annely Juda Fine Art, Kossoff's dealers for the last decade. I had hoped to interview the artist about his new work, but he politely insisted that I refrain from taping our conversation. I'm used to this – Kossoff's contemporary, Jeffery Camp, also forbade the machine. I rather admire this mistrust of the packaging of sound-bites, though this is something I've also striven to avoid in more than 20 years of interviewing artists, preferring a presentation that catches the flavour of an individual without processing them. With Kossoff though I have an additional restriction: he doesn't want anything he says to be quoted. As far as he's concerned, I should concentrate on writing about my own responses to his work.

Fair enough, but the artist makes the work, and a few observations are surely in order here. A small, slight man, dressed in black, clean-shaven and with a tendency to melancholy, Kossoff doesn't look his 84 years, and shifts heavy paintings around like a much younger person. He's not exactly lugubrious, but you sense that he is appalled by the challenge of communication, and that desperation is never far away.

It's clear that life does not rest lightly on this man. Anxiety pursues him, the business of painting is an all-encompassing struggle which makes a contented existence impossible; but on the other hand, not to paint is worse. He draws or paints most days, and regards painting as a form of drawing, an extension of it, as it were. Kossoff paints the same subjects: a few trusted and familiar sitters and a series of urban landscapes which have shed new light on the city in which he lives. He is a Londoner born and bred, the son of a Russian-Jewish immigrant baker, growing up in Shoreditch where one of the neighbourhood landmarks was Christchurch, Spitalfields, Hawksmoor's famous masterpiece, massive and dominating as an Egyptian temple. Kossoff began painting its magnificent facade in the late 1980s, and three paintings of it are included here. Other subjects have ranged from a children's swimming pool to Kilburn Underground Station and the flower and fruit stall at Embankment

Station. People hurry through his cityscapes, but in the figure paintings they are arrested, held up for our scrutiny. Kossoff refers to the paintings of people as 'heads' rather than 'portraits', and there is something distilled and essential about their construction which suggests more of a type than an individual. His latest heads look like ancient and abraded frescoes of matriarchs or priests – wise, modest, all-seeing, ascetic. There is a hieratic quality to their depiction, a certain fierceness and lack of compromise, yet for people who know who the sitters are (his wife Peggy and the painter John Lessore are favourite models), likeness also emerges from the pared-back forms.

Kossoff agrees with Euan Uglow's definition of a painting being 'a state of emergency'. He makes many drawings of a subject before he feels sufficiently familiar with it to attempt a painting, after which the actual painting may take months – or years – to emerge. Kossoff's practice is to paint and scrape off, paint and scrape off, until something tells him to leave the image. A morning's work might be left overnight, but then ruthlessly scraped back to the bare board, leaving just a ghost of what was painted, before he starts again. It's a kind of Sisyphean process of seemingly endless endeavour, lightened by moments of recognition, when the artist accepts that he has achieved something passable. Doubt is his constant companion, and disbelief in his abilities. Yet somehow, after Herculean exertion, he still manages to produce memorable and surprisingly positive images which look the reverse of laboured.

There are only 27 items in his new show, and five of these are charcoal drawings. All the drawings are studies of a particular branch of a cherry tree in his garden at Willesden, which has been propped up in an attempt to prolong its life. The drawings have led on to a series of nine paintings made between 2002 and 2008 which are marvellously varied evocations of age and infirmity, as witnessed in a London garden. The stakes which support the tree resemble pit-props in a mine shaft or crutches a person might use, and the literal image undoubtedly has a wider allegorical resonance. One of the finest paintings is the very first one Kossoff made, 'Cherry Tree, Autumn 2002', an amazing reconciliation of surface and depth, design and description. My other favourite is the last in the series 'Cherry Tree, and Tube Train 2007-8', a beautiful green painting that breathes tenderness and resolve. Kossoff is famed for his thick surfaces, for making images from heavy deposits of paint layered onto boards. These days he paints more thinly, but the worked and re-worked paintings nevertheless give the impression of a substantial impasto build-up. Over this body of paint, the main substance of the image, is another layer, a linear tracery of drips and runs of paint, which have fallen from the loaded brush in its urgent dash to get down a telling mark. This arbitrary-seeming pattern is more obvious in some paintings than in others – it is particularly noticeable and beautiful, as it sets up a poignant counterpoint with the weightier marks, in 'Christchurch, Spitalfields, 1999-2000'. The whipping lines of these paint trickles are reminiscent of the dancing rhythms in Kossoff's etchings (he is a prolific and inventive printmaker) and are as essential a part of the finished painting as any other mark.

The cherry tree paintings could be seen as a celebration of the dynamics of the diagonal, with the vectored energies shooting off at all angles through these powerful compositions. But for all their formal toughness, these are marvellously lyrical, even gentle, paintings, luminous and fluid, not betraying any of the hesitancy of their lengthy gestation. This is the end of this particular motif: the cherry's branch finally had to be removed or the tree would die. Thankfully it has recovered and was blooming again this year, but it has lost its appeal for Kossoff. He must turn his attention to other subjects.

KEITH COVENTRY The folly of ambition

27 November 2010

When I went to interview him, Keith Coventry (born 1958) had just won the John Moores Painting Prize, one of the most prestigious accolades in the art world. Now worth £25,000, the prize is awarded every two years at the Walker Art Gallery in Liverpool to the best work from an open submission, and is judged by a panel of experts. This year Gary Hume, Alison Watt and Sir Norman Rosenthal were among the judges. Since its inauguration in 1957, some of the big names of modern British art in the last half-century have won it: Roger Hilton, David Hockney, Euan Uglow, John Hoyland, Peter Doig. Also a number of artists unjustly neglected today, such as Henry Mundy, Myles Murphy and Mick Moon. Undoubtedly winning the John Moores can make a difference, but it does not guarantee immortality. But then not much does, except perhaps genius.

Coventry is pleased to have won the John Moores. It is perhaps a measure of the enviable international reputation he has established over the last decade or so, and a recognition of his remarkable versatility. For Coventry paints in a number of very distinct styles, and seems to embody the stylistic plurality so typical of our age. He makes what look like minimalist abstracts inspired by the layout of housing estates; he paints white on white abstracts which are actually scenes of typical Englishness, such as the Royal Family at public functions; he makes sculptures of snapped-off saplings or destroyed park benches from inner-city no-go areas; he paints black on black abstracts based on flower arranging or bright Mediterranean scenes by Dufy; and he reinterprets Sickert in a series of figurative paintings called 'Echoes of Albany'. Coventry's variousness, which disconcerts some critics, is deeply appealing.

His prize winning painting is 'Spectrum Jesus' (2009), one of a series of canvases inspired by a book he found in the London

Library on the notorious forger Van Meegeren. Coventry often goes to the London Library to research. 'I like research, but for a lot of people it's an excuse for doing nothing. I go there, spin myself around and then just pull books out, engage with them and sometimes something clicks.' This is where chance comes into his work, the necessary leaven for an artist who likes to have everything decided before he picks up a brush. The discovery of Van Meegeren's paintings was a chance event, though Coventry also recalls a Ladybird book he had as a child about Vermeer, Rembrandt and Rubens, which pictured the forger.

'Spectrum Jesus' is a very blue and atrabilious painting, Van Meegeren re-painted in the style and palette of Emil Nolde, but rendered inexpressive by its close toning. Coventry was brought up a Roman Catholic and there are echoes of the Turin Shroud in his picture, but it is really about distancing – as is so much of his work. This is art about art: Vermeer interpreted (badly) by Van Meegeren, reinterpreted through the filter of Nolde and then stuck behind glass to hold it even further away. Is it satire? Apparently not: 'I don't have a stance, I'm totally ambivalent. The viewer can make what they want of it, I just present it. With the white on white paintings, you can't be sure whether it's nostalgia for lost traditions or nostalgia for Modernism. There's a kind of sympathy for both.'

We met outside Coventry's studio, a small room with barred windows in a light industrial block in the East End. Here he puts in long hours, often forgetting to eat in his total immersion in the act of putting paint on canvas or canvas-board. He grudgingly admits to being a workaholic and mutters about displacement activity; no time to visit the two lap-dancing clubs that lurk on his doorstep. The studio is packed with paintings in various degrees of completion, and on a corner bookshelf are a number of oversize volumes. Two books on Churchill's paintings catch my eye. Why those? 'Because he did white on white paintings', says Coventry, 'a technique recommended by Sickert. I saw them at his studio down in Chartwell. I liked them, then thought of copying them myself as part of all that Englishness series.'

Some commentators have identified Coventry's work as a new and savvy form of history painting, managing as it does to encapsulate a dialogue between Modernism and English culture. He is seen as dealing with social issues, with vandalism and sink estates, drug abuse and prostitution. Another series of paintings, called collectively 'Anaesthesia as Aesthetic', is based on the treatment of shell-shocked soldiers by exposing them to soothing colours. (An idea he found in a book on colour by John Gage.) Yet another series re-interprets the colours and patterns of McDonalds' packaging as abstract arrangements of line and hue.

Coventry uses photography and found imagery, adjusts the image in his mind's eye and then turns to his real enjoyment: the application of paint. 'I don't want to have to change anything. The painting only develops in terms of the quality of the paint. I like to build up the edges of shapes until they're really thick, much as the way Sickert used to fill in an area with a green slightly different from the green underneath. It gives a kind of breadth to it.' The brush strokes are applied almost on a grid, either vertically or horizontally, to emphasize the two-dimensionality of the surface of the painting. 'It's a play between spatial illusion and the surface.'

Framing is important to Coventry, who presents his oils behind glass. 'I like the idea of a certain distance so that you can't quite take in a painting. Reflections slow down the process of consuming the picture. I read somewhere 30 seconds is the maximum that people spend looking at pictures.' Certainly Coventry wouldn't consider using non-reflective glass in his frames. He wants viewers to get a glimpse of themselves to help captivate them, to hold them in front of his pictures. Francis Bacon also liked the idea of the viewer's reflection becoming part of the experience of looking at a painting.

Coventry is beguilingly modest about his technical attainments. He doesn't think of himself as a sculptor, because his sculptures are found objects he takes to a foundry to be made into bronze. His first was a broken tree. 'I wanted to paint it like Caspar David Friedrich – an existential-looking snapped tree against the sunset, then realized I didn't have the skills.' But he has tried to develop his range as a painter – particularly in the 'Echoes of Albany' series. 'It's a big move from painting a rectangle to painting a figure, a real leap.'

'I remember something John Hoyland said when I was a student – you have to set parameters, because without them the energy that you have will just dissipate. I think that my parameters are quite tight; basically: don't do anything too difficult!' When I suggest that this doesn't sound terribly ambitious, Coventry ripostes: 'The thing is, it's how well you operate within that, isn't it? People who try to do ambitious things often fail. It's far better to know your limits and operate successfully within them. Then you can be more ambitious incrementally.' And that, it seems, is precisely what he is doing.

ALAN REYNOLDS Painter's progress
5 March 2011

At the age of 85, Alan Reynolds is enjoying a sudden and well-deserved flurry of interest in his work. A superb monograph has just been published on his art, written by Michael Harrison, director of Kettle's Yard in Cambridge, and to launch the book there's an exhibition at Annely Juda Fine Art (23 Dering Street, W1, until 26 March). This is Reynolds' 7th solo show at the Gallery, which has successfully represented him since 1978, and which has been responsible for promoting his work in Europe. The new work consists of white reliefs and pencil drawings, which continue Reynolds' exploration of the dynamic relationships between the horizontal and the vertical. The work can look a trifle austere at first glance, but the exquisitely balanced tonal drawings display a lyricism that leads you to the heart of his endeavour.

Reynolds' work has not always been so obviously abstract. In the 1950s, he made such a name with his landscape paintings that he was dubbed 'the golden boy of post-neo romanticism'. He was seen as the saviour of the English landscape tradition, heir to Samuel Palmer, Paul Nash and Graham Sutherland. His 1956 exhibition at the Redfern gallery was one of the most successful and talked-about of that decade, but within a couple of years he was moving away from landscape towards art that engaged more directly with poetry, music, harmony; in other words, he was becoming a geometric abstractionist. For just half a dozen years he was a painter of organic form, particularly noted for his ears of wheat and teazels. By 1958 he was working exclusively in straight lines and circles. What brought about this dramatic change?

In the first place, it's important to realize that Reynolds was never a straightforward realist. He made representational paintings, but as he says: 'I never painted landscape on the spot, apart from one occasion when our dear old drawing master took us out into the countryside and we did a few oil sketches.' It's clear that right from the start there was a great formality in his approach – an understanding of the essentially abstract construction of a painting – and when I suggest that Reynolds is really a formal artist, he agrees. 'Yes, I suppose I am. I got that of course through my baptism in Germany of modern art, after the war.' Reynolds was called up in 1944, aged 18, and volunteered for action with the Highland Light Infantry. 'When the war finished, my division was broken up. We were all sent off to different places and I finished up training as an army school master and eventually settled in Hanover for about a year and a half.' That was where Reynolds first encountered avant-garde art. 'It was the most important experience I had, I would think.'

Back in England it took time to understand the implications of what he'd experienced. 'I was on a high over what I'd seen in Germany but I didn't understand the philosophy. I call it that but for an artist to have an aesthetic philosophy is poisonous in this country – you can get shot for that. When I came back here I was totally baffled by the more sophisticated art circles in London. It was such a gloomy sort of set-up, partly as a result of the war I suppose, an indrawn nationalism. You can understand it: the country had been through a hell of a time and it had been cut off culturally, no question of that.'

The post-war years saw a gradual opening up and Reynolds can vividly remember the first Skira books coming out when he was a student. (He studied at Woolwich Polytechnic School of Art, 1948-52, then spent a year at the Royal College where he won a medal for painting.) Before that there had been no art books to speak of – a fact we tend to overlook with our glut of words and images today. Travel was limited: difficult to get to Paris let alone Hanover or Munich. 'The art world or art groups in Europe are much more open and accessible, and always have been, than in this country. France and Germany are big countries, and Germany especially has centres of excellence everywhere – a legacy of the old princedoms. It's not all centred on one place, like London, and it stops this dictatorship – the rule of the arbiters of taste that we have here.'

Reynolds' first one-man exhibition was at the Redfern Gallery in 1952 while he was still a student, and his distinctive silhouetted style, in which dark linear forms stand out against luminous backgrounds, caught on at once. He says his early success was embarrassing, though the financial rewards were welcome. The problem was that success created a demand for more of the same, and Reynolds knew his art had to develop. 'I was after something else, I had something ticking away inside me. I was lucky enough to read some things by Herbert Read, particularly his Faber book on Klee, and it was just like getting a pat on the back. It was marvellous – I thought "this man's been there". Read was a great scholar and an extraordinary man and he was British! I only met him twice but he gave me a lot of support.' Klee was evidently a crucial influence on Reynolds, more important even than other admired European masters such as Arp or Mondrian. 'What I really got from Klee was an aesthetic philosophy. He was a wonderfully accomplished musician – first violin for the Bern chamber orchestra, for a start – and he brought something of the insight of music into statements he made on visual art. He was incredibly articulate and also into metaphysics and that again is a German trait.' It was a European view of art that Reynolds now responded to, not a nationalist celebration of English landscape. As he says: 'I've been a European since the war finished. I think of myself first as a European and an Anglo-Scot after that.'

He has Scottish blood on his father's side, his mother hailed from Suffolk, and he grew up in Newmarket. As an adult, Reynolds settled in Kent, where he still lives. But instead of painting the Kentish landscape, he chose to eliminate the romantic figurative element and concentrate on art that dealt with balance and equilibrium. He found his true voice in mid-life and began to make contemplative work that is a distillation of the visual world. In 1967 he abandoned painting entirely to make constructed reliefs, and for the last 30 years he has made only white reliefs, tonal drawings and woodcuts. Yet there is great richness in the subtleties of his work.

It takes courage to abandon a lucrative career as a popular landscape painter in order to follow your instincts and make rigorous abstractions. Reynolds never again enjoyed the same degree of commercial success, and had to teach at art schools until he retired in 1990. These days, his reputation stands higher in France and Germany than it does in his homeland. Neglected by the English art establishment, he nevertheless stuck to his guns and continues to produce the most meticulous body of drawn and constructed abstract art, exploring rhythm, interval and volume through black and white, shadow and light.

As you look closer, the continuity emerges between the early landscapes and the current reliefs: there is no great change of direction, no sudden shift from organic to abstract. As Reynolds says, the geometric was always there: the white buildings in his early landscapes prefigure the all-white reliefs of later years. There's an unfounded art world rumour that he rejects his early work, but this makes him cross, for examples of it still hang on his walls at home and form an essential part of the narrative of his art. In Michael Harrison, Reynolds has found the perfect interpreter. Harrison trained as a sculptor, made his own wood constructions and understands the process inside out. He writes with refreshing clarity and charts the course of Reynolds' career with insight and understanding. His monograph (published by Lund Humphries at £40) is a model of lucidity: beautifully designed by Dalrymple and concisely illustrated, it reads extremely well. It's a testament to a lifetime of devoted effort, for which Alan Reynolds is now justly celebrated.

DENNIS CREFFIELD 'England's most closely guarded secret'

24 September 2011

'I'm a peripatetic architectural draughtsman', says Dennis Creffield, best-known for his magnificent series of charcoal drawings of the medieval English cathedrals, commissioned in 1987 by the Arts Council. He has indeed travelled the country, not only drawing cathedrals but also Welsh and English castles, the pagodas of Orford Ness in Suffolk (laboratories for testing the trigger mechanisms of atomic bombs), the stately pile of Petworth House in Sussex, and many aspects of London. He has also drawn and painted people, the living as well as the dead (Shakespeare, Queen Elizabeth I, Mozart), and done his fair share of landscape painting. But it is with dramatic, expressive charcoal drawing that his name is most often associated.

Creffield was born in south London 80 years ago, and studied with David Bomberg at the Borough Polytechnic from 1948 to 1951. He was only 17 when he started with Bomberg, one of the most charismatic and influential teachers of the century, and the experience was transforming. (Among Bomberg's other students were Frank Auerbach and Leon Kossoff.) Creffield's liking for charcoal was nurtured in Bomberg's classes, as was his ability to perceive what Bomberg called 'the spirit in the mass'. Creffield became a member of the Borough Group, whose aim was to promote Bomberg's work through exhibitions and his principles by example. Creffield later went on to study at the Slade where he was a prize-winner, becoming in due course an effective teacher himself and a substantial artist in his own right. He has had more than 20 solo exhibitions in the last 45 years, and his work is in public and private collections worldwide.

His latest exhibition is called 'Dennis Creffield. Jerusalem' and runs until 8 October at James Hyman Fine Art in Savile Row, W1. Hyman himself was the prime mover in this new body of Creffield's work. The exhibition really springs from a convivial lunch in 2007, and a conversation between artist and dealer in which Hyman proposed an exhibition with the theme of Jerusalem and William Blake. The work has been four years in the making, and brings together a very early drawing made prophetically in 1948, others done in 1993, paintings from 1994 and 1999, with the more recent commissioned material. The exhibition thus has something of a retrospective feel, but only to the extent of identifying a particular line of interest that has run through Creffield's career. Most of the work is new, and wonderfully vibrant and inventive.

'It was very difficult to find my way into the subject', recalls Creffield. 'I went up all sorts of wrong alleyways.' To get himself started, he bought a cast of Blake's life mask from the National Portrait Gallery, and this assumed an increasingly important role, becoming 'my main channel of communication and inspiration with him'. Although the heads he subsequently painted of Blake tended to emerge in bursts of creativity, Creffield established with this cast what amounted to 'a daily conversation through the act of drawing'. He entered into a sort of mystical communion with it, in which he feels he became a conduit for Blake's spirit; the resulting portraits of Blake were 'allowed to happen'. Wryly, Creffield acknowledges the difficulty of Blake's vision: 'in order to understand it you have to become a bit deranged yourself.'

In 1948, when Creffield made the earliest work in this exhibition, a charcoal drawing of King David dancing before the Ark of the Covenant, he was studying with Bomberg and the first Israeli Arab war was taking place. He still doesn't know quite why he chose that subject, but it lit a trail of thought and feeling that was only to find its proper conclusion in this exhibition. Creffield is a committed celebrator, a positive force among the often negative impulses of today's art world. This can be seen in the lyrical drawings of Jerusalem made on his first visit there in 1993, and in his interpretations of the city at sunrise in oil paint, made on a subsequent stay in 1994. These earlier works form the bedrock for the more visionary drawings and paintings that have recently preoccupied him.

He recognizes the challenge: 'The problem is that Jerusalem is more than a city, it is the spiritual home for Jews and Christians and a very important place to Muslims. It is both an actual place but also a part of their faith, imagination and dreams – dreams of the past and even hopes of the future. Devout believers of the three religions are buried in the Kidron Valley which they believe will be the site of the Last Judgement.... For the ordinary Christian it is not only the place of Jesus' death and resurrection but also "The Holy City, the New Jerusalem, coming down from God out of heaven, prepared as a bride adorned for her husband" (Revelation 21:2).'

Creffield's task was to interpret Jerusalem the actual place and symbol in parallel with Blake's exposition in the prophetic books. As he puts it: 'Blake's vision of Jerusalem contains all of this but he presents it to us as the London of his time – a brutalized suffering city place – Albion/London. His imagery is personal and esoteric and difficult to understand but it is clear that the message of the poem is that we must all forgive and love each – "*for all that lives is holy*" – inextinguishable hope of a New Jerusalem.'

From such complex sources, Creffield has distilled an art of rare presence and power. The drawings are immediate in their impact, the paintings unfold more gradually and deserve time spent in looking. The group of 27 small paintings of Blake, from an extended series of improvisations on the life cast, are arranged on the facing wall of the smaller room of Hyman's gallery in a potent group intended to echo an iconostasis in the Greek Orthodox Church. This immensely varied group, which ranges formally from abstraction to representation, from a simple outlined container like a jug, to a more recognizable evocation of Blake's features, offers a gamut of emotional expression, from the mute and glowering to the sorrowful or serene. The broadly swiped charcoal drawings of Blake's head take this investigation further still, at least one transcription recalling the features of the painter Francis Bacon. (It will be remembered that Bacon too was drawn to Blake's life mask and made several paintings from it.)

The great dome of Blake's forehead is, as Hyman points out, neatly echoed in the Dome of the Rock in Jerusalem and Wren's magnificent dome of St Paul's Cathedral. So are the various strands of this exhibition brought together and interwoven. Creffield moves easily from the literal to the metaphoric: from women with arms uplifted in attitudes of prayer, to the city as bride, angels dancing or Jerusalem in the form of a married couple. The word Jerusalem appears in Hebrew script here and there – 'it's the first time I've used any calligraphy in my work' – but the quality that comes across most strongly is the crackle of energy, both physical and spiritual. These images vibrate with life. As Creffield admits: 'I allowed Blake to encourage me to be more wild.' Has the draughtsman finally turned into a visionary himself? Meanwhile, in south London, another project is stirring. The collector Sarah Rose is a passionate enthusiast for Bomberg and his Borough Group. She has now decided to give her collection, which includes paintings and drawings by the master as well as Creffield, Cliff Holden (born 1919), Miles Richmond (1922-2008) and Dorothy Mead (1928-75), to the University of the South Bank, situated in Borough Road, SE1. Creffield is delighted by the appropriateness of this: the Borough Polytechnic sheltered Bomberg in the 1940s and 50s when he was unfashionable, and now it once again opens its doors when he is internationally famous and respected. A special display will be unveiled in 2012 to give local point and focus to this historic artistic alliance.

The distinguished American painter R B Kitaj once described Dennis Creffield as 'England's most closely guarded secret'. With this remarkable new exhibition, and the forthcoming Borough Group display, he should finally become securely lodged in the art public's consciousness.

JOHN HUBBARD   Natural Selection
3 March 2012

John Hubbard makes paintings about landscape which draw upon his early training in America and the influence of the abstract expressionists. But his pictures are far from abstract images: they are about the play of light through foliage or the surface of rock seen close to. They are concerned with atmosphere and the spirit of place – with earth, air, light and sometimes water interacting. He denies that these are aerial views, asserting that his paintings try to capture the experience of being in the landscape, rather than looking down upon it, and being in it over a period of time. 'I came to prefer an image that reveals itself gradually, by stages', he says, 'like so much of nature.' Hubbard was born in 1931 in Ridgefield, Connecticut, took his BA in English at Harvard in 1953, was based in Japan for his military service (1953-6), then studied for a couple of years at the Art Students' League in New York. His move from a general arts background to a career in painting was encouraged by working with Hans Hofmann at his legendary Provincetown summer school, even though (or perhaps because) Hofmann was highly critical of Hubbard's efforts. At that time de Kooning was Hubbard's hero, but in New York landscape was not thought a fit subject for painting. So in 1958 Hubbard moved to Rome and based himself there, painting still-life and street markets for the next two years, and travelling in Europe. Landscape painting began at last to seem a possibility. In 1960 he moved to England, marrying and settling in Dorset the following year. His work at this point was still very experimental, and the small de Stael-influenced landscapes he had made in the south of France seemed quite inappropriate to his new life. For the first time he had settled close to the subject of his work, and he moved into a style and scale more fitting to it. He made big paintings, calling on all the formal freedoms he had learned from the abstract expressionists. I went to meet Hubbard at Roche Court, an imposing 19th century country house set in Wiltshire parkland, in the village of East Winterslow, outside Salisbury. This is the home of the New Art Centre, a commercial gallery founded in 1958 in London, which re-located here in 1994. Between 1961 and 1975, Hubbard held nine solo exhibitions at the New Art Centre in Sloane Street. Over the following decades he continued to exhibit widely in Britain and America, showing in London with Fischer Fine Art and latterly Marlborough Fine Art. Now he is back at Roche Court, with a group of landscapes from the 1960s. This is not so much a retrospective as a re-examination of selected pictures after nearly half-a-century. One or two have been exhibited before, others have never previously left the artist's studio. The exhibition consists of half-a-dozen large oils on canvas and several much smaller oil-on-paper paintings. They are beautifully installed in a long light-filled gallery which links the house with an orangery in the garden. The subjects are general: coastal landscape, rocky woodland, light on a cliff-face, and correspond to the all-over paint application Hubbard favours, rather than identifying and focusing on a central image. Interestingly, the paintings that immediately preceded the ones here were more gestural, and more obviously abstract expressionist in mood and application. The actual making of the painting was more important in those pictures than the experience of the landscape. The group of works at Roche Court are much more involved with an interpretation of landscape which seems as passionately engaged today as when they were painted.

From the start, Hubbard showed a preference for the contained landscape rather than the scenic prospect: for quarries and caves, rocks and woodland. He liked to suggest water and sky in his paintings, though not always where the spectator might expect to find them (in a vertical strip rather than a horizontal one), but he preferred to concentrate on the textures of stone or foliage. This interest is reflected in his passion for gardens, not only to be seen in his later paintings of subjects fairly local to him such as Abbotsbury (Dorset) and Tresco (the Scilly Isles), as well as gardens further afield such as those of the Alhambra in Spain, but also in terms of his own garden at Chilcombe, near Bridport in Dorset. Although he would not want to be thought of as an artist-plantsman in the mould of Cedric Morris or John Nash, his garden is nevertheless essential to him, and reinforces the notion of a special and intense relationship with a particular stretch of landscape that is found in so much of his work.

Materials and their specific properties are important to him. He started these sixties' paintings by working in turpentine-thinned oil paint on fine prepared canvas. 'Sometimes you get a good beginning', he says, 'but sometimes a good beginning can be a snare and a delusion. You have to try something else.' Hubbard talks lucidly but in the most general terms about 'establishing the character' of a painting, or giving it 'a different life'. He tends to work thinly, though with selected areas of paint build-up, because he wants to keep in (literal) touch with the canvas, and thus with the reality of the picture as a painted surface, rather than a low relief sculpture in pigment. 'My painting idol is Rubens – in terms of how to paint, not subject matter. I love Rubens' sketches and the fluidity of his paint.'

Studied at close quarters, Hubbard's paintings have a marvellous textural range and vitality: he has applied the thinner paint swiftly, dripping it here and there, thrown or spattered it, and then administered it thicker with a palette knife. There are months of work in each painting, which might later be revised if Hubbard was unsatisfied with the final result. Formally, these are ambitious and impressive works, but they don't just exist in abstract terms. They are also intimate and searching explorations of the nature of landscape as it changes under variable light, and as paintings of place they are remarkable. Seen from the garden through the glass wall of the gallery, their subjects change and become more elemental: distance brings out different emphases in their structures. Here be waterfalls, storms, mountains, spring torrents, great blocks of alpine air. And yet they are actually more local images, the kind to be experienced by driving along the coast roads of Dorset. By 1968 Hubbard was getting restless with painting the English landscape. A commission to design decor and costumes for the Dutch National Ballet helped to free him up. Then in 1969 he made his first visit to Morocco and the Atlas Mountains, and his work changed again. For the next 40 years, he pursued an elusive goal, going ever deeper into landscape, exploring structure and pattern and detail. All his life John Hubbard has been searching for a sense of place: not one particular place, but a recognition of the special qualities of a series of places which have intrigued and beguiled him through a long and distinguished career. These 1960s landscape paintings mark the point at which his mature vision really took off.

CHURCH PATRONAGE

20 December 1997

For centuries, the Church was the chief patron of the arts. Then, after the Renaissance and the gradual secularisation of the state, and with man-the-measure-of-all-things supplanting God at centre stage, patronage was increasingly colonised by the great families and the mercantile rich.

The nature of art changed: the personal portrait replaced the altar piece. Landscape painting graduated from background to foreground. Very few people painted fresco cycles on the lives of the saints, and, if they did, they tended to be third-rate artists. If the Church was spending money on the arts, it was the architects who benefited most: new churches and cathedrals had to be built, but they didn't necessarily have to be adorned. Or at least, not beautifully.

There have been various attempts to revive this flagging Church patronage, but few have outlived their initiator's enthusiasm. One notable bright spot in what is otherwise a rather lamentable history is the career of Dean Walter Hussey (1909-85). Beginning at the Parish church of St Matthew, Northampton, where he commissioned the likes of Henry Moore and Graham Sutherland to produce work for the church, Hussey became a considerable patron of contemporary art. He was a collector in his own right, and continued to commission new things when he moved to Chichester Cathedral. Chichester has an attractive mix of art these days, ranging from a beautiful and rare Romanesque stone carving to John Piper's bright altar tapestry. The sculptor Geoffrey Clark cast a pulpit in aluminium, Graham Sutherland's painting 'Noli Me Tangere' hangs in a side chapel and Chagall designed a luminous stained-glass window. As an example of enlightened patronage, it shows what can be done. A few years ago, a sculpture by Leonard McComb of a gilded nude youth caused quite a stir. It was only on temporary exhibition in Lincoln Cathedral but it certainly raised the whole question of whether nudity was permissible in a place of worship. (It was swiftly removed through pressure of public opinion.) You would have thought that nothing would be more acceptable in the eyes of God than the unclothed human form, free from all vain encumbrance. Yet our traditions are such that the loincloth must at all times remain in place.

When 'The Messenger', a video by Bill Viola, was commissioned and exhibited in Durham Cathedral, it was at once pointed out that the man in the film was naked. Indeed so. The video consisted simply of this character rising and sinking through great depths of water. What could be more expressive of the trials and tribulations of a particular soul? It is a deeply moving piece, and it is also remarkable for its essential purity.

Nevertheless, by many it wasn't considered quite proper to show in the house of God. Half-proud, half-relieved, Durham Cathedral sent it on tour round the art galleries instead. Religious authorities should have the courage of their convictions. Admittedly, as with any other large organisation, a choice has to be approved by endless committees and bureaucrats, and many an imaginative scheme must have been quashed by Dean and Chapter. But to vacillate once a good artist has been approached to lend or give work, or has even been commissioned (in these cash-strapped days), is the height of pusillanimity. Particularly as, in recent years, religious art has experienced something of a resurgence. Various exhibitions have examined the kind of art that now appears in churches, debating whether or not it is appropriate, and just what is meant by the word 'spiritual'. Coincidentally, at the same time Sister Wendy Beckett, writer and broadcaster *extraordinaire*, appeared on our screens, as if to prove that the Church could move with the times and not only understand but actually appreciate modern art.

A great deal of abstract art has been identified as spiritual in intent, Rothko usually being cited in this connection. But, as with all abstract art, it's impossible to prove the point – it could mean absolutely anything. That's its great strength and its weakness. Figurative art has always fared better with the public, but quite often there is resistance. The more rigid among the congregation will disapprove of any art, but modern art in particular. A stark but stately marble altar by Henry Moore caused much dissension in a Wren church in the City. You can't please all of the people all of the time. On the other hand, one artist whose work does seem to arouse almost universal praise is Craigie Aitchison.

Aitchison has been painting the Crucifixion since about 1958, long before it even occurred to him that one of his pictures might hang in a church. He began to paint this particular subject because it is the greatest human event he could imagine, not from any specific religious belief. Along with still-lifes, Bedlington terriers and portraits, it has remained his chief subject matter. Until recently, nearly all his Crucifixions have remained in private collections, bought as much by connoisseurs of contemporary art as the religiously minded. This summer, however, Aitchison was asked to paint a picture for Truro Cathedral.

Looking at possible sites within the Cathedral he chose the Chapel of St Margaret, where he would have to fill four blind Gothic arches. Aitchison decided to paint Christ between the thieves, which takes up three panels, but what to do in the fourth? The artist resolved the situation in typically inventive and poetic fashion. The fourth panel, on the extreme right, contains simply a tree with one branch reaching up towards the moon above it. Although austere, it offers a breath of hope: the possibility of redemption has entered the world. Aitchison's inspirational handling of this subject is at once refulgent and contemplative.

This commission was made possible by the generosity of the Jerusalem Trust, a charitable organisation set up by the Sainsbury family. Last year Christopher Le Brun and Adrian Wiszniewski were commissioned by the Trust to do a pair of paintings each for the Anglican Cathedral in Liverpool. The romantic symbolism of the one contrasts well with the busy idealisation of the other. In addition, above the main entrance to the Cathedral is placed an Elisabeth Frink sculpture of Christ. At the other end of the country, the Hampshire Sculpture Trust arranges temporary exhibitions at Winchester Cathedral, most recently of an ancient piece of bog oak carved by the young sculptor Tim Harrison. In the crypt stands an Antony Gormley lead figure in prayer, more often than not dramatically up to his knees in water.

In fact, there's a great deal more contemporary art in churches than one might at first expect. Look at the series of 14 powerful watercolour Stations of the Cross by Norman Adams in St Mary's Church, Mulberry Street, Manchester, the oldest Catholic church in Britain. Or the recently installed glass-pierced bronze doors on the theme of the tree of life by Bryan Kneale at Portsmouth Cathedral. Returning to Craigie Aitchison, the Jerwood Foundation has just presented his prize-winning 'Crucifixion' (1994) to King's College Chapel in Cambridge where it will hang near the great Rubens 'Adoration of the Magi', familiar from so many Christmas cards. Yet these considerable achievements are not being much trumpeted unless they cause controversy. But if as religious art they are quietly doing their job, bringing serenity or peace of mind or arousing the light of faith, what more should we ask?

UPDATE by the Editor, August 2012

Re-reading this piece, I am struck by the phrase 'cash-strapped days': it seems some things never change. Bill Viola is still making video works, Sister Wendy is still out there somewhere, Leonard McComb has enhanced the mosaic glory of Westminster Cathedral by means of two golden saints, and Durham goes on adding to its contemporary collections with Paula Rego's St Margaret and the Transfiguration window by Tom Denny. Craigie Aitchison, alas, has departed, but his spirit will linger long in S W London, where the church of St Mary the

Boltons has installed a stained glass window in his memory. Following a design set out by Craigie, incorporating Christ on the cross flanked by a cypress tree and a Bedlington terrier, the window was completed after his death and now stands as a memorial to this luminous artist.

LEAVE IT TO THE PEOPLE

11 December 1999

In a recent Spectator article about the collection of high art, low art and ephemera assembled over more than half a century by the Pop artist Peter Blake (Arts, 9 October), I suggested that in the fullness of time this unique omnium gatherum should be left to the nation. To my mind it should be kept together and preserved as a museum to the collecting spirit and the working methods of one of our key post-war artists. But who would bankroll such a worthy project? Would the artist himself have to provide the necessary funds? (Sounds a bit like vanity publishing.) If the state were bequeathed Blake's studio contents – of considerable value in themselves – would it be too much to expect the running costs to be met by local or central government?

The popular portrait and landscape painter Graham Sutherland ran into problems on just this issue. In 1976 he gave a sizeable and representative collection of his work to Picton Castle, near Haverfordwest in Wales, hoping that it would form a lasting memorial to his achievement in the country that had so inspired him. But who was to pay for its upkeep? Sutherland soon found himself out of pocket and tried unsuccessfully in the last year of his life to move the museum to more suitable quarters. The collection remained at Picton, increasingly strapped for cash. Running costs escalated. Eventually the National Museum of Wales took over responsibility for it in 1989, but by 1995 it was threatened with closure. Its future remains uncertain. What are we to make of this cautionary tale? Perhaps Sutherland's need to be remembered impaired his common sense. If you plan to set up a museum nowadays it has to have a solid and practicable foundation, and probably the subject of the museum is not its best instigator. You would expect a professional collector to be more tough-minded altogether, and recent events seem to bear this out. Take the example of Sir Denis Mahon (born 1910). This distinguished art historian had built up an unparalleled collection of 17th-century Italian paintings, which he reckoned cost him around £50,000 to assemble and which is now worth £25 million. He had never intended to sell these pictures, but had always wanted to safeguard their future. Mahon offered to trade his collection for a government assurance that no charge would be made for museum access and no work of art sold from a museum's existing collection.

In 1998 he got his way and left the bulk of his collection to the National Art Collections Fund which will lend the pictures to various English museums, as well as keeping a sharp eye on their policy and procedures. In June this year it was announced that 28 Italian baroque masterpieces, including works by Guercino, Guido Reni and Domenichino, were to join the National Gallery on indefinite long-term loan. Mahon's behaviour can hardly be termed anything as crude as blackmail, yet the subtle arts of bargaining and diplomacy can here be seen to have achieved a desired result which will be a real benefit to the nation.

The NACF has an important role to play in the administration of collections and the allocation of loans. When in the 1980s the philanthropist Charles Kearley took an interest in the newly opened Pallant House Gallery in Chichester, it was through the NACF that he decided to act. Dean Walter Hussey, the greatest church patron of modern British art, had already established Pallant House by promising to leave practically all his pictures to it if a gallery were started. As he so succinctly commented, 'And that blackmail did it'. Hussey's collection comprises work mostly by the artists he knew and commissioned – Moore, Sutherland, Piper and Ceri Richards, for example – and it is both complemented and extended by Charles Kearley's bequest. Kearley had collected the likes of Piper and Hitchens but also bought major works by European modernists such as Severini and Léger. A very definite character has been created by these bequests, and the substantial holdings of 20th-century art at Pallant House now look set to receive an even greater boost.

Colin St John Wilson, best known as the architect of the British Library, has been collecting art for more than 50 years, and has gradually amassed an impressive group of museum-standard works by modern British artists. A selection of these is on show at Pallant House, together with the plans and models of a proposed extension to the gallery. A new wing is planned, designed by architects Long and Kentish in association with Wilson himself, which will enlarge the gallery to more than six times its present size, and enable the entirety of Pallant House's existing collections to be shown concurrently. It will also be the display case for the Colin St John Wilson collections, which will find their permanent home here if the extension is built. All that is now needed is the money.

The good burghers of Chichester and its environs should not hesitate to dig deep into their pockets, for a Pallant House enlarged as planned would indeed be a jewel in the glittering tiara of the South East. Among the works on show at Chichester are a magisterial late Thames painting by Michael Andrews, artwork by Peter Blake for the inner sleeve of *Sgt. Pepper's Lonely Hearts Club Band*, the world's best-selling album, and Richard Hamilton's relief work (with real car door) 'Swingeing London '67', which depicts Mick Jagger and Robert Fraser handcuffed after a drug bust. This last is particularly at home in Pallant House as the groovy pair were actually arrested just outside Chichester all those years ago. Further key paintings include Bomberg's 'Last Landscape', excellent things by Patrick Caulfield and Prunella Clough, an early Lucian Freud self-portrait and Sickert's large oil of Gwen Ffrangcon-Davies in *The Lady with a Lamp*. Among the other artists are Auerbach, Coldstream and Hodgkin. R B Kitaj is represented by a number of works including a superb double-portrait of Wilson and his wife, of 1981, entitled 'The Architects'. The collections are particularly strong on drawings – there was a trailer exhibition of Wilson's drawing board at Pallant House in 1997 – and include several preliminary studies for finished works. Any museum would be proud to add this significant group to its permanent collection.

Both Hussey and Kearley bought and sold to the end of their collecting lives, and Colin St John Wilson reminisces in the elegant catalogue of his collection (*The Art of Drawing and Painting*, £9.95) about the compulsion to trade-in pictures for better things. Indeed, what good collection is static? Charles Saatchi is probably the single more important collector in Britain today, exercising a profound (though not necessarily always benign) effect over our younger artists. But he appears to vary his collecting with dealing: by buying in bulk (which many collectors would claim vitiates the particular pleasure of acquisition) and by off-loading in bulk those artists he tires of. This would seem to be taking the responsibility of collecting rather too lightly. It would seem, in fact, to be more about market forces than art. There is doubtless some aspect of power-play in all collecting, but the truly gracious gift of work to the nation – such as Janet de Botton's recent benefaction to the Tate of a quarter of her collection, including Warhols, worth more than £2 million, or indeed Colin St John Wilson's handsome offer – reaffirms that there are still those around who want to share culture, not attempt to direct it.

UPDATE by the Editor, August 2012
In 2008 eighteen paintings, ranging from a Zoffany and an early Gainsborough to works by Monet and Freud, were left to the National Gallery and the Tate by Simon Sainsbury, great-grandson of the

founder of the grocery empire. That same year the dealer Anthony d'Offay handed over almost his entire collection of postwar and contemporary art to the nation, to be managed jointly by the National Galleries of Scotland and the Tate. Of course they came with a price tag, £26.5m, their original cost, but it was philanthropy of a sort as their current value was estimated to be £125m.

The task of keeping collections together and available to the public is not helped by straitened circumstances and the unforeseen consequences of the phrasing of legislation, but while there have been some distressing cases such as that of the Wedgwood Museum, there have been some triumphs. The William Morris Gallery in Walthamstow is back on its feet, and Pallant House goes from strength to strength.

The effect of the Olympics as an absorber of public funds has yet to be quantified, but the demands on the general purse will always be with us, as will the fact that works on loan are no guarantee of an abiding stay. All praise then to those who determine that even a small collection or number of pieces be left to a particular gallery. It helps to tailor your gifts to the intended beneficiary. Contrast the successful 'placing' of £2m worth of work by sculptor Niki de Saint Phalle with Glasgow Museum of Modern Art, a transaction brokered by the Contemporary Art Society on behalf of Eric and Jean Cass, with the still unresolved fate of the Saatchi collection.

FILMS OF ARTISTS Seeing But Not Believing

27 May 2000

How the advance guard becomes accepted and acceptable! With news of fashion-world glossies finally latching onto the glamour potential of young British artists, the Saatchi generation has come of age. Contemporary art is big business, but it's also cool – we'll no doubt be seeing many more advertising hoardings with the now not-so-young stars of BritArt splashed across them, endorsing everything from alcohol to hairspray. Damien, Tracey *et al* are the new establishment, even if they do behave badly. But that's part of it – the myth-making. The public still has a soft spot for the notion of the artist as bohemian, unconventional, immoral, possibly drunken, preferably self-immolating. Even in this age of the artist as professional, when restaurant design and co-ownership can make you a millionaire even if your art doesn't, the public still wants to think of the artist as outsider, as rebel, safely beyond the pale.

Biographies of artists tend to be written for the specialist market, and though general interest in art is increasing all the time, few heavyweight art books make it to the bestseller lists. There is, however, a category of writing which more closely engages the popular imagination, and this is the fictionalisation of an artist's life. Particularly if such novels are later adapted for film, they can do much to direct popular conceptions of artistic behaviour. How many people still think of Kirk Douglas when they summon up an image of Van Gogh? The film in which he starred, Vincente Minnelli's *Lust for Life* (1956), was based on the novel of the same name by Irving Stone; as Carol Reed's 1965 film about Michelangelo (strainingly impersonated by Charlton Heston), *The Agony and the Ecstasy*, was based on another of Stone's books.

In these instances, both novel and film were in the blockbuster class, and suffer the over-simplifications and intense dramatisation of the genre. However, there are subtler examples of the artist-novel; *The Bridge* (1986), Maggie Hemingway's poignant story of Philip Wilson Steer's adultery, *Summer in February* (1995) by Jonathan Smith dealing with the rumbustious early years of Alfred Munnings, and those two brilliant evocations of the artist's life *My Name in Asher Lev* (1972) and its sequel *The Gift of Asher Lev* (1990), by Chaim Potok. But novels about artists deserve an article to themselves. Films which are, even loosely, based on the lives of real artists, can serve to acquaint a wider public with those artists' work, and may indeed encourage some to seek out the original paintings or sculptures. Rarely, however, is the artist's actual work allowed to be used in such a fictionalised portrayal if it is still within the copyright control of the estate. The makers of three very different recent films – *Basquiat* (1996), *Surviving Picasso* (1996) and *Love is the Devil: Study for a Portrait of Francis Bacon* (1998) – were all denied permission to film the original work of the artist in question. Why? Because the estates – those supposed guardians of the dead artist's reputation – evidently considered that only a travesty could result. Unless, of course, greed came into it.

Both *Basquiat* and *Love is the Devil* are shaky when it comes to the art, and purvey deeply compromised and superficial views of their protagonists. I have just watched the video of *Surviving Picasso*, and, while I cannot say I was entirely convinced by it, it did have its moments. Anthony Hopkins is a fine actor, but he is not Picasso, nor anything like. Here he was altogether too puckish to be convincing, showing none of that implied power he so brilliantly evoked as Hannibal Lecter. This was partly the fault of the chirpy dialogue by Ruth Prawer Jhabvala. 'You are now in the labyrinth of the Minotaur,' intones Hopkins to Natascha McElhone, mis-cast as the young Françoise Gilot, soon to become Picasso's lover. 'Aren't you afraid you'll never get out?'

Well, it was funny from time to time, but it certainly wasn't sexy; Picasso must have been sexy, though maybe it all went into his work. (The Surrealist Eileen Agar, who holidayed with Picasso in the 1930s, maintained he was more gallant than flirtatious.) Anyway, there were good supporting roles from Joss Ackland as Matisse and Peter Eyre as Picasso's long-suffering secretary, Sabartes. But what was the point of this Merchant Ivory entertainment, released by Warner Bros? The storyline was intended to be based on Gilot's own book *Life with Picasso* (1964), but she refused to be involved with the project and, with her son Claude Picasso, tried to prevent it being made. The principal source for the film then devolved onto Arianna Stassinopoulos's sentimentalist and much criticised *Picasso: Creator and Destroyer*. The end result is that we have Picasso the ruthless womaniser, surrounded by a few daubs and bits of twisted junk which are supposed to be works of genius.

For it is the art that really lets the film down. John Richardson, the great Picasso authority, quotes one of the film's art department employees responsible for these atrocious daubs as saying: 'Can you imagine a critic in front of these things? He's going to have a nervous breakdown.' Quite. And at the other extreme, anyone unfamiliar with Picasso's work will be given a totally erroneous impression of its quality. This is the trouble with so many art biopics. John Maybury in his Bacon film *Love is the Devil* tried to surmount the issue by recreating the 'action' of Bacon's paintings with all the ready tricks of the pop promo – slow motion, soft focus, distorting mirrors. But that still didn't cope with our desire to see what actually happens on the canvas. And herein lies the irony of all films made about artists: if it's not that interesting to watch paint dry, it's not much more riveting to see it applied. Not unless it's done by Picasso himself, as it was in Henri Clouzot's 1956 documentary *Le Mystère Picasso*. Perhaps the only solution is to work with the artist's estate, and make the official version. Might rule out some of the romance, though.

CURATING AN EXHIBITION Vistas of the Imagination
9 September 2000

Euan Uglow is dead. It has to be said that a light in English painting has gone out. Not everyone, thank God, liked his painting – that would probably indicate ineptitude or worse – but there are few who didn't admire his rigour and dedication, let along the sheer beauty of his work. I find it hard to write about him: I was not a great friend of his, but I loved him. I used to go to his studio once in a while, and shared with him the finest wines I have ever drunk. At the time he reminded me that we probably weren't worthy of drinking them. I wasn't, but I know he was. He was a painter of extraordinary vision, who had the ability to make pictures which reminded people of the beauty of the world. We forget this too much. For some reason we are prepared to deny not only the natural beauty of our planet, but also our responsibility for it. We do worse, and risk destroying it utterly. Euan was prepared to take on the kind of responsibility others shun; indeed, it could be said that he felt it was his duty as part of the notion of public service he held dear. Through his celebration of, for instance, a new skylight in his studio (there is actually a painting called 'Celebration of a New Skylight'), he renewed and rejoiced our visual apprehension of the world. It is a great privilege to have known him, and also to have seen him in action. (By that I don't mean literally putting brush to canvas or board, but just generally being around when a painting was under way.) As Hazlitt said: 'Pictures are scattered like stray gifts through the world; and while they remain, earth has yet a little gilding left, not quite rubbed off, dishonoured, and defaced.'

This lengthy preamble is by way of being an introduction to a small landscape exhibition I have just curated. Euan is one of the 12 artists in it. He is not often thought of as a landscape painter, being better known for his still lifes and nudes, but he occasionally turned his hand to the rendition of countryside, particularly when it was beautiful to him. Why do artists make landscapes? Perhaps it is simply that – a response to a visual stimulus which they respect. I asked George Rowlett, another of the artists in this landscape show, what were his reasons. 'Making a painting in the landscape is the most physically and intellectually direct way I know of engaging with nature, the earth to which we return and from which comes our life, culture and history. In a joyous struggle to unite history with present experience, luck, cunning and courage may combine to make an authentic painting. There is nothing better; it is the equal to love and sex.' Fairly comprehensive, I think you'll admit. Landscape painting is not a category admitted to the modernist canon – the figure is the key component of modern art – yet painters still keep returning to it as a subject. And personally I'm very glad. When I first sat down with Michael and Oya Richardson of the Art Space Gallery in Islington (their premises are on the corner of Noel Road and St. Peter Street), and began to talk about putting a landscape show together, I drew up a preliminary list of 40 artists. And that was only the living. But there had to be some basic guidelines, chief of which was that all should be contemporary artists who made what could be interpreted as landscape pictures. At once, one of my favourite painters, Prunella Clough, was excluded. (Sadly she died on Boxing Day last year.) But the worst part of selecting a mixed show is the exclusions you are forced to make. You can't simply put together a group of friends and acquaintances and hope to have a coherent show. The thing has to have its own internal logic.

With that preliminary list of 40 names I reviewed the situation. The main consideration was one of space. The Art Space Gallery is a building of character, with exhibition rooms on two floors, but it is not vast. Without packing in the pictures from floor to ceiling, it was clear that I could hang only a dozen artists if their paintings were to be allowed sufficient space to breathe. And because some artists paint big pictures, there might be room for only one picture by each artist. So, I needed a minimum of 12 paintings which would work together (there are actually 24 pictures in the show), and 12 artists whose work when hung together would not only make sense, but strike new resonances.

I hit on the idea of subdividing the 12 into four groups of three because one or two obvious groupings emerged at once. Uglow and Rowlett and Anthony Eyton are bound together through ties of teaching and common interest, based around Camberwell School of Art, though their work is sufficiently varied to look well together.

All paint out in the landscape, in front of the motif. Uglow was a cool, architectural painter using very thin paint, Rowlett slathers on the pigment in vibrant heaps, and Eyton practises a very personal and vivid form of impressionism. I wanted to hang Graham Crowley with John Craxton and Julian Perry because both Craxton and Crowley had written about Perry's work, but none had exhibited together before. Would their very different visions (Craxton's Celtic/ Byzantine linearity, Crowley's *grisaille* sociology with stunning colour accents, Perry's masterly evocations of the spirit of the place) sit happily together on the wall, or shriek in discord? Well, I invite you to go and see for yourself, but I'm pretty happy with the result.

Of course, the actual installation of the show was not all plain sailing. You select an exhibition in your imagination, never actually able to see the pictures together until they come to the gallery. There are geographical considerations. I couldn't get to see the latest work of Craxton because he's making it in Crete, but I did manage to visit Karl Weschke down on Cape Cornwall. There are the inevitable compromises. But once everything is delivered to the gallery, then comes the task of making visual sense of the exhibition. However much you may have imagined how things will look together, surprises are in store. I was immeasurably assisted by the expertise of Michael and Oya Richardson, who have been hanging shows in their gallery for 15 years now, so have had a fair bit of practice. Once we had established the first room, with a big landscape by Weschke playing brilliantly against a radiant red hill by Ken Kiff and an exquisitely luminous painting of the surface and depth of water by Ian Welsh, I thought we had cracked it. I was too sanguine.

The remaining three rooms were not nearly so easy to hang, and I was forced to sacrifice my neat groupings into threes (which just goes to show how neatness doesn't always make for coherence). However, the results are, I think, impressive. The show looks good. I cannot forget how superb is the juxtaposition of Adrian Berg's large colour-filled painting of Kew Gardens and Euan's tiny panel of Lake

Lugano. Equally inspiring is the vista through the galleries the other way of another Berg, of Beachy Head, against some of Jeffery Camp's small, odd-shaped vignettes of the same locality. And I am haunted by the sheer painterly gorgeousness of Laetitia Yhap's seascape. I can't help being enthusiastic: these pictures and these artists look well together. I wish Euan hadn't died, but he said he'd had a good life, and at least he's survived by his art.

VALENCIA Valencian virtues

25 May 2002

Valencia is Spain's third city (after Madrid and Barcelona), but has as yet been mercifully overlooked by tourists, though recent travel articles extolling its party-style night-life may be set to change that. Certainly it is not an obvious destination for art lovers, yet it has a very decent fine arts museum (with memorable things by El Greco as well as Goya and Velasquez), a bizarre ceramics collection with one of the wildest facades in museum history, and a currently evolving but already dramatic 'City of Arts and Sciences' designed by local boy Santiago Calatrava, which when complete will comprise an arts complex with planetarium, interactive science museum and oceanographic park.

When I visited in late April, the temperature was soaring and the jacaranda trees were flowering in the streets, sending wafts of fragrance over the passing pedestrians. Valencia is the capital of the Levante (the land of the rising sun), that region between Catalonia in the north and Andalucía in the south, and traditionally the garden of Spain. It is the birthplace of paella (the special rice for the dish is grown locally) and famed for its oranges. Some claim it as the pyrotechnic capital of the world, and it's renowned for its spring festivals. The Holy Grail is kept in the cathedral, which has an alabaster-glazed lantern. The city also has IVAM (correctly pronounced 'ee-bam'), the Valencian Institute of Modern Art, an attractive modern museum purpose-built to showcase its noteworthy permanent collection, and to mount temporary exhibitions.

The permanent collection includes an immensely distinguished body of work by Julio Gonzalez, the great sculptor who taught Picasso so much about working in three-dimensions. Although Gonzalez does not hail from Valencia, a previous director of IVAM was far-sighted enough to buy his work and encourage donations, and the museum now houses the largest concentration of his sculpture and drawings in the world. His brilliantly witty cut metal masks are displayed in IVAM's beautiful spaces to great effect. To complement this strength is a good collection of modern art, including a strange Delaunay relief made from casein, cork and sand, a fine Helion from 1933, a couple of Schwitters reliefs and a Cornell box, and a mass of lesser-known works grouped inevitably around the highpoints of such Spanish masters as Saura, Tapies, Millares and Chillida. There are a couple of very colourful early Ad Reinhardts and a large resin floor piece of axes and chopped logs by Tony Cragg called 'Clearing'.

Another gallery is devoted to the Valencian Impressionist Ignacio Pinazo, a sort of Spanish Jeffery Camp in his exuberantly tender dabbing on small panels; wonderfully informal and immediate. Of the temporary exhibition spaces, there is an annexe a short walk away called the Centre del Carme, a building of considerable historical interest dating back to the 13th century, once a religious foundation, and consisting of courtyards and cloisters and cool white high-ceilinged rooms. The current exhibition there, until 30 May, is a vast survey of the recent paintings and sculptures of Markus Lupertz, one of the generation of German neo-expressionists which includes Baselitz and Penck. Sadly, this will be the last exhibition organized by IVAM in these elegant surroundings, as the galleries are being reclaimed by the Museum of the 19th Century, which is concurrently showing works in the other half of the building from the Sorolla Museum in Madrid; Joaquin Sorolla being the other Valencian Impressionist of note beside Pinazo.

Back in the main IVAM building on Calle Guillem de Castro is a splendid sculpture hall on the ground floor for temporary displays, hosting during my visit a show of architectonic plinth-like pieces by the American Tony Smith (1912-80). But upstairs is the *piece de resistance* and principal reason for my visit, the newly-remodelled top-lit galleries in which is hanging an impressive Ben Nicholson exhibition until 7 July. Curated by Nicholson expert Jeremy Lewison, the show spans the entirety of the artist's career in a display of some 60 pieces, chosen with care and intelligence to illustrate the artist's trajectory from traditional still-life painter to abstract master. Not that Nicholson was ever entirely abstract as this exhibition demonstrates - he was too interested in still-life and landscape, carrying with him a much-loved collection of vessels and utensils he continued to draw and paint, and the memories of many different landscapes from Cornwall to Switzerland.

Nicholson's earliest works on view are talented exercises in the manner of his father, Sir William, although one of the paintings - 'Blue Bowl in Shadow' of 1919 – seems to have lost all the sparkle I remember and to be on the point of vanishing altogether into the shadows. The next ten years or so see him working through the various 'isms' until he found his own voice in the relief paintings of the early 1930s. Some of his experiments were more European than others, as he explored cubism and even - tentatively - surrealism (which explains why 'Painting' of 1932 is so curiously unresolved), while others, like the gorgeous little landscape of Dymchurch done while staying with Paul Nash, are essentially English in character. But Nicholson was soon homing in on the square (or rectangle) and the circle, making himself master of the incised line and the well-orchestrated texture, and mingling drawing and painting to make his very distinctive landscape/still-lifes. This beautifully selected and installed exhibition, which draws authoritatively on so many public and private collections, looks superb in IVAM's lovely light-filled spaces and reminds us how truly international Nicholson's mature art is. It seems incredible that despite being heavily promoted by the British Council during his lifetime, and represented in collections nearly everywhere else as a consequence, Nicholson remains unrepresented in a single French or Spanish museum. Jeremy Lewison tells us this (and a great deal more about the somewhat puritanical Nicholson) in the handsome hard-back dual-text publication which accompanies the exhibition. Perhaps IVAM's show will change that. I can think of no more fitting sequel than the acquisition for Valencia of a quintessential Ben Nicholson to enhance IVAM's permanent collection. Any donors forthcoming?

ON ART SCHOOLS Quick-fix solutions
24 May 2003

Here's a random sample of my postbag: an invitation to a mixed exhibition of nine artists' interpretation of 'focus' through painting, photography, digitisation and computer manipulation; notice of a show of photo-text, photo-document and photo-juxtaposition-cum-montage pieces about HIV and place; and the press release for an installation of scarlet mobility scooters which is supposed to be 'a reflection on age, youth and contemporary Britain'.

Clearly Britain is in a bad way. A watered-down conceptual art is the current orthodoxy. Much of what looked new and radical when it first emerged in the 1960s is now being run past us again, and it's limping badly. And so much of it is the same. It really looks as if art students were issued with a pattern book of how to come up with a show – six ideas on the back of an envelope: good tried-and-tested old concepts that won't cause anyone too much trouble. How has this come to pass? The decline of one of our greatest glories

– the art schools – has much to answer for. The artist Ian Welsh (born 1944) is ideally situated to comment on the situation. Besides making his own work (Welsh is a distinguished painter specialising in the depiction of water and reflections), he taught for 25 years in the public and private sectors because he believes that art schools can offer a unique education. He himself studied painting at Chelsea School of Art (1963-66), when it was in its heyday under the enlightened direction of the painter and art historian Lawrence Gowing. He then studied sculpture as a postgrad with George Fullard (1966-67) after which he began to teach himself. He returned to Chelsea to do an MA in printmaking in 1976 and was finally appointed head of printmaking there in 1992. He gave up teaching in 1993, utterly disillusioned with the way art schools were now administered and structured.

So what has changed so much? The pressure is on the student to be instantly fully formed, successful and original, because the art school has to be seen to perform in order to justify its existence. This kind of context is inimical to the slow but steady development of talent and understanding which art schools are supposed to nurture – that particular combination of thinking and acquired skills which needs time to mature.

'All this really started when art schools were swallowed by polytechnics, which began in the 1970s,' says Welsh. 'The emphasis changed then. The idea that courses had to have results at every stage was introduced. Coupled with the ever increasing concerns about finance within higher education, the very thing I fell in love with when I went to Chelsea, and which made me want to teach as well as be an artist, was undermined. And that was people truly finding out who they were through the process of working and acquiring knowledge and skills, and putting those things together to stumble their way through to making something that they could recognise as their work. 'Nowadays, art schools have less and less space, less and less teaching, fewer and fewer craft skills available, because they're expensive both in space and time and staffing. How do you, as a department or college, maintain the output? By encouraging conceptual work, which is a way of coming up with the goods which doesn't require the space, the money, the materials or the range of workshops. But you have to abandon a lot of the things which are fundamental to the process of making work and replace them by a series of dogma and quick-fix skills.

'Anybody can pick up a video camera and it doesn't matter if it's shaky or lit properly or audible because that's part of what it's supposed to look like as "an art video". Most of it doesn't carry any meaning except that it looks vaguely contemporary. I don't have a problem about what people use to make their work, but it has to be thought through properly and it has to have the appropriate skills to make it work. I suspect that all this has been short-circuited. And I still don't think that such a large percentage of young people are naturally drawn to conceptual work, but it's virtually the only thing they can do with the system.'

Welsh recalls a very different situation 35 years ago. 'When I first started teaching there were about 20 kids on the Foundation course at Harlow, and there was a very good chance that three of those would be fine artists and the rest designers of one sort or another. At that time there were something like 28 disciplines in design you could do a degree in – there was Foundation Design, for instance, which was for undergarments, corsetry and so on. Later, when I was at Norwich Art School running the Foundation course, the then shadow minister for the arts came to talk to the senior staff of the Art School and the University Art History Department. He looked around at us and said, "The trouble with you lot is that you all live in ivory towers." Where do you go after that?

'The sad thing is that he missed the point. In the mid-Seventies, when the British car industry was disappearing fast down the plughole, there were something like 200 senior design posts in the car industry throughout Europe. Of those 200 key people, 180 had been through the Royal College of Art – which has a very fine course in automotive design – but they were working in Europe and not the UK. The government was looking at art schools and thinking they were full of painters – people who sit around smoking dope waiting for inspiration – whereas 75 per cent were design students, like the graduates in furniture who went to Milan. The quality of British art schools has been completely missed by those in positions of real authority. 'The moment that institutions of higher education had to become businesses it was the death-knell of education. It's a contradiction in terms. And that's from somebody who actually ran a little independent art school as a business.' Welsh ran his own private art school from 1986 to 1989, the Mill House Atelier, in the Suffolk village of Weybread. 'We set it up as a way of surviving, not as a flourishing business. What we did was to allow people time and space with as much skill-help as possible to make work that was to do with them, whether they were housewives who wanted to paint the landscape or people who wanted art as a career.'

Unless there is a full-scale revolution in the funding of higher education, which seems unlikely, hope for the future probably lies with these private art schools – if you can still find the people to run them.

UPDATE by the Editor, August 2012

Speaking to Ian Welsh for an update on this piece, it seems he detects something of a sea change over the past ten years. Based on his experiences with graduates from London colleges, he thinks that art schools in general are re-developing and cultivating their own personalities once again, and this is leading to a much broader, and more interesting and understandable, mix of work. There is one noticeable exception, Central St. Martins, where good work seems to result from students influencing each other rather than from any real teaching. Apart from raising the question as to what students are actually getting for the hefty fees they are paying, Welsh observes "If you're not in an environment that allows talent to float to the top, it happens less readily." If CSM is stuck within the confines of its own image and brand, then others such as Chelsea and Wimbledon, are moving with the times. Wimbledon for instance now runs a well-structured and focused MA in Drawing.

Last word perhaps to the students themselves, in their own inimitable style. On the one hand: "At CSM the chances are you'll get lost in the masses and from what I've been told there ain't a lot of tutor/pupil teaching going on so you'll be pretty much on your own". And on the other: "You dont want or need tutors breathing down your neck the hole time... St. Martins give you this freedom with exceptional support when you need it at one of the most predigious art courses in europe."

ARTISTS AT WORK Getting to know them

21 May 2005

I had intended to devote this article to the subject of artists on film and in particular to a newish archive, the Artists on Film Trust, which was founded seven years ago by Hannah Rothschild and Robert McNab, and affiliated this February to the newly created University of the Arts, London. Under this inelegant umbrella (it used to be The London Institute) are huddled most of the capital's art schools – Camberwell, Central St Martins, Chelsea and the London College of Communication (formerly the London College of Printing) – because university status is an essential means of self-protection and funding in an increasingly aggressive commercial world. Likewise for the Artists on Film Trust: partnership with a museum would not safeguard its future – education is the way to survive. The first national collection of film dealing exclusively with artists – primarily at work and in conversation – now has its headquarters on Millbank, the new campus of Chelsea College of Art and Design, handily situated next to Tate Britain. Both Rothschild and McNab are steeped in arts broadcasting. Rothschild made the highly acclaimed 2001 *Omnibus* film on Frank Auerbach, working with the artist's son Jake, and McNab began his 25 years in the business as an assistant to Kenneth Clark. Their plan is to bring together all the recorded film of artists, which is currently dispersed through the archives and libraries of the world, and make it accessible to students and the general public. This process will take time, and not just in terms of transferring material to a digital format ready to be accessed. Although it's at a turning point in its development, the Trust will need the best part of a decade to become fully operational. McNab estimates that within a year 100 hours of material will become available for viewing, but stresses that public accessibility is currently restricted.

So perhaps it's not yet the moment to be writing glowingly of this new resource, when it is still something of a twinkle in its organisers' eyes. I will return to the subject when readers can visit the Trust and view footage of Degas or Renoir, Monet or Stanley Spencer. In the meantime, the work continues off-site as it were, with a worldwide series of lectures and symposia to focus on and complement the collections. McNab describes the Trust's activities as 'a mixture of a roadshow, a plan and an installation', with the roadshow so far visiting such varied venues as Hay-on-Wye, the Getty in Los Angeles and the Courtauld Institute. This spring, a series of films and lectures under the Trust's aegis took place at the Prince's Drawing School in Shoreditch, on such subjects as Duchamp, John Virtue, Marc Quinn and Avigdor Arikha.

There is often strong magic in the footage of artists at work. The film of Jackson Pollock dripping paint in arabesques of great beauty is a far cry from that arch performer Picasso, half-stripped for the camera and doing the painter's version of card tricks, but both are revealing. Unsurprisingly, not all artists are keen to be filmed. Some, like Craigie Aitchison, are allergic to cameras. He hid behind dark glasses throughout the shooting of the Arts Council documentary on his work, pretending they helped him to 'see the colours better'. In Jake Auerbach's recent film *Lucian Freud: Portraits* (available on DVD from the National Portrait Gallery bookshop), the artist only appears on screen in photographs or self-portraits, until the closing sequence when he stalks across the studio set like a man exiting, not entering a room. But then Freud has cultivated enigma for years, directing the limelight to his activities – or withholding it – with the hand of a master. In a way, it's surprising that he permitted this film to be made at all.

For it's the kind of documentary which goes behind the scenes in just the way one imagines that Freud dislikes most – interviewing those intimate with him about the experience of sitting for their portraits. The film begins with the writer Francis Wyndham, who sat two or three times a week for a year and described the process as 'not tiring – all you have to do is be there'. Others, including various daughters, had different experiences to recount. Ex-lovers were also interviewed. The most harrowing testimony came from the painter Celia Paul, who seemed flayed by events and ruefully characterised the experience as being about 'power and desire'. Best value were the Duke and Duchess of Devonshire. She described Freud as 'a will-o'-the-wisp', while he, referring to the artist's 'misogynous' portraits of women in contrast to his rather 'conventional' depictions of dogs and horses, concluded, 'I'm not sure how much he loves women.' After he'd finished speaking, the camera lingered uncomfortably just that moment too long, which gave an unexpected weight to this opinion.

If there weren't any scandalous revelations, there were plenty of insights into Freud's intensive studio practice – painting long hours by day and by night – and lots of pictures to compare with the sitters. Not so much a 'portrait of the artist' though there were stray comments about his driving, his gambling and his charisma, but then it should be the art that counts. Public curiosity about the personalities of artists is best titillated rather than satisfied: it helps to keep up interest in the work.

One artist whose myth has in recent years tended to outstrip knowledge of her paintings is Frida Kahlo. The Tate is poised to remedy that by mounting a substantial show of her work, opening on 9 June. Consider that date for a moment. Glorious June (well, we can hope) means it's time for that old gladiator the Royal Academy *Summer Exhibition* to enter the fray once more. That opens on 7 June. On 8 June, the V&A unveils an interesting exhibition entitled *70 Years of Penguin Design*. Less than a fortnight previously, on 26 May, three major shows open: Reynolds at the Tate, *Colour after Klein* at the Barbican and Rebecca Horn at the Hayward. Is a pattern starting to emerge? Yes. Exhibitions are now like buses: they all come at once. It's bad enough that there should be so many shows competing for public attention (of course, in one way it's very welcome, though many of them are simply designed as museum revenue-raisers, and are often of very dubious academic or aesthetic value), but that they should all open at the same time is totally ridiculous. It means there's either a glut to review or a drought. Why don't museums and galleries get together and plan things better? Or are they all trying to cut each other out? Sometimes it feels just like that.

CHARLIE MILLAR Meditation for Lent
4 March 2006

For Lent, the artist Charlie Millar (born 1965) has installed a pavement of 308 resin casts, like transparent bricks, arranged in a rectangle on the floor of the Eastern Crypt of Canterbury Cathedral. Millar casts these bricks himself, embedding within them an eclectic mix of objects. Each in itself is an individual work of art, but combined they make an image-rich meditation for Lent, a series of tableaux which are infinitely suggestive, and throw the viewer back upon his or her own resources and responses, in a quest for meaning. By focusing upon the detail of such unconsidered trifles as riverbed detritus, builders' rubble or ordinary dust, Millar opens the way for speculation of a larger, more spiritual order. The Dean of Canterbury and all those responsible for this original and rewarding commission are to be highly praised for the initiative.

A good place for a pilgrimage, Canterbury. But Chaucer's pilgrims set out from Southwark's Tabard Inn in April 'when the sweet showers fall', not in the last wintry days of February when I wended my way to London Bridge. Thence by train through the desolate suburbs of south east London, out past the dormitories of Orpington and Sevenoaks, through the pillared Martian emptiness of Ashford so-called International, to the unmanned halt at Canterbury West. By foot from there, on the approach to West Gate and then into the rather tawdry pedestrianised shopping precinct that was once a main street. The cathedral is at no point visible above or beside the enclosing shops and offices. Then you glimpse it down a side street, turn in through Christ Church Gate (where you will be asked for an admission fee) and confront the building – large, but by no means at once awe-inspiring.

The first church was established here by St Augustine in 597. It was rebuilt in the 1070s by Archbishop Lanfranc, a century before the place really got famous when Thomas Becket was murdered in the Cathedral in 1170. Over the next ten or 15 years the Quire was rebuilt, and the Eastern Crypt – our destination today – added. The soaring spiritual genius of the building itself, captured so memorably in the closing sequences of Powell and Pressburger's poignant film *A Canterbury Tale* (1944), is not our immediate concern, though its encompassing identity establishes the context for Millar's installation. Down the steps, therefore, to the Crypt, a still place, the perfect setting for a work of art which seeks to rouse, as the artist says, 'the individual visitor's highly tuned and unique sense of nostalgia, memory and encounter'. Here let me quote from that remarkable novel *Shamrock Tea* by Ciaran Carson:

> In the *Confessions*, Augustine speaks with awe of the vast cloisters of his memory, which is an immeasurable sanctuary for countless images of all kinds. Perplexed by time – since the present has no duration and past and future do not exist – he concludes that the measure of time must be memory; hence a long past is a long remembrance of the past.

Of course, it is a different Augustine from the founder of Canterbury Cathedral, but the sentiment holds true nevertheless. And 'an immeasurable sanctuary for countless images of all kinds' is the perfect description of Millar's installation. There are those among us who will claim that loss of contact with our past is precisely the cause of our decay as a civilisation. Certainly, a general and particular knowledge of the past can lead to greater understanding of any current predicament, and our individual and collective identity can only be augmented by this kind of awareness. Yet many shun it in a misguided attempt to recreate themselves, in a self-vanquishing urge to be 'of the moment'. Millar's art deals with the resources of the past (one friend described his objects as full of 'longing'), and re-presents them for our enlightenment. His collection of occupied resin casts is somewhere between a cabinet of curiosities and a box of delights – where museum meets magic.

Charlie Millar is a painter of innovative abstract images which relate closely to music and architecture, a skilled topographical watercolourist and a maker of objects. His work with resin casts finds the artist in his role as collector and curator. Objects he has found on his travels and brought back, imagery from his paintings and photographs, specimens from the natural world – the man-made mingles with the organic in these bricks. Each block of resin contains souvenirs of Millar's past, reinterpreted and recomposed, and structured in terms of line and form and colour in much the same way as a painting is made. This particular grouping for

Canterbury, which was made specifically for the site in the Eastern Crypt, is designed to have as much contrast between the blocks as possible, to show up in a variegated, tessellated pattern a taste of the visual richness of the world we inhabit all but briefly.

Millar is no stranger to this medium: he made 1,000 smaller blocks before the Canterbury commission, and became adept at the gradual setting of objects in this kind of resinous aspic. As I wrote in 2004, they are like the 'cobbles or setts from a vast pavement that, being unattached and discrete, can be reconfigured in innumerable ways'. I also likened them to freeze-frames and memory cells, densely packed with information and resonance. Associations should spark and develop in the mind of the beholder as the viewer's own experience of life is brought to bear on these carefully selected aspects of existence.

London is Millar's home and where he works, so much of the raw material incorporated in these setts is of London origin. He keeps bees in the gardens of Lambeth Palace (there are traces of honeycomb in some of the images) and goes mudlarking by the Thames. (Peach stones and bones are part of the river's contribution.) The gardeners at Lambeth Palace entered into the spirit of the exercise and donated fragments of stained glass and an old clay pipe bowl dug up in the flowerbeds. Blossoms and other organic material were also gathered there.

The process of assembling these setts is one of collaging, the juxtaposition of previously unrelated objects arranged in layers in a much more interesting three-dimensional way than is usually achieved with flat collages. Printed papers, layers of salt or grain, grass seed or petals coincide with a clinical thermometer, lengths of thorny stems, small metal boxes or cotton reels that look like baby parsnips. A dragonfly larva makes a guest appearance, as does a graphite-coated wooden spoon. Crucifix-sized nails in a bunch, an INRI cartouche, palm crosses – the imagery makes specific references, and indeed began with the Parable of the Sower. In one block, an Apostle spoon cradles a medicine capsule. But Millar deliberately opened out the frame, and a silvered oak leaf and a phial of honey suggest a 'pagan' presence as well. Even popcorn makes an unblushing entrance. The banal rubs shoulders with the exotic. A weaver's house in Mali is wound round with cotton in horizontal bands; a photo of this is juxtaposed with an orchid bloom. A vast array of objects is brought together in stillness and transformed into art, as the dried crocus bulb bursts forth into new life. Take my advice and hasten away, on Lenten pilgrimage, to Canterbury.

Charlie Millar: *All Flesh in Grass* is in the Eastern Crypt, Canterbury Cathedral

PUBLIC CATALOGUE FOUNDATION A Pevsner for paintings
23 June 2007

There is a remarkable project of great enterprise and diligence in progress throughout the land - a plan to catalogue all the oil paintings (as well as those in acrylic or tempera) in national collections. This gigantic task is being undertaken by a charity called The Public Catalogue Foundation, which is publishing its findings in single volumes dedicated to different areas of the UK. The aim is to give a county-by-county account of pictures in museums and other public collections. As I write, I have in front of me five of the Foundation's catalogues: 'West Yorkshire: Leeds', 'Cambridgeshire: Fitzwilliam Museum', 'East Sussex', 'North Yorkshire' and 'Imperial War Museum'. Obviously some places are more dense with pictures than others, particularly a metropolitan centre like London. So far, the Foundation has only published 'The Slade and UCL' and the 'Imperial War Museum' catalogues to represent the capital's rich and varied collections, though more volumes are forthcoming.

Meanwhile, zealous researchers tally and tabulate among the dusty inventories of provincial institutions, recording their findings in this beautifully-produced series of books.

Museums - particularly in these cash-strapped times, when the meagre elegant hang is favoured over the full-bodied floor-to-ceiling display - actually put on show at any one time a tiny percentage of their holdings. Members of the public can sometimes gain access to particular pictures in store, if they make an appointment sufficiently in advance, but until now it has not been possible to browse these hidden collections. The PCL's affordable catalogues, with images printed in colour, nine to the page, offer something which is more than a thumbnail illustration, and they demonstrate the full range of a museum's holdings. Occasionally, forgotten collections come to light. Thus the unknown Roebuck Collection (in the North Yorkshire volume), which contains a modest but interesting sampling of Modern British (amongst other things), emerges from the gloom. Representing the taste of 'quite a playboy' (in Mr Roebuck's own words), the collection was left on his death in 1988 to the town of Skipton and is now in the process of being transferred to Craven Museum and Gallery.

Leafing through that North Yorkshire volume, the Harrogate Museum, famous for its Friths, strikes the eye with a strange early Bomberg, a lovely Robert Medley and a couple of dark Christopher Wood landscapes. In Scarborough are five John Armstrongs, donated by Tom Laughton, hotelier brother of actor Charles. The National Railway Museum in York is distinguished by the hyper-realist train paintings of Cuthbert Ellis (1909-87), while at the University are three early John Hoyland landscapes, rare figurative works from this passionate abstractionist. York Museum, in case you'd forgotten, has a seemingly endless array of Ettys, yet there's also a tough portrait of Sir Herbert Read, apostle of Modernism, by Bryan Kneale, better-known these days as a sculptor. This mixture of old and new, expected and unexpected is typical of these catalogues, and one of their principal charms. These are essentially picture-books, with perhaps a short text about the history of a museum, particularly if a whole volume is devoted to one institution, as in the case of the Fitzwilliam, which has a brief introduction by Duncan Robinson. Here's a volume to linger over. There are so many scribbled notes on my bookmark it's difficult to know what to mention first. I'm always happy to encounter old friends in new contexts, so to find a striking portrait by Yolanda Sonnabend, one of our foremost stage designers, was as pleasant a surprise as the discovery of a Karl Weschke landscape also in this eclectic accumulation. I mustn't however give the impression that our museums are stuffed to the gunnels with British art only, when continental delights are also thick on the reserve racks. The Fitzwilliam is a case in point, with excellent things by Seurat and Vuillard, Degas and Cézanne, Matisse, Renoir and a couple of oddly effective stylised still-lifes by Picasso. Not forgetting Rubens and the simply magnificent pair of panels by one of my favourite artists of the Italian Renaissance, Domenico Veneziano.

The latest volume details the collection of the Imperial War Museum, with its compelling mixture of imaginative art and straight recording. Here are the high art achievements of Paul and John Nash, for instance, side by side with the accurate documentation of Leslie Cole, Philip Connard, Charles Cundall and Charles Pears. This is a book for all libraries, public and private, a reminder of man's modern inhumanity to man, with a roll call of great names, some of them, like Albert Richards and Isaac Rosenberg, lost on active duty. (The only limitation of these catalogues immediately apparent is the fact that they only deal with oil paintings, and thus a great war artist like Eric Ravilious, who worked exclusively in watercolour, is excluded and could possibly be overlooked by anyone who considered this book to be exhaustive.) A particular pleasure is discovering new things: Dick Lee's series of 'Catch 22' paintings, the sculptor Frank Dobson's luscious oil 'The Balloon Apron', Julian Trevelyan's fearsome 'Premonitions of the Blitz'. This is a book to return to. The first PCF catalogue I saw was the Leeds volume back in 2004. Since then they've been appearing thick and fast, and there are now a dozen available in hardback (£35) or paperback (£20). (You can order them direct with an additional £5 postage per volume on 0870 1283566.) The project is financed by private and public funding, and catalogue proceeds will be held in trust for future use in the restoration and conservation of paintings. The Foundation's slogan is 'Discover the Paintings You Own'. Through its industry and initiative, we are beginning to get an idea of just what treasures lie (often) hidden in our museums. The extent of this heritage is both exciting and heart-warming. The PCF aims to create a 'Pevsner for Paintings', revealing the previously unsuspected wealth of pictures in public ownership, and making them available - at least in reproduction, and eventually on the Internet - to art lovers everywhere.

UPDATE by the Editor, August 2012

The PCF tally now stands at 38 volumes with over 1600 collections having been catalogued and photographed. Edinburgh 1, the first of three planned for the city, and The Arts Council Collection are the latest to be completed. The good news is that the collections are now available online, 'Your Paintings' is a joint venture with the BBC (www.bbc.co.uk/arts/yourpaintings). As I write there are 145,613 paintings which can be searched, either by collection, artist or subject matter, with a target of 200,000 by the end of 2012. The PCF's own lively website www.thepcf.org.uk puts the spotlight on different collections each month, as well as having changing artists and paintings 'in focus'. The benefits for participating collections of this imaginative project are manifold, the benefits to the public incalculable. And they are still only on the oil paintings...

CHARLES MAHONEY A well-kept secret

27 October 2007

One of the great things about having an area of specialism is the discovery of a new aspect to it. Since my teens, I have developed a particular interest in 20th century British art, encouraged initially by a brilliant art teacher and by the writings of Sir John Rothenstein, quondam director of the Tate Gallery. Well, it's a big area to cover, so for me new things are emerging all the time as my knowledge extends and my tastes change and develop. Charles Mahoney (1903-68) is one of those artists who had somehow slipped through the net of connections and cross-references I have gradually built up over 30 years of reading and research. Looking back, I realize I had come across his name from time to time but without the artist coming into focus. And this was principally because I hadn't seen his work anywhere.

It's impossible to see all the exhibitions that are on in London (never mind the provinces) at any one time, and write articles and books as well. So I had managed to miss the Charles Mahoney exhibition staged by the enterprising dealer Paul Liss at the Fine Art Society in 2000. (In these infuriating days of postal strikes I am still awaiting the delivery of the catalogue from that show, which is the principal source of information about Mahoney.) What really alerted me to his presence was a not very good book about the artist Evelyn Dunbar (1906-60), best-known now as an official war artist, who'd been a close friend and colleague of Mahoney, and with whom she'd written and illustrated the delightful volume *Gardeners' Choice*, published by Routledge in 1937.

From being an unknown quantity, Mahoney suddenly began to register as an artist and assert his continuing existence through his drawings and paintings. First I began to see reproductions of his work in catalogues, then the real thing at an art fair. I rather liked what I saw: a precise and quirky delineation of the real world (Mahoney was not only a passionate gardener but also a knowledgeable botanist), and a quiet but compelling way of looking at things. I heard stories about him - how his baptismal name was Cyril, but the irrepressible Barnett Freedman (1901-58), a fellow-student at the Royal College, re-christened him Charlie and the name stuck; how he had lost his teaching job at the Royal College of Art because he insisted on giving the then impoverished student John Bratby extra supplies of paint; how he was himself a perfectionist who often found it difficult to complete his work. And that he had painted the finest cycle of mural paintings in England since Stanley Spencer's Burghclere masterpiece.

Really? I hear the gentle reader murmur. Then why has no one heard of them? As Sir John Rothenstein wrote in his 1975 tribute, Mahoney is perhaps best remembered as a teacher because one of his most ambitious works was destroyed by bombing during the war, and the other was left incomplete. The first was a mural for Morley College in London, lost to enemy action at the same time as adjacent murals by Eric Ravilious and Edward Bawden. The second is a mural cycle for the Lady Chapel of Campion Hall, the Jesuit College in Oxford. It was this unfinished group of paintings that had earnt such high praise and yet was so little known. My curiosity aroused I contacted Campion Hall and made an appointment to visit.

The comparison with Stanley Spencer's masterly murals at Burghclere, near Newbury, is not a helpful one. I had been down to visit them in August and been deeply impressed by the breadth and invention of their imagery. Spencer was a very odd man but he was a remarkable painter, and his powers of pictorial organization are breath-taking. The Oratory of All Souls (the Sandham Memorial Chapel) is now administered by the National Trust and contains an intense cycle of paintings which flood the walls with movement; not only a movement of the senses, but also of the spirit. Here humanity is depicted with singular generosity: the subject is the

First World War, and Spencer conceived the design of the murals while on active service. He managed to marry ordinary everyday activities like scrubbing the floor and sorting the laundry with war-specific events like the arrival of a convoy of the wounded or 'Stand-to' in a dug-out on the Salonika front. The end wall of this surprisingly small building (though it has height) is dominated by a great Resurrection of the Soldiers. Other subjects include a marvellous 'Reveille' full of mosquito nets and 'Tea in the Hospital Ward' which features one of Spencer's most favourite things: bread and jam.

Spencer's achievement at Burghclere is stupendous. The ordinary becomes sacramental and the resurrection is presented as a natural part of life's pattern. The painting is of the highest quality, in terms of conveying a story (or series of events) in the most effective and economical way, and as a decorative scheme with a distinctive emotional and spiritual resonance. It is a mural cycle of great power, and there is nothing like it in England. When the Master of Campion Hall, Father Martin D'Arcy, decided in 1939 that his Lady Chapel should be decorated with murals, it's hardly surprising that Stanley Spencer should be proposed for the job. Spencer visited the Hall and stayed for a month, but refused to submit cartoons for his proposal. This was deemed a serious drawback with the somewhat unpredictable Spencer, and the matter was let drop.

Two years later, John Rothenstein suggested that Charles Mahoney be approached, and in December 1941 he accepted the commission. Mahoney was a meticulous craftsman, making many preliminary drawings for his paintings on the life of the Virgin, most of which were destroyed in the act of tracing them onto the plastered walls of the chapel. For Mahoney had decided to paint directly onto the walls in the approved Italian manner, undeterred by the dampness of our climate. (Spencer, for instance, had painted on canvas which was later affixed to the walls at Burghclere.) Mahoney also made a number of colour studies for his compositions. He worked slowly, only painting in the long summer vacation and part of the Easter holiday (when he was not teaching), and insisting on natural light. He continued thus for 10 years, his last regular summer session being in 1952.

Then something went wrong. Apparently Mahoney didn't feel that his efforts were sufficiently appreciated, the funding ran out and work ceased. Although he visited the chapel again about a year before he died, he was too ill to do more than a little re-touching. As a result, a panel to the left of the Sacristy door and two other panels, on either side of the altar, are unfinished. Drawn in grey underpaint, they look surprisingly graceful: spiritual and unaffected, they do not detract from the completed murals. From a technical point-of-view it's interesting to see how he constructed his images, and the lack of colour does not impede response. In fact, the grisaille effect is not inappropriate for the subject of 'The Dormition', which depicts Mary's death.

Campion Hall was designed and built by Lutyens. The chapel proper contains a marvellous wooden baldacchino and Stations of the Cross by Frank Brangwyn lithographed onto sycamore panels, and the prevalence of wood continues into the Lady Chapel. Mahoney's paintings had to compete with the Sacristy door, and he was ingenious in his solution to this problem. He painted the Flight into Egypt above the door (Rothenstein relates that he spent two weekends drawing a donkey borrowed specially) and framed the scene with a big spreading oak tree which also cleverly encompasses the door beneath it. This theme is continued in the scene depicting the Coming of the Shepherds, who find the Baby Jesus in the open air embowered by trees rather than in a stable, and given another twist in the Betrothal, where two male figures are seen breaking branches over their knees. The paintings develop a magnificent interplay between red and blue and derive a great deal of their effectiveness from the exquisite patterning of fabrics and garments and the detailing of flowers and plants. Mahoney the botanist comes into his own here, illustrating his belief that the flowers and trees were as important in the great scheme of things as the figures. His designs have a classical dignity enhanced by the beauties of the natural world - the springing vines and ivy, the hyacinths, primroses, poppies, the lily and the Christmas rose. Our Lady of Mercy is shown with the most wonderful array of roses and an affectionate frieze of cherubs. 'God is in the details', as another architect, Mies van der Rohe, said.

Charles Mahoney's murals were never officially unveiled or publicly launched simply because they were never finished. They've remained something of a well-kept secret ever since. Although not open to the general public, they can be seen by appointment, and well repay a visit.

EILEEN AGAR Independent spirit

25 October 2008

It's possible that my life would have been quite different if I hadn't met the literary agent Jacintha Alexander at a party in 1985. At the time I was an impoverished researcher and aspirant writer, with a specialism in 20th century British art. As we chatted of this and that, it emerged that Jacintha had a project that might interest me – working on the memoirs of an artist who'd already written quite a substantial text but needed help to prepare her book for publication. The artist in question was the distinguished surrealist Eileen Agar, and I jumped at the suggestion that I might work with her.

I remember our first meeting, at a group exhibition of English surrealists. Eileen was tiny but immensely chic, wearing black and white and red, with a beret and dark glasses. She was imperious and carried a stick. Desmond Morris, himself a surrealist painter as well as a popular behaviourist, came and stood over her in his white raincoat in a wonderful display of body language that (on another occasion) I'd have loved to have heard him analyse. Nothing daunted, Eileen held her ground and soon escaped. She showed me examples of her work on the gallery walls and we agreed to meet at her flat and discuss further the idea of working together on her book. I duly presented myself at her eyrie in Melbury Road, Kensington. Eileen had already written a lengthy tribute to her late husband, the Hungarian man of letters Joseph Bard, but the various publishers who'd been shown the typescript all made the same response. They wanted to know more about Eileen and less about Joseph. One famous editor asked specifically for details of her sex life. It became clear that she wasn't averse to writing about herself (indeed was rather gratified that people should want to know), it was simply that unaided the task seemed rather daunting.

So this was my role: to act as catalyst in the creation of Eileen Agar's autobiography; not to be a ghost writer, but a collaborator who would ask the right questions to set Eileen recalling her past. I interviewed her on tape and transcribed the results, I encouraged her to write short sections of text and I wrote some myself in her style. These various components I then attempted to weave together into a seamless narrative of her life. And what a life it had been. Born into a wealthy English family in Argentina, she had not only decided to be an artist (very unsuitable) but had then run off to marry a fellow Slade student, much against her parents' wishes. Her life had been thrown into further disarray when she met and fell in love with Joseph Bard in 1926. They were to remain together, despite flagrant and at times sustained infidelities on both sides, until his death in 1975.

Eileen had led a full life, working hard as a painter, but also playing hard, holidaying with such sacred monsters as Evelyn Waugh, Ezra Pound, Picasso and Lee Miller, and enjoying affairs with the French poet Paul Eluard and the English painter Paul Nash. All this was perfect material for her autobiography, and I learned a great deal about the art world through which Eileen had risen.

As I spent more time looking at her work, I began to recognize its fundamental independence of spirit. When the organizers of the 1936 surrealist show had visited her studio, they told her she was a surrealist. Her very proper response was 'Am I?' It suited Eileen to exhibit with the surrealists - with such international figures as Max Ernst, Rene Magritte and Joan Miro, not to mention Salvador Dali – but she was never really a card-carrying surrealist.

This is the point I have tried to make in the Agar exhibition I have been organizing for Pallant House Gallery in Chichester (it opens on 25 October and runs until 15 March 2009). Eileen's work comes out of the great English Romantic tradition, its origins lying in medieval manuscript illumination, which reached one of its highest points in the work of William Blake. She was heir to the distinctly English gift for fantasy and invention, so apparent in the work of Lewis Carroll and Edward Lear, and didn't need to draw inspiration from European surrealism. She was always her own boss.

When Eileen was about to move house in the summer of 1987, she told me about a painting in the attic she hadn't seen for years. It was seven feet long and painted on hardboard. She said it was too big to fit into her new flat, and might have to be sawn in half. I suggested that we had a look at it first. It proved to be a masterpiece of her early period, became the centrepiece of her next exhibition and the Tate bought it. My selection for the Chichester exhibition began with a request for this picture, and I'm delighted to report that 'The Autobiography of an Embryo' (1933-4), as it's called, is now on loan to Pallant House for the show.

There was another early work I'd re-discovered in Eileen's attic which I hoped to secure for my selection. This is 'Angel of Mercy' (1934), a decorated plaster head, and a benign counterpart to her more famous 'Angel of Anarchy' (also in the Tate, but too fragile to be lent). Around these two key pieces I built a selection of Eileen's paintings, drawings and collages which reflect her great strengths as a colourist and inventor of evocative shapes. Eileen's works nearly all involve collage or the allied strategy of layering, and this became the theme of the show. I also wanted to demonstrate how vital a role abstraction played in her work, and how some of her paintings from the 1960s and 70s relate to abstract expressionism.

Selecting an exhibition is always a balance between including a few familiar works that art lovers will recognize and trying to locate less-known works which will illuminate the subject rather than confuse it. I decided not to include one of Eileen's most famous objects, her 'Ceremonial Hat for Eating Bouillabaisse', because it could lead all too readily into the area of Surrealism and Fashion, extensively covered by the V&A in a recent exhibition. But I did borrow three exhibits from the Tate, one from the National Galleries of Scotland and another from Leeds. In contrast to these more public works, I managed to unearth a number of collages and drawings from private collections that hadn't been exhibited for some time (if ever). In addition, Eileen's family lent an array of pictures, most of which will be unfamiliar even to those who know her work. The revival of interest in the 1980s inspired Eileen to embark on a late flowering of collages of undiminished inventiveness and wit. It was important to me to end on this high note, partly because I witnessed some of these works being made. The fact that the show is such a fine representation of Eileen's long career (born in 1899, she lived until 1991), is due entirely to the generosity of lenders. I'm particularly glad to see again two small works which used to hang in her flat and which I always enjoyed: 'Bug of Genius' (1943) and the joyful 'Beach Scene' (1952), full of dancing figures. It's a great pleasure now to be able to thank Eileen and celebrate her life with such a glorious display of imaginative art.

WHEN POEM MEETS IMAGE

30 May 2009

Illustrated books are one of the glories of a library. Looking over my own shelves I find assorted delights ranging from *The Story of My Heart*, the unorthodox vision of the naturalist Richard Jefferies fittingly partnered with woodcuts by Ethelbert White, to David Gascoyne's poems decorated rather sombrely by Graham Sutherland, and The Traveller by Walter de la Mare, accompanied by colourful landscapes by John Piper. The pairings of writer and artist are often intriguing: Wyndham Lewis and Naomi Mitchison, William Beckford and Marion Dorn, Samuel Johnson and Edward Bawden. One of my favourites is an anthology called *The Poet's Eye*, selected by Geoffrey Grigson and illustrated superbly by John Craxton. A more modest project altogether is the charming series of pamphlets produced in two series by Faber & Faber in the 1920s and 30s and then in the 1950s, called the Ariel Poems. These brought together a single poem and an artist in often magical conjunction. I'm thinking of Paul Nash and A E (George Russell), John Nash and Wilfrid Gibson, and C Day Lewis and Edward Ardizzone. Unforgettable.

I long for a publisher to produce something as enterprising and inexpensive today (the second series were priced at two shillings and came with an envelope ready to send to a loved one), but some of the most interesting current word and image collaborations are appearing at the other end of the market, up among the pricey limited editions. The Royal Academy of Arts has just published an extremely handsome book, pairing its leading printmaker Norman Ackroyd with the poet Douglas Dunn. The result is called *A Line in the Water*, and is a splendid large landscape format hardback of 159 pages, featuring 75 etchings by Ackroyd and 15 poems by Dunn. It's available in three different editions: the standard is priced at £60, a limited edition containing a separate signed Ackroyd etching is

£250, and the deluxe edition containing the etching and an extra signed volume of poems is £400. These prices suggest an appeal to print and fine book collectors, not to the general public. This is not the sort of volume to tuck into your pocket when off for a country ramble. Not unless you've got very long pockets.

The initial idea for the book was Ackroyd's. He had already collaborated with Dunn on a limited edition of unbound etchings and poems in a solander box under the title of *The Pictish Coast* in 1988, so the two had worked together fruitfully before. This new book is an extension of that interest, in the ancient, once-inhabited islands off the west coasts of Ireland and Scotland. 'I didn't want to do the normal monograph', explains Ackroyd, 'I wanted to do a book looking forward, not back.' He relishes Dunn's self-deprecating wit, the 'humour hanging about between the lines', his ability to do the job with style. 'We're on a similar wavelength', he says.

Norman Ackroyd (born 1938) is a Yorkshireman, but he sees himself very much as 'a resident of a group of islands on the edge of Asia really, as well as the edge of Europe. Fantastic things happen visually out on that edge.' He is fascinated by the people who lived on these edges in the 9th and 10th centuries, the beleaguered communities of monks who inhabited islands with no pier or easy access, who built chapels and beautifully corbelled cells. 'Who were these people?' he asks. Monks who chose an island in the Atlantic instead of a hermitage in a wilderness or a column in a desert? Dunn tries to supply an answer in his poems.

Douglas Dunn (born 1942) is, according to Melvyn Bragg, 'among the finest of our poets'. He is interested in the musical effects of formal verse, and despite a busy career as an academic (from which he lately retired), he has published a notable string of books since *Terry Street*, his first collection of poems, in 1969. He has collaborated on projects with other artists, but clearly enjoys working with Ackroyd, who he refers to as 'a force of nature'. Dunn also says of Ackroyd: 'He responds to poetry perhaps more immediately than I respond to visual art.' Although Dunn's intimacy with Ackroyd's work informs his poems, he made a conscious effort to get back to first principles; as he confesses, 'I was more responding to the places.'

Both artist and poet research their subjects through books, maps and archaeological magazines before making field trips. In fact, they only journeyed together once, to the Shetlands in early spring. Ackroyd stresses that he is not just interested in the scenery, but in its historic inhabitants. His principal subject is topographical, but, as he says, 'the sense of place on the western shore is inextricably tied up with weather. The ocean dominates'. Some of Ackroyd's best images are not at all literal but approach the abstract in their veils of aquatint. They are also devoid of people; the human element is clearly his collaborator's province. 'I tried to introduce a population', comments Dunn.

Much of the appeal of the book is due to the expertise of the designer, Isambard Thomas. Ackroyd gave him 140 reproductions of his etchings and trusted him to make the best choice. (The etchings were made over the last three decades: the earliest in the book is dated 1987, and 44 were made since 2000.) As a direct consequence of this, Dunn's poems are not illustrations to specific images so much as a response to the flavour of Ackroyd's work. This suited Dunn. Otherwise, 'a writer can end up doing captions which is not very satisfactory'.

Poems can be commissioned but not easily written to order. After the idea for this book had been proposed, discussed, and some preliminary work achieved, Dunn fell under the cosh of writer's block. This desperate state held up the book for a couple of years, and meant that the project has been some five years in the making. Dunn calls poetry 'hand-knitted truths and sense / That search for a melodic intellect / In the turbulent mind-mess'. He maintains that a good poem should work in the mind, the heart and the ear simultaneously. When poem meets image, the eye too must join the party. Ackroyd's beautiful monochrome etchings (but with what a wealth of colour in their tones) marry successfully with Dunn's thought-provoking and evocative poems to make a new and distinct entity.

STANLEY SPENCER 'All must be safely gathered in'
(this article relates to Stanley Spencer's pen and ink 'Study for Joachim among the Shepherds', reproduced in The Spectator)
19-26 December 2009

Stanley Spencer (1891-1959) is a rare figure of international standing among British 20th century artists. As the painter and critic Timothy Hyman has observed, Spencer can be ranked alongside Munch, Bonnard, Kirchner, Beckmann and Guston, for his extraordinary work exploring the relationship between the self and the world. He was a wonderfully original and inventive artist whose work has paradoxically suffered because of his unconventional private life. People remember that he loved bread and jam and was obsessed with rubbish, that his sexual compulsions drove him to divorce the love of his life and marry a man-hating and gold-digging tease, and amid all this detail the tremendous seriousness of his work can be lost. Undoubtedly Spencer made art out of his life, which accounts for some fairly strange nudes and odd allegorical pictures, but his paintings and drawings must be seen as art and not literature. They are not diary entries but marvels of pen and brush. Spencer was a superb draughtsman, always preferring drawing to painting, considering the real work over when the compositional drawing was complete, and likening the addition of colour to knitting. The pen and ink 'Study for Joachim among the Shepherds' is in fact far more accomplished and pictorially interesting than the oil Spencer made from it in 1913. The best of his paintings, however, achieve a fully-realized integration of paint and image, the paint bringing something to the iconography that drawing alone could not supply. Here we have shepherds, a solitary sheep and the father of the Virgin Mary – not a bad start for a Christmas painting. I have chosen this beautiful drawing rather than say Spencer's 1912 painting 'The Nativity', partly for its greater clarity and lucidity, but also because it stands slightly to one side, aslant from the Nativity theme. Spencer himself, with his uncompromising beliefs and intensely personal religion, was himself always at a slight angle to the accepted norms of human behaviour, and it seems fitting to represent him here with a less expected subject for Christmas contemplation.

The drawing was inspired by Spencer's love for the paintings of Giotto, which he knew through reproduction in such books as the sixpenny *Gowans and Grey* series, and Ruskin's *Giotto and his Works in Padua*. Illustrating the fresco 'Joachim retires to the Sheepfold', Ruskin described how Joachim determined to withdraw from bad company and go to the desert places among the mountains, calling about him his flocks and shepherds and departing with them to the hills. Spencer chose to depict the moment when Joachim appeared to the shepherds, inevitably foreshadowing another, more momentous, appearance to shepherds, when glad tidings of great joy were brought.

The pair of shepherds with their backs towards us have just arrived. Joachim is the distinguished-looking bearded gent on the right, materializing round the fence as if emerging from the wings onto the stage of the drama. The place in which they are depicted is a strange mixture of confined outdoor and threshold indoor space. The reed fence or wall on the right of the drawing suggests some form of habitation (the fact that the sheep seems to be happily resting nearby indicates security), yet the main part of the picture space is overgrown with thickets and briars. What appears to be a young fig tree shades the recumbent sheep. In the distance a tree-lined hedge encloses an open space beyond the foreground foliage. The four main figures are surrounded on all sides, shut in by a combination of natural and man-made barriers. Instead of this being a landscape format, spreading out horizontally as might be expected of a pasture, it is a tight near-square composition, focused closely on the figures it contains. Revealingly, none of them make eye contact. There is a consequent tension to the drawing's structure, a build-up of emotional power that stops just short of menace, but suggests a certain complexity or ambiguity of feelings.

The scene can be identified as the water meadows beside the Thames at Cookham, the Berkshire village that was Spencer's beloved home. Some years after he made the drawing he explained his way of working. 'I like to take my thoughts for a walk and marry them to some place in Cookham. The "bread and cheese" hedge [a country name for hawthorn] up the Strand ash path was the successful suitor. There was another hedge going away at right angles from the path and this was where the shepherds seemed to be. We had to walk single-file along this path and the shadows romped about in the hedge alongside of us. And I liked the hemmed-in restricted area feeling in that open land.' Here is Spencer's lifelong fascination with boundaries and barriers, and, of course, transgressing them.

Spencer talks of the path to Strand Castle in Cookham as the place 'where the shepherds seemed to be', as if he had seen them there in a vision. And indeed there is something visionary or mystical about his early work, which has much in common with the pastoral and Romantic vision of Samuel Palmer. It is a spiritual, inhabited landscape, full of Spencer's 'feeling for things being holy'. He identifies with the Bible stories, transposes them to Cookham, and enters fully into them. The setting of this drawing has all the hallucinatory sharpness of a waking dream (note the crisply-delineated shapes of the foliage), a holy place of the imagination.

The First World War expelled Spencer from the earthly paradise of Cookham, and though he returned there afterwards, things could never be the same, for he had lost his innocence. He never again made such sense of life as he painted before the war. Although he was to go on to produce some of his greatest masterpieces, including the magnificent cycle of mural paintings for the Oratory of All Souls at Burghclere (1927-32), he was never to recapture the purity of feeling – the sense of communion between man and his environment – that he had once so effortlessly celebrated. His vision grew darker and more personally tormented, filtered through the anguish of broken relationships and frustrated hopes. His religious feelings became inextricably bound up with his desires, and he planned a great installation of his paintings in a special building to be called 'Church House', in which the visitor would be encouraged to 'meditate on the sanctity and beauty of sex'.

There is much to be said in favour of a fusion of the domestic and the sacred, but Spencer was never quite able to reconcile the various impulses that drove him. His ambitions were all-inclusive ('I am on the side of angels and dirt', he proclaimed), and his robust celebratory art is essentially a generous and nurturing vision. As Spencer said to fellow-artist David Jones: 'All must be safely gathered in'; Jones subsequently remarking, 'a more apt expression of the artist's business I never heard'.

JOHN CRAXTON In Arcadia

20 February 2010

Last year, within the space of five weeks before Christmas, I lost two friends who had illumined the world for me and made it a more enlivening place. Both were artists, both were in their eighties and both were determined individualists who recognized each other's work without being in any way close allies. John Craxton was the first to die, in hospital on November 17th after a short illness. Just over a month later, Craigie Aitchison dropped dead of a heart attack. I hope to write about Aitchison when some of his distinctive work on the theme of the Crucifixion is on show. This is a tribute to John Craxton.

An artist with a particular interest in the inhabited landscape, Craxton could summon up the spirit of place with a wit and ingenuity that left most painters of his generation standing. Aware from youth that there is no art without other art, he sought out essence rather than originality, but achieved an original vision by the depth of his understanding and interpretation. John detested labels and pigeon-holes, principally because they encouraged unjustified assumptions and lazy thinking, and he is frequently quoted as disliking the term 'neo-romantic' which was attached to his own work of the 1940s. It was the 'neo' he objected to particularly, being proud to admit his indebtedness to the romantic vision of William Blake and Samuel Palmer, just as he would be the first to claim the inspiring influence of Byzantine art.

Bryan Robertson, the brilliant director of the Whitechapel Gallery who gave Craxton a retrospective in 1967, noted the enduring appeal of John's work – its qualities of clarity, incisiveness and abstraction. He wrote:

> 'The great allure of Craxton's work in general, for me, was the sophistication of its references to Miro and Picasso and the crisp, clean vitality of its design. Above all, perhaps, the colour seemed more tonic, cleaner and fresher, than the prevailing mood of English painting then. Picasso affected everyone, of course, but Miro was exotic ground for speculation in this period.'

Robertson made the point that Craxton painted only for pleasure and did not seek out a public career – so much so that in later years I would encounter many an art lover who thought him already dead because he was so little visible on the exhibiting circuit. In fact he spent much of his time in Crete, and had long before reached the firm decision that life was indisputably more important than art, that in fact life (in Noel Coward's words) was for living. This was a revolutionary position to take up in the outwardly dedicated art world. The artist is supposed to be utterly committed to his art, with no time for the distractions of social life or extra-curricular activities, the contemporary model for this being Frank Auerbach or Lucian Freud. Craxton begged to differ, delighting in the art of conversation (at which he was a past master), travel (often by motorbike), parties (grand or impromptu), food and all the many possible seductions that others might dismiss as time-wasting but which he regarded as time well-spent. He knew how to enjoy life, and in the process he enriched countless other lives as well as his own. Who is to say that the wealth of knowledge and experience he derived from living, and which he dispensed to friends and acquaintances with a liberal hand, was not equally as valuable as his more visible and tangible legacy, his paintings?

It is often maintained that Craxton's work declined from its early eminence, that he never fulfilled the promise of his evident talents. I think he did, but he chose not to channel it simply into his art, he diversified his genius into his life. Not everyone has the gift of being happy, but he did, and he offered his own happiness to others. There is perhaps a lesson here.

John's memorial service took place at St James's Church in Piccadilly. Craxton was probably a pagan, or an Arcadian as he would have preferred, but like most interesting people he was a bundle of contradictions, so a church service with hymn and prayers was not in fact inappropriate. Craxton was very English: he observed the forms of society, finding it unnecessary to flaunt his homosexuality or his artistic nature – preferring to save his powder for something more important. He would grow incensed about the treatment of art or individuals, the disrespect with which our society treated something or someone he held dear. In Crete, his own Arcadia, he shook his stick just as much at thoughtless tourists as at the neglect of historical monuments. The church was packed and the congregation bellowed out 'Jerusalem' before settling down to hear Philip Gammon play two preludes by Shostakovich and an excerpt from Ravel's ballet Daphnis and Chloé. Gammon, who was taught by John's father, Harold Craxton (who gave the first recital of Debussy's piano music in England), played superbly. There followed a beautiful passage from Ecclesiastes, read by a young member of Clan Craxton, 'To every thing there is a season, and a time to every purpose under the heaven...' Then Sir David Attenborough gave a perfectly judged and very moving address. Oboe music by Benjamin Britten followed and the service ended after prayers and a blessing with Philip Gammon's rendition of 'Wish Me Luck (As You Wave Me Goodbye)'.

The best of John Craxton's paintings and drawings will long continue to give pleasure, but the inestimable benefit of knowing him is more difficult to quantify. John had an awful tendency to puns, a linguistic tortuousness that goes under the general heading of Anglo-Craxton. He had an exceptionally well-stocked mind, and was blessed with a degree of natural scholarship that was not just the result of wide reading, but of independent thought and a life spent looking and enquiring. It will be a challenge for any biographer to do justice to Craxton's life as well as to assess his work. For his life was, in some respects, his greatest achievement. The measure of the artist has rarely been more bound up with the measure of the man. It is that totality we now celebrate.

TATE ARCHIVE Treasure trove

27 November 2010

One afternoon in the winter of 1992 I was on a bus traversing London's Millbank when an extraordinary sight caught my eye. A bright red Triumph Spitfire had been driven up the imposing front steps of the Tate Gallery and abandoned there. Not for the first time in my life I wished I had a camera with me. Only later did I learn that some disaffected artist or taxpayer had committed this spectacular act as a protest against the Turner Prize.

Nearly 20 years later, it's Turner Prize time again, though perhaps passions are today more jaded. But what prompted this memory was the publicity material for the 40th anniversary of the Tate Archive, which includes – among notebooks gorgeously illustrated by famous artists, old posters and revealing holiday snaps – a couple of slides of the offending Triumph.

The Archive is an invaluable resource which since 1970 has been busy collecting all sorts of material documenting artists' lives and then making it available to the public. Not just obvious items such as letters and diaries, but complete artists' photographic collections (photos taken by Eileen Agar, Paul Nash and John Piper, for instance), Keith Vaughan's suicide diary entry, a lime-green table mat designed by Terry Frost for Heals, Sickert's cream linen painting overalls and Turner's metal paint-box. These are the things that bring the past to life. An exhibition of such wonders may be seen at Tate Britain (until 13 February) or visit http://www.tate.org.uk/reserch/research services/reading rooms.

PAUL NASH Intimations of infinity

18/25 December 2010

Paul Nash is one of the best-loved English painters of the last century, a great imaginative artist, always trying to discover the appropriate form for what he wanted to say. Nash was a philosopher-poet who expressed himself best (though he was a good writer) in visual terms and chose landscape painting as his primary vehicle. Although he died prematurely, in 1946 at the age of 57, his work stands easily above most of his contemporaries, and its originality and inventiveness have continued to inspire painters and beguile the public. He saw nature as a creative mystery and painting as a way of offering insight into it. The act of making a painting was for him essentially twofold: an emotional response to a subject and a process of solving visual equations between shapes. He tended to paint elemental forms distilled from nature rather than any kind of more rigorous abstraction. Nature was much more than textbook geometry.

Nash preferred painting trees to people and his landscapes are usually empty though pregnant with mysterious possibilities. His places are temporarily deserted, as if the inhabitants had just that moment exited our field of vision. He did not depict the natural world topographically, from the outside, as the *plein air* realist might draw it, sitting on an old stump and attempting to describe the surroundings. Nash painted *from within*, the artist making a kind of mystical identification with the landscape, offering an insider's interpretation and thus proposing a different order of relationship with the viewer. Nash had a vision to communicate rather than visual facts. He wanted his audience to feel for themselves the importance and relevance of what he was painting.

In the First World War, Nash served in the British army in France and then worked as a war artist. His experiences at the Front affected him deeply and after the hostilities he went to live at Dymchurch on the Kent coast (1921-25) in order to recuperate from a breakdown ascribed to war strain. There is a notable emptiness to his work at this time. The flatness of the coast and nearby Romney Marsh may have recalled the plains of Flanders, and Nash apparently derived solace from gazing at the sea. He painted and drew the sea wall at Dymchurch and made of this rather stark subject many memorable images. One of the most moving and complex is 'Winter Sea' (1925-37), begun in Kent but completed many years later in London.

This extraordinary painting, with its long recessive planes and distinctive triangular shapes, its reduction of foaming waves and spray to stylized folds and geometric facets, presents an archetypal sea rather than a particular one. It may be based on Dymchurch –

there are indeed suggestions of sea wall – but the artist's intention was evidently to make a larger and more general statement, of what an early Nash chronicler Margot Eates called 'the very pattern of all seas from everlasting to everlasting'.

The phrase strikes the right note of spiritual insight for Nash's slightly melancholy Romantic Cubism. Dusk has fallen on the wintry waves. The moon is only suggested, shadowed forth through a bank of snow-laden clouds, but what we are shown is a moon-path of reflections on a night sea. Upon that path a spectator might take the first tentative steps of the mind or heart's voyage into the infinity of faith. The first steps before being brought up sharp against a wall of dark cloud above the horizon. Here is a striking metaphor for the physical limitations of earthbound existence versus the infinite freedom of the spirit. Nash paints the limits not the soaring of the spirit; this will come later as his work gains more assurance, when in his final years the sunflower was transfigured by flight and became a symbol of hope and resurgence. In the meantime, the sea with its soft luminosity and yet apparent iron hardness (which has something of the armoured style of Wyndham Lewis), supplies a measured release for the soul.

Nash's relationship with the sea was an involved one. Intended by his father for the Navy, he failed to pass the entrance exam, although commentators in later life persisted in finding traces of a seafaring past in his mien. John Rothenstein described Nash's exceptional blue eyes thus: 'The steadiness of their gaze, and the habitual closeness of the pupils to the upper lid gave them the far-ranging look of the eyes of sailors.' And the art critic Herbert Read observed: 'He carried over, with his actual career, some of the swagger of the rejected career – art, for him, was to be the Senior Service.'

Winter Sea epitomizes for Nash a lifelong fascination for all things maritime and refers back in particular to a very early drawing, now in the Tate Gallery, called 'The Pyramids in the Sea' (1912). In this, the triangular forms seem almost to be part of the water, rather than landward pyramids in the process of being engulfed by the tide. And to take an example from his later career, 'Winter Sea' relates closely to 'Totes Meer (Dead Sea)' of 1940-1, now also in the Tate. This is an immensely potent image of the massed hulks of crashed German planes gathered on a dump at Cowley, just outside Oxford. It is an iron sea of wreckage, an ocean of twisted metal, wings and fuselages. Here all movement is arrested, apart from a white owl gliding over the ghostly scene. The flood of planes is frozen, defeated, the threat of the sea confounded.

In the 1920s, and perhaps as a direct result of his war experiences, Nash was attempting to find an image for God. He did this consciously in an extraordinary series of twelve woodcuts he made as illustrations to the Book of Genesis, published in 1924 by The Nonesuch Press. Intense contemplation is bodied forth in powerful dark images: the woodcut relating to the division of the waters and dry land looks like a combination of 'Winter Sea' -and 'The Pyramids in the Sea', though possessed of a different kind of flexed serenity.

According to one interpretation, 'Winter Sea' goes beyond the human and subjective into a cold realm of objectivity and perfect forms. I don't find the image that extreme: the rectilinearity of the structure is gentled with scarcely suppressed curves, the severity of its palette is redeemed by warmer tones – pink in the brown, green in the white. The interpenetration of shapes is important, and the sense of metamorphosis: the liquid becoming solid, the sea interchangeable with the land. Nash, in this tough but surprisingly tender image, was seeking to make an equivalent for nature, not a copy, and in doing so was trying to understand the forces that shape us all.

CY TWOMBLY The outsider

16 July 2011

With the passing of Cy Twombly – who has died of cancer aged 83 – a beacon light of rare civilization has gone out in the western world. An elusive artist, with a highly developed faculty of challenge and response, he developed a pattern of investigation into the visual which was part philosophical enquiry and part sensual celebration. Despite close association with Robert Rauschenberg and Jasper Johns, recognition came late. He remained something of an outsider: an esoteric American artist who settled in Italy in 1957, and grew obsessed with Classical antiquity. He cultivated various literary muses – Catullus, Pound, Rilke, Pessoa, Virgil, Archilochus – and made gloriously expressive abstractions from their inspiration. Best known for employing calligraphy and script in his paintings, Twombly is no more 'Cy the Scribbler' than Pollock was 'Jack the Dripper', though the non-art press love nicknames to make them feel at home with anything that threatens to be profound.

Twombly called himself a Romantic symbolist showing things in flux. Other artists see him differently, as the following extracts demonstrate. The sculptor Nigel Hall (born 1943) finds landscape and music in Twombly's work. 'The paintings seem comparable to desert or arid wastelands which on first encounter appear unrewarding when contrasted with more lush or scenic landscapes. However, they reveal themselves slowly. What at first seems impoverished or ill-formed, has by its very paucity an eloquence. The sculptures take a more concentrated form with the stillness and silence evocative of whitened ruins. They seem the visual equivalent to the spare and tentative explorations of Miles Davis' music of the late 50s and early 60s. Like Davis, they evoke a feeling of melancholy and an awareness of the passage of time.'

Allen Jones (born 1937) recalls first seeing Twombly's paintings when he started going to New York in the 1960s. In those days,

Twombly was exhibiting with Leo Castelli, and Jones was interested to note how Twombly's very individual work sat with a gallery of mostly Pop artists. It was clear to Jones that Twombly had carved out his own niche somewhere between the very different territories of Pop Art and Abstract Expressionism, and that while he didn't subscribe to Pop's involvement with consumer culture he nevertheless imbued his own mark-making with meaning apart from its purely formal, abstract values. Thus when he used words on the surface of a painting, they were meant to be read as writing, not just as shape and gesture.

The first time I looked at any great concentration of Twombly's work was in 1987 when a museum show that was travelling Europe reached the Whitechapel Gallery. I loved the dramatic freedom of it, the originality and mesmeric flow of mark, the occasional stutter and awkwardness disrupting what might otherwise have been too elegant in its assured occupancy of the picture space. But I also remember feeling slightly excluded when I heard Twombly eulogized as a 'painters' painter'. Now I think the 'painters' painter' tag is too restrictive, and one of the things that's so attractive about his work is its breadth of cultural reference. Gillian Ayres (born 1930), for instance, is drawn to Twombly's Europeanness. As she says, it's just that quality of culture that's needed nowadays, and is so hard to find amongst the self-referential young. 'I think he's a sort of hero, unmistakeably, one of the things you really look up to – like Beckett as a writer.'

Ian Welsh (born 1944), a painter who seeks visual expression for scientific observation, feels strongly about the issue. He writes: 'In an age when perhaps too much attention and respect is paid to the self-obsessed doodles of some contemporary artists and writers, it is with relief and anticipation that one returns to the work of Cy Twombly. He is an artist whose very personal language is used to construct works which are at one and the same time both timeless and intensely contemporary, mining as they do the creative energies and cultural offerings from all the known history of sophisticated man and responding to the immediacy of the modern environment. A profound joy!' Welsh stresses that artists can make totally personal and individual work without indulging themselves in autobiographical maunderings; that in fact the business of trying to make direct and telling marks in painting demands an ability to distance oneself.

Veteran realist, Anthony Eyton (born 1923), proves that Twombly's appeal is not limited to abstractionists. 'Like Turner, Cy Twombly was a visionary with a sense of the cosmos. They are both poets remembering a place or experience and re-creating the memory later on. Both are fond of words: Turner with verses attached to his paintings, Twombly with words actually inscribed on the painting. Both had an enormous respect for the support, Turner in his watercolours especially, and Twombly in the light inherent in the paper or canvas so that white to him was a source of magic to be chastised or caressed. He was a master of spontaneity, letting himself go to roam free in associations in his imagination, free of the tyranny of visual fact. To this extent he was like a Zen poet.' Maggi Hambling (born 1945) is a passionate admirer of Twombly's work. 'It is as if his paintings are being made in front of me', she says, 'they are not dead finished things. The juxtaposition of life and death is finely balanced in every mark: the paint breathes. I am taken into unknown territory that is made at once familiar. He advanced the language of paint from late Titian, through Rembrandt, van Gogh, Rothko and Pollock, and so takes his place among the elite. The courage of his work lives on.'

Lorcan O'Neill, a leading art dealer in Rome who first got to know Twombly when working for Anthony d'Offay in London, has this to say: 'Cy Twombly is one of the truly great artists. He had a profound understanding of the human condition, and his spirit – of such intelligence, humour, and delicacy – is visible in all his work. I was always aware of what a privilege it was to have been around him, he was like one of the giant granite columns in front of the Pantheon; ageless, strong, and forever impressive. His courage and independence as an artist are a constant inspiration to many people. His passing is a shock because you can never prepare for the void that, at whatever age, the departure of such a man leaves.'

SET ART FREE

22 October 2011

The casual observer of London's art scene, or even the devoted reader of exhibition listings, might be forgiven for thinking that the range of shows available throughout the conspectus of the nation's museums was of a healthy vigour and diversity. In fact, it could be effectively argued that there are still too many different blockbusters simultaneously competing for box-office success, with museums forever chasing revenue by putting on displays of tried-and-tested favourites, and not actually serving the public in the best possible way. A museum's dual responsibility is to its collection and to its public, and too often the permanent collection remains hidden, in cellar and off-site storage, with only the tip of the iceberg ever going on display. The Tate is a notable case in point.

For several years now a cherished project of mine has been to select and mount a full-scale survey of English painting since 1945. Just an exhibition of painting, in all its glorious variety, celebrating the richness of our national achievement over half-a-century. Initially, I was approached about this by two arts world luminaries who had themselves hatched the idea but felt the need for a third party to help implement it at a suitably inclusive level. I was completely convinced by their enthusiasm (one, I must admit, I already shared) and whole-heartedly joined the team, compiling enjoyable lists of artists and then remembering favourites inadvertently overlooked. The other two, carrying a greater weight of years and experience than your humble columnist, were the ones who approached the institutions we thought might be interested in such a venture, and it was they who repeatedly had to break the news that no one was prepared to take it on. Several people expressed interest, but it never went further than that. This was extraordinary, for we even had the promise of sponsorship to sweeten the proposal.

Why this wholesale rejection? You may well ask – as indeed did we. An answer was eventually volunteered by one eximious museum director, who agreed that the exhibition was a good idea and that it would be very popular with the public. The problem lay with the museum's curators, who would not like it at all – and who would prove to be the stumbling block. I can understand the paid officials of an institution resenting the intrusion of freelance outsiders, but the issue is not one simply of competition. The curators would apparently not approve of our proposal because *it had no argument.* Every museum exhibition these days is structured around a curator's interpretation or theory, and quite often the art is made to fit the theme, rather than being the real reason for the show. Curators use exhibitions – and their weighty accompanying catalogues – to further their own careers, rather than serving art and the public. The idea of presenting a major survey and celebration of painting is thus anathema to them, for *painting* is central stage, not a curator-controlled theory of what painting is or should be.

As you may have detected, I disapprove of the self-aggrandisement of curators who stand in the way of art. Of course, not all are like this, and some few are prepared to put art first. But the majority spend their time elaborating concepts to impress their colleagues and prospective employers, rather than searching out artists who've been unfairly neglected, or simply not seen for a while, and putting forward their work for reassessment. I would much prefer to see the Tate organizing a whole series of small exhibitions devoted to individual artists, drawn largely from their own collections, rather than the endless programme of blockbusters that are usually too big to be either properly enjoyable or really instructive. Yet this is precisely what doesn't happen in museums. As a consequence, the commercial galleries have had to supply the shortfall, and the kind of high-quality focus exhibitions that public galleries should be arranging are being put on in the private sector. All praise to the galleries who manage to do this – very often by mixing museum-quality loan works with a smattering of items for sale to defray the costs of mounting such a display. Hazlitt Holland-Hibbert (38 Bury Street, St James's, SW1) is a gallery which has staged a series of such shows in recent years, including impressive displays of Lucian Freud and Barbara Hepworth. Currently they are showing (until 4 November) a sumptuous group of still-life and landscape paintings by William Nicholson (1872-1949), to mark the publication of the catalogue raisonné of his oil paintings. Besides borrowing famous works from private collections, they have also managed to obtain loans from the Tate, the Towner Art Gallery and the Fitzwilliam Museum. Along with much-loved favourites there are a couple of paintings not exhibited for decades: 'The Lustre Bowl' and 'Rose Lustre'. Inclusions such as these make the exhibition priority viewing.

In this column I have regularly lamented the lack of a museum focusing on modern American art, but at least the dealer Bernard Jacobson in Cork Street mounts exhibitions of distinguished American artists of the highest quality. His latest foray is 'Robert Motherwell: Works on Paper' (until 26 November), and very good it is too. Motherwell (1915-91) was the youngest member of the New York School, and came to Abstract Expressionism through European Surrealism. Honouring Mallarmé's dictum, 'describe not the object itself, but the effect it produces', he made wonderfully inventive drawings of great imaginative freedom, exploiting the surrealist strategy of psychic automatism, or 'artful scribbling'. A revelation. In November, Jonathan Clark & Co (18 Park Walk, SW10) are showing early sculpture by Eduardo Paolozzi, dating from 1946 to 1959. Arguably his best and most original work, any assessment of Paolozzi's reputation must begin here. From a brief preview of the catalogue this looks to be a classic loan exhibition in a commercial gallery. Recommended.

William Nicholson also features among the 27 artists I have selected for 'A Critic's Choice' at Browse & Darby (19 Cork Street, W1, until 11 November). Limiting myself to British art 1900-1950, I have brought together examples by artists whose work I care about. This is a celebration of painting, drawing and printmaking (with a couple of sculptures thrown in) which makes a few links between the artists but has no thesis to propose or axe to grind, apart from my own passion for the art of the period. Thus I include very old favourites such as Paul Nash, Frank Dobson, Wyndham Lewis and Ivon Hitchens, neglected younger brothers John Nash and Gilbert Spencer, and more recent enthusiasms such as Algernon Newton and Allan Gwynne-Jones. Then there are the unjustly undervalued, such as Leon Underwood and John Armstrong, and the genuinely unfamiliar, such as Thomas Hennell (1903-45), friend and contemporary of Edward Bawden and Eric Ravilious. The resulting mix is a very personal choice, but never intended as anything else. I hope you enjoy it.

TWO TEMPLE PLACE Buried treasure

26 November 2011

In recent years there has been a surge of interest in the treasures hidden in our public art collections, many of them rarely if ever on view. The Tate Gallery is perhaps the principal offender here, only showing a tiny percentage of its glorious and wide-ranging holdings of British art, but attention is now being directed towards our provincial galleries and museums. Since 2003 the Public Catalogue Foundation has been recording and publishing the oil paintings held in galleries and civic buildings, county by county, and issuing invaluable volumes of colour illustrations to show us what usually remains invisible. By its calculations, a shameful 80% of these paintings are not on view. This unknown resource is finally emerging into the light, and in London will have a venue for its public exposure: the grand building just off the Embankment known rather anonymously as Two Temple Place.

Built in the 1890s as an estate office and London pied-à- terre, it was commissioned by William Waldorf Astor (later 1st Viscount Astor) to be a house which would 'personify literature'. It thus contains such details as sculptures of characters from 'The Three Musketeers' carved by Thomas Nichols to decorate the newel posts on the great staircase, a frieze of figures from Shakespeare, and silver gilt panels by George Frampton on the door of the Great Hall upstairs depicting Arthurian heroines. After its sale by the Astor family, the building was for many years the head office of the Society of Incorporated Accountants and Auditors, before being acquired in 1999 by The Bulldog Trust, a charitable foundation that specializes in educational grants. The Trust has spent the last decade or so deciding what to do with this magnificent pile and has finally decided to turn it into an art gallery.

The interior space, despite its grand battlemented Portland stone facade and gilded weather vane of beaten copper depicting Columbus' ship the *Santa Maria*, is actually not extensive, though it is extraordinarily ornate. The architect was John Loughborough Pearson (1817-97), a medievalist considered to be the founder of the Gothic Revival, and noted for his attention to harmonious detail, proportion and contour. John Betjeman described him as one of 'the three most remarkable pioneers who thought and constructed in Gothic rather than imitated' (the other two being Butterfield and Street). Pearson was primarily a church architect (best known for Truro Cathedral), and passionately interested in vaulting, though his excursions into domestic building show considerable versatility.

In Betjeman's view, Two Temple Place was 'one of the most attractive late-Victorian private houses in London'. Today it is worth visiting in its own right as an architectural gem. But there is another good reason to seek it out: the first in a series of exhibitions which will bring the treasures of regional galleries to the heart of our capital.

The current exhibition is 'William Morris: Story, Memory, Myth' (until 29 January 2012), and may be visited every day except Tuesdays when the building is closed and certain days when it is booked for private functions (check the website). Admission to the house and the exhibition is free, there's a cafe and a bookshop, and the whole experience is a very civilized one. The house gives the impression of great solidity from the moment you enter: it is well-grounded, substantial, a thing of carved stone, ornamental ironwork and much oak panelling. The hall floor is laid with a geometrical pattern of marble, jasper, porphyry and onyx, forming a richly coloured focus to the building, offsetting the mahogany sculptures and the pillars of ebony around the gallery above. The labels for the exhibits have been well designed and are easy to read, and a handsome, small but appropriately solid catalogue accompanies the exhibition, priced at £7.50.

On the ground floor is the Lower Gallery, where the Morris exhibition begins, with a series of five marvellous embroideries on the theme of The Romance of the Rose, a medieval French allegorical poem reinterpreted by Morris and his great friend Burne-Jones. These are done in silks, wools and gold thread on linen, and are immensely subtle in effect, their colours being mostly duns and greys, with a little deeper brown and blue. 'Love Leading the Pilgrim through the Briars' is an especially fine embroidery, with figures floating amidst an intricate filigree of thorns and tendrils. These beautiful panels have been recently conserved by the Royal School of Needlework, and this is their first outing. They are on loan from the under-visited William Morris Museum in Walthamstow, which is currently closed for renovation but is scheduled to re-open in July 2012. Upstairs, the exhibition continues around the gallery and then into the Library, with Morris designs for such beloved items as his Brer Rabbit furnishing fabric, in blue or brown, and some lovely tiles telling the stories of Cinderella or Beauty and the Beast (decorated with an exquisite swan border). Move through into the Great Hall and the architecture takes over: hammer-beam roof, panelling galore, great carved fireplace, stained glass. 'The Woodpecker' tapestry and an embroidery on the theme of Pomona just about hold their own, but most of the exhibits up here are inevitably somewhat overshadowed. In life, William Morris and John Loughborough Pearson were rivals over the restoration of Westminster Hall, a contest Morris lost. In their present confrontation Morris gets to invade Pearson's building, but the match is pretty much a draw. I wonder how other exhibitions will fare in this highly ornate space. I can't see modern paintings working here at all (though I'd like to see someone try an installation of abstracts), but a collection of Cathedral treasures or Tiffany glass (from the Haworth Art Gallery in Accrington, for instance) might complement rather than conflict with the setting.

The aims of the Bulldog Trust are threefold: to raise awareness of the unknown riches in the country's regional art galleries; to promote the architectural wonders of Two Temple Place; and to encourage and provide opportunities for up-and-coming curatorial talent to organize exhibitions. I can see that the last objective fits neatly with the Trust's educational work, but I fear that it may bring a certain timidity to the exhibition programme. Why not also employ, from time to time, independent scholars of more experience than the up-and-coming, men and women who in these times of swingeing cutbacks may no longer be employed by other museums? Two Temple Place is such a remarkable cultural asset that it deserves the very best, and youth is no substitute for hard-earned knowledge and the wisdom of experience.

JOHN LEECH An ideal Christmas

17 December 2011

Christmas approaches, and my thoughts with reassuring inevitability turn to Dickens. As the nights draw in and the winter winds blast across the fields of East Anglia, the counter-urge is for the comfort of a good book, to be read preferably by the fireside in a snug armchair. Dickens is the high priest of cosiness, forever creating situations in which the fire and wine within are contrasted with the cold and storm without. In his novels, hearth and home are crucial images of goodness, comfort and continuance, and nowhere more so than in his first and greatest festive story, that indisputable classic, *A Christmas Carol.*

Dickens, always an intensely visual writer, sets the scene: 'The fog came pouring in at every chink and keyhole, and was so dense without, that, although the court was of the narrowest, the houses opposite were mere phantoms. To see the dingy cloud come drooping down, obscuring everything, one might have thought that nature lived hard by, and was brewing on a large scale.' In the cold darkness is the pale glimmer of Scrooge's mean fire over which he huddles and eats his gruel. Evidently, he has yet to honour his fireside. Here, as a prologue, he is visited by the ghost of Jacob Marley, his deceased partner, who appears dragging a chain of moneyboxes. John Leech's etching of the scene is surprisingly gentle, but it deftly catches the ordinariness of the setting into which is injected the extraordinary and supernatural. Marley has come to save Scrooge. To this miserable old sinner's home is brought a drama in three acts as the Ghosts of Christmas Past, Present and Yet to Come visit him and show him scenes which he finds inexpressibly moving. The shadows of the past and of the future overwhelm his ingrained misanthropy. The miser is thawed and his moral regeneration achieved: rejoicing breaks out in his heart, and the selfish, avaricious killjoy is replaced by that generous celebrant of life, the Dickensian figure of an ideal

Christmas, in which all the world becomes an extended family and feelings of benevolence are engendered by an awareness of one's own good fortune and comfort.

Although Dickens drew unforgettable pictures with words, from the start his books were accompanied by a range of illustrations by some of the best graphic artists of the day. Chief among these was the distinguished Punch cartoonist, John Leech (1817-64), who became a good friend of Dickens, along with Mark Lemon and Henry Mayhew, joint founding editors of Punch. These men, known as the Punch Brotherhood, spent a great deal of time together, and Leech often accompanied Dickens on the restless writer's trips in England or abroad. It was with Leech and Lemon that Dickens visited Norwich and Yarmouth in 1849, afterwards walking from Yarmouth to Lowestoft and back, an excursion which so fired the writer's imagination that it resulted in key episodes in *David Copperfield*.

Leech was a master of what might be called 'delicate' satire, and was instrumental in leading Punch away from radicalism towards conservative commentary. His work was immensely popular – Trollope said Punch's success was due to Leech more than any other individual – and he was probably the best-known English artist of his time. When he died, Millais said of him: 'Very few of us painters will leave behind us such good and valuable work as he has left. You will never find a bit of false sentiment in anything he did.' (And Sickert tartly observed: 'Millais had the benefit of Leech's friendship, but his example taught him nothing...') Leech's gentle irony infused a visual language that was deliberately measured and thus readily acceptable to the average Victorian householder. It was not savage and explosive satire, but subtle and well-judged. Leech, who had briefly studied medicine, possessed satire's equivalent of a soothing bedside manner: he was the reassuring GP rather than the surgeon who wielded the knife. Although *A Christmas Carol* was published by Chapman & Hall, Dickens' dissatisfaction with the company led him to take on himself the expenses of the production. Perhaps unwisely, the first edition was a rather lavish affair, illustrated with four full-colour etchings by Leech with an additional four black-and-white woodcuts. It sold well but did not initially make Dickens the fortune he had hoped.

Leech excelled himself in these illustrations. The etching of 'The Last of the Spirits' is a superb and moving image. Leaving aside the character and economy of the drawing, Leech's use of colour is highly effective: the midnight blue of the Spirit's robe both darkens and warms the composition, adding emotional depth but also a suggestion of hope. The greys and blacks of the night graveyard are gentled with touches of brown and green (intimations of spring and rebirth), while patches of paler blue at the top suggest the approach of dawn. The tiny huddled figure of Scrooge is penitent before the awful inhuman presence of the Spirit with its down-pointing finger. (Surely a witty reference to the upward-pointing gesture of Old and New Testament prophets in Renaissance iconography.)

The plot of *A Christmas Carol* was constructed while Dickens roved the streets of London for as much as 15 or 20 miles a night. He was deeply involved in the actual writing of it and confessed that he wept and laughed throughout the six weeks it took him. When the book was published it sold 6,000 copies in its first day. Thackeray, uneasy friend and close rival, told Dickens that it had done a 'national benefit, and to every man or woman who reads it a personal kindness'. Lord Jeffrey, literary critic and founder of The Edinburgh Review, wrote to Dickens that he had done more good than the Christian church could in a whole year. And apparently an American factory owner gave his employees another day's holiday after reading it. Over 100 years ago G K Chesterton wrote: 'Whether or not the visions were evoked by real Spirits of the Past, Present, and Future, they were evoked by that truly exalted order of angels who are correctly called High Spirits. They are impelled and sustained by a quality which our contemporary artists ignore or almost deny, but which in a life decently lived is as normal and attainable as sleep, positive, passionate, conscious joy. The story sings from end to end like a happy man going home; and, like a happy and good man, when it cannot sing it yells. It is lyric and exclamatory, from the first exclamatory words of it. It is strictly a Christmas carol.'

Scrooge is the embodiment of accountability: his behaviour can alter society for better or for worse, and the book's conclusion is so heartening because his personal redemption means the improvement of the condition of others. The material is not opposed to the spiritual in the book, only the wrong attitude to material things is shown to be harmful. When matter and spirit work together, the outcome is seen to be joyful. In part Dickens' tale of a redeemed miser is effective because he himself understood so clearly the power of money, being a self-made man from an impoverished background. There's definitely an element of 'there, but for the grace of God, go I' in his delineation of Ebenezer Scrooge.

At Christmas begins the cycle of life. The Christian year starts with Christ's birth, and the celebration of this special event builds upon the foundations of the midwinter pagan festival of lighting bonfires and decorating the dwelling with evergreens, to ensure the return of spring. In Dickens' version, the rules of both pagan and Christian festivity are observed. Christmas is not just a time for feasting and shutting out the dark, but also for praying and considering others – a singular combination of religion and merry-making. Dickens composed an appeal for charity and mirth and delivered it through his Christmas stories to his readers, intimately and directly, seated as they were before their festive logs, digesting turkey and plum pudding. Its powerful emotional impact mixes fantasy, religious mysticism and popular superstition. And thus we begin to understand what Chesterton meant when he wrote that 'Dickens did not strictly make a literature; he made a mythology'.

JACKSON POLLOCK Wrestling with paint and demons
28 January 2012

In his centenary year, the status of Jackson Pollock (1912-56) looks assured: a self-created American hero who is now accorded all the reverence due an Old Master. The most famous of the Abstract Expressionists, nicknamed Jack the Dripper because of his trademark style, his emphasis was on paint and process: the surface of the canvas was an arena in which the artist could externalize his feelings through action. Some have called Pollock the father of Performance Art, but his primary involvement was with pure painting – creating a complex abstract imagery that was intended to engage with Jungian archetypes and thus have access to deep meaning. Of course not everyone was convinced, and for many Abstract Expressionism could not remotely approach the realities of the human condition. As Francis Bacon put it: 'Jackson Pollock's paintings might be very pretty but they're just decoration. They look like old lace...'

After a slow and untalented start, Pollock struck upon a way of working by dripping the paint in long threads and trails onto a large canvas laid flat on the ground, rather than applying it traditionally with a brush. Max Ernst had already experimented with a similar procedure by piercing a hole in a can which was then swung above a canvas and released paint in a wide or narrow arc. But Pollock was the first to turn a strategy into a technique and exploit it to its full extent. He applied his paint by hand, letting it run off the brush or flicking it in great long spatters, as he moved athletically around the canvas, rhythmically dripping and hurling the paint in a kind of ritualized dance. The term Action Painting was coined to describe this style of work, because of the physical exertion it demanded. After his second solo exhibition in March 1945, the influential critic Clement Greenberg hailed Pollock as 'the strongest painter of his generation'.

Pollock's moment of glory was short-lived. For five years he was able to ride the whirlwind of his success, during which time he not only wrestled with the paint but also with his demons. He had been declared emotionally unstable (with 'a certain schizoid disposition underlying the instability') by his psychiatrist when it came to fighting in the war, and he resorted to alcohol to contain or calm his fractured nature. Drink achieved neither, and made him inarticulate and aggressive. Of course, deprived of his inner conflict it's entirely likely that Pollock would have had nothing to paint about, and therefore nothing to justify the great struggle with paint. If a psychiatrist had been able to 'cure' him, we would not have had the paintings. Instead the result was a series of extraordinary and very beautiful works of art, unlike anything before or since, and an increasingly off-the-wall artist.

As John Updike has observed, America loves an emblematic life, and Jackson Pollock's life-narrative of 'long struggle, high triumph and swift fall' fits the bill rather neatly. The Abstract Expressionists are still viewed by many as working on a heroic scale and making heroic stylistic breakthroughs, of which Pollock's 'epic' drips are perhaps the most engaging. His paintings certainly encourage an elemental subjective response in the viewer: abstract pools and lines suggest space and its limits, openness and closure, symbolic themes of the utmost gravity. Line is disassociated from its traditional role of describing the outside of things, from holding a composition together, and deployed instead to blow it apart. But actually line still does hold Pollock's paintings together, in a rhythm which is also a pattern, like a snaking net, or a braided thread.

Pollock was the first American artist to become really famous, which can be seen as a triumph of need over skill. His early work was muddy and undistinguished, and he was more in love with the idea of being an artist than in actually making art. He studied briefly under the Social Realist painter Thomas Hart Benton and liked the work of Albert Pinkham Ryder and the Mexican muralists.

Later, he was impressed by Picasso, primitive art, Miro and the other European surrealists. Kandinsky was an important influence, and Pollock's mature art might with some justification be called Abstract Surrealism, even though the depths of exhilaration and despair provoked by excessive self-reflection eventually required a decidedly Expressionist outlet.

At the time it was made, Pollock's art was considered wild and violent, threateningly transgressive. Today it looks elegant, even serene, and beautifully modulated, the colours and tones exquisitely controlled. The energy remains but it is corralled, lassoed by Pollock's whirling lines. The myth states that the struggle took place spontaneously, that Pollock fought and wooed the paint in one great session of love-making, and a major painting resulted. The reality wasn't quite like that, and he would often retouch the drips later with a brush to improve them. Pollock was not a natural draughtsman, but his lines achieved new grace when he threw his paint through the air – as if metamorphosed by the different element. His method transcended his own inabilities and turned him into a great artist.

This transmuting of base metal into gold is such a rare event that it makes him a dangerous role model for young artists. The fact that it worked for Pollock is no guarantee that the magic will ever work again. His was an intensely personal solution, and it's the intensity of the art that lingers and convinces, not the myth. He created a form of all-over painting that challenged all norms and preconceptions and shook up how people thought about art. As de Kooning admitted, it was Pollock who 'broke the ice' for American painters.

In Arnold Newman's moody photo-portrait of Pollock, taken in 1949 for the Life profile that proclaimed him the greatest living painter in America, the artist, his face corrugated with pain, stands against the gappy wooden wall of his painting hut. Next to him on a shelf reposes a human skull, while in front of him is a table cluttered with paint pots from which protrude a thicket of brushes and sticks. The skull and the brushes seem to hem him in, to pin him against the wall. Pollock looks more like a miserable garage hand or mechanic than an artist. But this was part of the macho non-arty image he espoused, a lifestyle that in his case led to alcoholism, long bouts of inactivity and destructive self-doubt.

Between 1948 and 1950, when his reputation was really taking off and the photographers were coming to call, Pollock was mostly sober. He started drinking again as soon as the famous 1950 filming session with Hans Namuth was over, perhaps disturbed by the thought that the whole thing had been set up for camera, and was thus phoney. He hated and feared phoniness and the best of his art has exceptional freshness and authenticity. Namuth's film, of the quintessential Action Painter in action, is remarkable, but it probably triggered Pollock's rapid downward spiral. He had betrayed his muse by faking his procedures and he had to suffer the consequences. Or, looked at another way, how could he keep on venturing into the unknown, deep within the self, without the process exacting a terrible cost?

Pollock's art got stuck around 1950 and in his depression he took more and more to drink. His death in a driving accident at the age of 44 was probably the only solution he could see.

DAVID JONES Sacramental vision

(This article relates to David Jones's 'Sanctus Christus de Capel-y-ffin', reproduced in The Spectator)
7 April 2012

As the focus for an Easter meditation, David Jones's 'Sanctus Christus de Capel-y-ffin' (1925), a small heartfelt painting in gouache on paper, could scarcely be bettered. The Crucifixion takes place in a luminous landscape with the bird of hope in attendance. This is the world of medieval illuminated manuscripts and ivory carvings, a highly sophisticated spiritualized and classicized vision of existence which is sometimes dismissed as primitive. A Welsh hill pony is set off against a chapel, trees and a bridge over running water in an arabesque design quivering with natural and spiritual life. Rhythm is crucial. As Jones said: 'I don't care how static the subject is, but it must be fluid in some way.' He recognized the strong rhythms of the Welsh hills and the counter rhythms of the brooks, and made of them a new unity, a new beauty.

David Jones believed that the artist's primary function was as a 'rememberer'. In 1959 he wrote: 'My view is that all artists, whether they know it or not, whether they would repudiate the notion or not, are in fact "showers forth" of things which tend to be impoverished, or misconceived, or altogether lost or wilfully set aside in the preoccupations of our present intense technological phase, but which, nonetheless, belong to man.'

Myth and religion were two of the things he strove through his art to elucidate to the contemporary mind. He was lucky to have been born at a time of late flowering in Catholic culture: not only were the writers G K Chesterton, Hilaire Belloc, Evelyn Waugh and Graham Greene superbly active, but Eric Gill and his circle of artists were Jones's intimate friends, while the spiritual overseers included that notable Jesuit Father Martin d'Arcy, together with Douglas Woodruff and Tom Burns, successive editors of the influential Catholic weekly, 'The Tablet'. In such a sympathetic climate, Jones could thrive and give rein to his very particular themes and obsessions. His friend and fellow-poet Kathleen Raine identified the three strands in Jones's work which defined his place in civilization: Wales and the Romano-British roots of our ancestral heritage; the Catholic Church and its liturgy; and the army. David Jones (1895-1974) was born in Kent of Welsh extraction, his father hailing from Flintshire, while his mother's family came from Rotherhithe. He was four when he first visited his grandparents in Wales, and from his earliest years, drawing made more sense to him than anything else. He studied at Camberwell School of Art under A S Hartrick, and then on 2 January 1915 enlisted in the Royal Welch Fusiliers, fighting as a private in the trenches of the Western Front from December 1915 to March 1918. The camaraderie of the army was one revelation, another was the mystery of the Eucharist, first glimpsed during the war through a crack in the wall of a barn while Mass was being celebrated. After much soul-searching he was received into the Catholic Church in September 1921, and in 1922 he joined the community set up by Eric Gill at Ditchling in Sussex, to concentrate on establishing a career as an artist-craftsman. To this end he learnt the technique of line engraving.

Gill left Sussex and gravitated to Wales, re-establishing the community in 1924 at Capel-y-ffin in the Black Mountains. In 1925, Jones joined him there, staying on and off until 1927. These were crucial years in his development, witnessing his first works as a mature artist, among which his small but potent Crucifixion must be numbered. Just across the valley from the community was Y Twmpa, or the tump, a conical mountain which features in many of Jones's paintings of this period, becoming a motif rather like Cézanne's Mont St Victoire in its importance to the artist. It appears here in the background of the Crucifixion, to the right of the Cross.

Jones loved lettering – an enthusiasm he shared with Gill – and became an expert maker of inscriptions. In the painting he has lettered the legend 'Sanctus Christus de Capel-y-ffin' around the figure of Christ in the top half of the painting, arranging the script to make both horizontal and vertical patterns of strikingly original simplicity. His was a sacramental vision of celebration and praise, based on an understanding that transient natural beauty was but a reflection of eternal things. As Auden wrote of William Blake, he 'heard inside each mortal thing / Its holy emanation sing'. In his art, David Jones proceeded from the known to the unknown, rediscovering the sacred in the ordinary. Although Jones was one of those rare figures who excelled in more than one discipline, and is widely known and respected as a poet (Eliot placed him with Pound, Joyce and himself as one of the four significant writers of his generation), he thought of himself as essentially a painter rather than a writer. Ironically, he is still somewhat underrated as an artist, whereas his reputation as a poet is more assured. But in whatever he attempted, his profound historical imagination was evident, much preoccupied with the layering of metaphysical, mythical and metaphorical meaning. For Jones, man made things of mysterious and sacred significance, which were both timeless and yet also of their age, possessing what he called a 'requisite nowness'.

Jones hated the way daily life was deprived of spiritual meaning. What would he have made of our secular society? As Kathleen Raine so poignantly put it: 'The ugliness of the world without any sacred dimension, proliferating and submerging the landmarks of the soul, was more than he could bear'.

At the Solemn Requiem for David Jones held in Westminster Cathedral, the poet Peter Levi delivered a sermon which began as follows: 'David Jones understood better than the rest of us the sacrifice of the lamb. His experience in the 1914 war was terrible and it was deep. He understood and he needed what is offered at the stone of this altar and what is shared at the table of this altar and what is said and what is sung in the petrified forest of this church. His need was quite innocent, merely human, to do what has already been done once and for all on another hilltop, outside a different city, and also done many times from the beginning of mankind. In its reality and in its meaning that long series of sacrifices has not ended'.

There is in his serenely joyful painting a sense of a world washed clean and a new beginning for mankind.

MILTON AVERY

Waddington Galleries, 11 Cork Street, London W1
15 September 2001

Milton Avery (1885-1965) is a painter who stands up remarkably well to contemporary taste. For instance, an echo seems to be struck between his work and the gorgeous colour harmonies of Craigie Aitchison. Though Aitchison was quick to distance himself from the American, there does appear to be a similar sensibility informing their work.

The impressive selection of Avery's late landscapes and seascapes currently at Waddington Galleries looks surprisingly fresh and full of vitality; also full of relevance. It is easy to see why he exercised such an influence over the American Abstract Expressionists and Colour Field painters – particularly Mark Rothko and Barnett Newman. As Hans Hofmann said, 'Avery was one of the first to understand colour as a creative means. He was one of the first to relate colours in a plastic way', while Rothko is known to have called Avery the greatest American painter, much to the sceptical amusement of Alfred Barr, eximious director of the Museum of Modern Art in New York. Critics might have complained that Avery wasn't radical enough because he never embraced complete abstraction, but that didn't prevent his work from being a lasting inspiration to artists. In this case, the artists certainly knew best.

A prolific worker who usually produced a painting a day – it is said that he didn't do anything else but paint – Avery was largely self-taught, taking Matisse as his role model, and exploring pure colour in glowing combinations. Avery applied his turps-thinned paint in flat areas, staining the canvas as if with watercolour. The inky richness of 'Morning Sky' is actually painted with oil, but examine it closely and it really does look like watercolour. In fact, Avery did create actual watercolours. His practice was to make drawings with colour notes directly from the landscape, then watercolours, while the oils were done back in the studio. He could be just as effective working in oil on paper. 'Weirs' has some of the strangeness of a Prunella Clough invention, while 'Southern Sea' has all the extravagance of a major painting.

Avery is an extraordinary colourist, most notably here in the pomegranate and turquoise of 'Sunset Sea', but as a draughtsman he is rather limited. Look at the blank faces and limbs of the figures that sometimes stray into his pictures. The sketchiness of their treatment is scarcely convincing. When a composition features a horse or a cow, as do two paintings in this show, Avery is more interested in the pictorial use he can make of a large white shape than in accurately evoking an animal. Generally speaking, his brushmarks are less descriptive than textural for colour is the real subject here.

The most abstract pictures are thus the most successful. When Avery can indulge freely in calligraphic swirls and scratchings and sustain the wonderful brushy quality which animates his rather dry surfaces, then he is a painter of real presence and originality. A painting entitled 'Blue Forest' could easily be a seascape – the subject matters less than the poetic deployment of colour. (In this lack of specificity, Avery again recalls Aitchison. In any number of Aitchison's pictures of the Crucifixion, the animal that bears witness to the Passion could be read as a dog or a goat or a sheep.) What matters about 'Blue Forest' is that its surface has the variety and inventiveness of texture more readily associated with the Surrealists. It looks almost *printed*, rather than painted; printed in some singular and ingenious way. Yet it's simply a masterly bit of painting. Similarly, the pulsing central brown-and-green rhythm of 'Autumn', all flowing horizontals like a river in spate, is expertly varied in other parts of the picture by free hatching and swift, brisk vertical strokes.

A measure of Avery's skill is the way in which he manages to maintain a pictorially tense balance between simplicity and sophistication. Although his pictures seem entirely spontaneous, they are in fact very carefully considered. Look at the brilliantly judged and exquisitely disposed green patches in 'Dark Mountain'. Avery knows and loves the idea of land or sea, and this knowledge of its essence allows him to employ a visual shorthand far more effective than straightforward description. This abbreviated phrasing gives us such successes as 'Pink Meadow' or 'Mountain and Lake'.

Avery achieves an unusually convincing kind of pictorial space, the reverse of traditional perspectival space, perhaps because he arrives at it intuitively through the sure placing of colour. As Rothko wrote: 'Avery was a great poet-inventor who had invented sonorities never seen nor heard before. From these we have learned much and will learn more for a long time to come'. In the end, it's the focused naturalness of Milton Avery, the inevitability of his colours and forms, that wins the day.

Slow Glass: New Work by NAOYA HATAKEYAMA

Impressions Gallery, 29 Castlegate, York, until 3 August
13 July 2002

Last year the award-winning Japanese photographer Naoya Hatakeyama underwent a four-month residency in Milton Keynes as part of the Japan 2001 festival and year of the artist. I use the word 'underwent' with some deliberation. The only occasion on which I have visited Milton Keynes was in the company of the painter Maggi Hambling, and we traversed what seemed the entire length of the town on foot in search of the art gallery, walking down the central reservation of one of the grid roads, risking life and limb at every junction or roundabout. Milton Keynes is a town entirely devoted to the motorcar, and we had made the mistake of trying to walk through its concrete purlieus. Any slight inclination towards melancholy in either of our personalities may be dated to that grey and rainy afternoon of pedestrian temerity. It is thus deeply appropriate that Hatakeyama should have concentrated on depicting Milton Keynes seen through a car window in the rain. Well, that was his intention on first arriving in this (to him) unknown town in a land where it always rains. In fact, it did not rain much during the early summer last year, so Hatakeyama had to find another subject. He lighted upon the new housing estates in this new town, and photographed them from a height of three metres, thus making them appear slightly smaller and even more ridiculous than they actually are. This series of photographs - called still life - is actually fairly ordinary, though beautifully lit and composed, the most impressive being a wide shot of houses in the distance from the other side of a lake or river.

Luckily Hatakeyama was lent a Suzuki jeep by the Milton Keynes council, so he could get about car town without being run over, though the council logo on the vehicle's door did for some reason attract a certain amount of unwelcome attention. He seems to have enjoyed himself bombing about in the sunshine, all preconceptions of English weather subverted, listening to the car radio and nosing out sites of the genteel new brick-built vernacular architecture. Ah, but when it did finally rain, the streets were transformed and Hatakeyama was able to put his first plan into action - photographing the course of raindrops as if looking through a windscreen or window pane. The backdrop is the city at night, in and out of focus. Some features are just recognizable, such as a set of traffic lights or a multi-storey car park, but in fact the more abstract the images, the more effective they are. The runs and clusters of water droplets, like polished pebbles of light, work well with the fragmented views of the town. Intensely coloured and almost abstract, these long-exposure rain images - the slow glass aspect of the exhibition - are highly original and strangely beguiling. I saw the show in Winchester, on the second leg of its three-venue tour. The large rain photographs are framed unobtrusively in grey-white wood, unglazed, the prints on foamboard and aluminium remaining exposed in all their fragility to the atmosphere. This has the effect of making them even more engaging and immediate. The images are not titled individually, but can be purchased for £3,000 each. The exhibition is accompanied by a handsomely illustrated book, priced at £12.50. Ironically, there are no plans to take the work to Milton Keynes itself. A shame really: Hatakeyama's raindrop photographs make the town seem quite beautiful.

CEDRIC MORRIS AND LETT HAINES: Teaching Art and Life

Norwich Castle Museum and Art Gallery, until 5 January
9 November 2002

The East Anglian School of Painting and Drawing was founded in 1937 by two remarkable artists, Cedric Morris and Lett Haines, and was described by them in a prospectus as 'an oasis of decency for artists outside the system'. Based upon the 'free rein' approach current in French academies – which both artists had enjoyed while living in Paris (1920-6) – instruction was kept to a minimum, the atmosphere being more that of a family of artists striving for a common cause. The school's first incarnation was at Dedham, and Lucian Freud was among the earliest students. In July 1939, this building was destroyed by fire. Local arch-traditionalist Alfred Munnings had himself driven back and forth before its smoking ruins gloating over the destruction of such a dangerously radical tendency. Imperturbable, Cedric suggested the students draw the fire-blackened wreck.

Cedric and Lett, as they are familiarly known, had met on Armistice Night, 1918, at once fallen in love (though Lett was married), and remained together despite numerous lovers until

Lett's death in 1978. Both had little formal art training, which in part explains their own freedom as teachers. From the start, it was evident that Lett was the more avant-garde of the pair, exhibiting in New York with such artists as Picasso, Gris and Miró, and working for a while in Brancusi's studio. In fact, Cedric was often described as 'the painter' but Lett was 'the artist'. After a much briefer period of experimentation, Cedric established his mature style by the mid-1920s, and continued to paint with clarity and directness in a form of heightened realism until in 1975 blindness stopped him working. By the late Twenties Cedric's pictures had become fashionable – particularly his flower paintings – and Lett determined to put his own artistic career on hold in order to promote Cedric's. They returned to live in England, and eventually to found their art school.

After the accidental destruction of the Dedham premises, a new school was sought. Towards the end of 1939 Lett and Cedric discovered Benton End, a rambling 16th century house with gardens, a sequestered paradise on the outskirts of Hadleigh in Suffolk. For the first time, the artists could live and run their school (also accommodating their students) in one place. Lett was the 'father' of the community, responsible for its daily administration and for producing two vast meals a day, while Cedric got on with his life as painter and internationally renowned plantsman. In fact, from 1940 to 1980, Cedric was perhaps better known as a breeder of irises than he was as a painter. His early reputation had dissipated, and, although he didn't stop painting until his sight failed, it's only over the last two decades that his true artistic worth has been properly registered. Lett, who had given up his own career to promote Cedric's art – not his garden – was understandably enraged. He came to hate the garden, and turned to cooking as his primary creative outlet, rather as Lee Miller did when she gave up photography. Lett's cooking was sophisticated and experimental for the time (Elizabeth David was a good friend), but could it ever compensate? The school's heyday was in the 1940s and Fifties, when Benton End was a powerhouse of art and literature, good food and lively conversation. Ronald Blythe describes it as 'robust and coarse, and exquisite and tentative all at once. Rough and ready and fine mannered. Also faintly dangerous'. By the 1960s it was no longer really functioning as a school, and Lett was able to do more of his own work again, particularly the small sculptures, his 'weirdies' or 'humbles', made from rubbish and kitchen scraps. These are his most original and witty creations – whether a fetish made from bones, or a strapped-up baked carrot, tearing skyward like some phallic totem. Lett, who described himself as a surrealist, was a good draughtsman in the Gaudier-Brzeska/Wyndham Lewis mode. He should have been better, but he gave up art at the very moment when he needed to consolidate his potential.

Cedric, on the other hand, was a very considerable painter, and this exhibition confirms that. The best of his portraits are shocking in their directness (look at the strange images of Glyn Morgan, Betty Addison or Mary Butts), quite different from the sensuality of the flower paintings, or the gentle freshness of the landscapes. But it is as an inventive colourist that Cedric excels. Take, for example, the pungent colour combinations in 'Nasturtiums' from 1975. They are intuitive rather than analytical, and therein resides Cedric's great natural gift.

The exhibition, which includes paintings by the school's more distinguished pupils such as Freud and Maggi Hambling (showing two powerful studies of Lett), will travel to the National Museum and Gallery, Cardiff (25 January – 27 April 2003), and is accompanied not just by a useful and well-illustrated catalogue, but by a book as well. Benton End Remembered (Unicorn Press, London £25) is a profusely illustrated compilation of 31 memoirs of the Cedric/Lett circle, and is full of fascinating anecdote and precise appreciation. It looks as if finally these richly creative outsiders – who so brilliantly demonstrated how painting could be a way of life – are being given their due.

EVA HESSE

Tate Modern

7 December 2002

Many consider Eva Hesse to be one of the most important sculptors of the second half of the 20th century, but on the evidence of the current Tate show – the largest ever of her work – she appears to be less of a real sculptor and more of an all-pervading influence. To put it another way, Hesse only lived to be 34, and was just beginning to produce relatively mature work in the last four or five years of her life.

The facts that she experimented widely with informal materials such as latex and fibreglass, that her work was often sexually suggestive in subject matter, that she died young and that she was a woman working successfully in a hitherto male-dominated preserve, all helped to make her a cult figure with art students. Her appeal is still largely to the young and, since her tragically early death in 1970 from a brain tumour, Hesse the iconic rebel has been virtually canonised, with her merest scribble elevated to the status of holy relic. The lavish Tate catalogue duly attests to this reverence, which is seemingly propagated by art historians. The trouble is that only a small percentage of Hesse's work deserves such attention. However, no doubt reassured by the blanket acceptance of her oeuvre by those who should know better, the young people flocking to this exhibition showed no signs of being able to distinguish the good from the weak and derivative.

In 1936, Eva Hesse was born in Hamburg of Jewish parents. Escaping the Nazis, her family came to London and then emigrated to New York. She graduated from the (High) School of Industrial Arts in 1945 before entering the Pratt Institute of Design to study advertising design. In 1954 she enrolled at the Cooper Union, graduated in 1957 and entered the Yale School of Art and Architecture to study painting under Josef Albers. In 1960 she worked part-time as a textile designer, and in 1964, when she returned to Germany for a year at the invitation of a rich patron, Hesse had a studio in an abandoned textile factory. The history of design experience in particular relation to textiles was to exert a lasting influence over her thought. In the old German factory she drew machine parts and pieces of cord, and moved definitively away from her early Expressionist self-portraits with heads like golf clubs. She began to make hybrid objects such as the corded and painted reliefs, which developed into the probing tubes and dented receptacles, the ropes and nets and shards of skin for which she is famous.

Hesse's best work has a frenetic tactility, though of course nowadays these objects cannot be touched (and will probably never travel again for exhibition) because they're so fragile. She claimed her subject was 'the total absurdity of life', a good example of how she illustrated this being 'Hang Up' of 1966. It consists of an 11ft rod describing an uneven loop from a vast empty frame. It's going nowhere, doing nothing – a closed circuit, like so many of Hesse's early drawings, such as the too-tidy zipped-up diagram 'Untitled' of 1965, now in the Tate collection. This negativity led inevitably to its logical conclusion. 'I now remember I wanted to go to non art …' she said in 1969. All too probably she succeeded.

One gets the feeling that Hesse was more interested in breaking bounds, in a youthfully transgressive way, than in extending art's territory. She was well aware that the materials she was using would not last, and that their effects were ephemeral. Latex hardens and perishes; fibreglass discolours and becomes brittle. Yet these changes were not essential to her art. An artist like Dieter Roth, who made work which was intended to decay and change its nature over time, was actually being more honest about his intentions. Should copies of Hesse's most fragile sculptures now be made? A copy could never be more than an inauthentic three-dimensional reproduction, for Hesse wanted the artist's touch visible in her work. So why didn't she make more permanent art? Perhaps because she lived in an adolescent dream world. She claimed she wanted to go beyond what she knew and what she could know. Art of any real stature achieves that by its very nature, but Hesse never came to realise that. If she had lived longer, she might indeed have developed into a considerable artist, a sculptor of rare accomplishment. As it is, she remains a dangerous role model for self-obsessed youth, for those who yearn to be different and original – like everybody else.

JOHN PIPER IN THE 1930s: Abstraction on the Beach
Dulwich Picture Gallery
5 February 2003

John Piper (1903-92) was one of the pioneers of modern art in Britain whose centenary falls this year. Others include Graham Sutherland, Barbara Hepworth, Eric Ravilious and Ceri Richards – a powerfully talented generation, but none of them more genuinely popular in the widest sense than Piper. Articulate, prolific and prepared to purvey a brand of modern art containing enough reassuringly traditional elements to satisfy the conservative public, Piper was to become by the end of his long life a Grand Old Man, the kind of figure much loved by the British because he was not too radical. Yet this exhibition concentrates on his work of the Thirties when he was making the most extreme and abstract statements of his whole career – a decade which would exert a formative influence over his subsequent development and mature style.

Piper was something of a late starter as an art student, five years older than his coevals, delayed by a period studying law in accordance with his father's wishes. This age gap made him 'a bit sophisticated' and, by his own account, arrogant and not at all humble, according to his biographer Frances Spalding, writing here in her catalogue essay. Piper was well-informed about contemporary art and swiftly developed an independence of spirit which resulted in him leaving the Royal College of Art in 1930, before gaining his diploma. Some of the earliest work in the exhibition shows him adroitly employing collage (doilies to represent curtains and provide pattern stencils) to soup up his compositions. The subjects are mostly simplified interiors and landscapes with a seaside bent. Picasso and Braque were his heroes, and other influences included Ben Nicholson and the biomorphic shapes of Hans Arp. Abstraction was in the air, but Piper still clung to the representational.

Soon, however, he was experimenting with wholly abstract geometrical drawings and constructions, making reliefs like electrical diagrams out of dowelling and metal rods, sand, gauze and glass. The second room of the exhibition is devoted to this stuff, all done in 1934, and soulless doodling it seems too, all design and no art. At its best it's highly elegant – such as 'Abstract Collage' – but absolutely meaningless. The paintings in the next room are a slight improvement, the finest being one from the Tate, 'Abstract I' of 1935, and a smaller picture from a private collection simply called 'Painting'. Here Piper is developing a language of vertical planes like flats in a stage set – a brand of abstraction that was to prove fashionable with a certain clique, but not saleable.

The work of the next year, 1936, shows increased assurance of handling and greater inventiveness of colour. At the same time we are reminded of Piper's antiquarian interests by a small display of eight of his eloquent black-and-white photographs of Anglo-Saxon and Celtic sculpture. He was an architectural historian of some note, specialising in churches, and it was this strain in his nature – the picturesque and topographical - which was soon to assert itself over pure abstraction. Piper was essentially a Romantic representational artist who benefited from an invaluable abstract training.

The heart of this exhibition is the room of beach and coast collages Piper made between 1936 and 1938. They have an energy and invention which suggests Piper's own relief at returning to depictive imagery; at the same time they have a formal freedom conferred by his recent experiences with abstraction. Their zestful shorthand is immensely evocative, as roughly cut or torn pieces of paper jostle with smudged and overprinted sections of music sheet, patches of gouache colour and fresh, speedy ink drawing. Their directness is compelling and heart-warming. In many respects this is Piper's finest hour. The last room of the exhibition sees Piper approaching the style for which he is best known – essentially a Romantic view of landscape, a sort of abstracted topography, relying on technical dexterity and atmospherics, very knowing.

Was it a sell-out to make accessible art that could be readily enjoyed by large numbers of people? The development of abstraction had long been associated with the pursuit of political freedom, so when Piper wrote in 1938, with his country on the brink of war, 'abstraction is a luxury', did he mean that political freedom was also a luxury? Apparently not. Look at his stage design for Stephen Spender's play *The Trial of a Judge*. Here the geometrical rigidity of the set is intended to indicate oppression, which is the reverse of the notion that abstraction equals political freedom. David Fraser Jenkins, the authority on Piper, states unequivocally that 'The function of Piper's abstraction, at its close, was to illustrate political tyranny'. So abstraction must be generally eschewed. Piper's shrewdness, however, lay in never completely abandoning it.

A word on the selection, which relies heavily upon loans from private collections. Besides indicating Piper's continuing popularity with individuals who are prepared to pay large sums for his work, the preponderance of little known pictures makes the show all the more fascinating. Mixed with a few better known images from public collections, the result is an exhibition of considerable impact and flavour. This is Dulwich Picture Gallery's first show of a 20th-century classic. They've shown plenty of contemporary artists – such as Lucian Freud and Paula Rego – whose work has related to their permanent collection, but not an independent modern. This show is so well-selected and presented that I very much hope there will be more on similar themes. If by chance you miss it in London, it travels to the Djanogly Art Gallery, Nottingham, in July.

BURIED TREASURE: Finding Our Past

Room 35, British Museum

29 November 2003

As a child, various hobbies and enthusiasms haunted my spare time in a rather cyclical fashion. My interests would wax and wane with the seasons, so ornithology would give place to a short-lived mania for collecting stamps, or coins, or foreign banknotes. One long summer I yearned for a metal detector, which would guide me to hoards of Roman coins, or precious rings which had slipped from the fingers of amorous couples on the sandy banks of the lazy Surrey river nearby. My father, perhaps judging all such enthusiasms to be of a temporary nature, counselled against such a purchase, and gradually the dream faded, though a certain romance still attached itself to the adventures which might have been possible with a metal detector. The new exhibition at the British Museum on the emotive subject of buried treasure has a curious double effect: it both enhances the mystery and banishes it forever.

That statement might at first appear contradictory, but let me explain. Most of the exhibits have been found not by archaeologists but by amateurs with metal detectors. (Apparently this group can now lay claim to some 90 per cent of all treasure discoveries.) For instance, the beautiful Ringlemere gold cup, found two years ago in a Kentish field, was located by an enthusiast with a detector. At some point it had been crushed, probably by farm machinery, but had remained buried since about 1600 BC. Once the find had been reported, the archaeologists moved in and started excavating the site. It often seems that the site then becomes the chief focus of interest. It's as if archaeologists would much prefer to deal with earthworks and aerial photographs, with maps and plans and rotted posts, than with such exquisite artefacts as the Ringlemere cup. Aesthetics seems almost to be an embarrassment to them. Certainly, this is the impression conveyed by this determinedly ugly exhibition in one of the BM's unsympathetic new Great Court galleries. The display is dominated by vast lime-green-lined vertical display cases with very little in them, and by huge information panels, three of which are set into the floor. The precious exhibits are dwarfed. Of course, a lot of these objects are tiny anyway – coins or rings or amulets – but there must be better ways of displaying them. However, I was impressed that the public can get to handle various items, under expert supervision, and learn about them from more direct experience. (A Roman cosmetics grinder – a sort of canoe-shaped metal pestle and mortar – seemed to arouse particular interest.) But, for the most part, the objects seem oddly remote and inaccessible, though the exhibition's curators have been at pains to stress accessibility and to amuse children at all costs.

Even the magnificent Mildenhall treasure is mediated through the wall-mounted words and images of Roald Dahl and Ralph Steadman (they collaborated on a book about the subject), while the actual plates and dishes have fake food scattered over them so that we can no longer see their intricate designs. Is this supposed to make them more real, or instruct lame-brains of their purpose? Much more telling is the information that the treasure's finder, Sidney Ford, who quite understandably wanted to keep it for himself, and did so for several years, used the Great Dish for fruit at Christmas. Perfect! What better use for it? The fact that it is an exceptionally fine example of Roman silver tableware of the 4th century AD only adds poignancy to the story.

There are other fine things to be seen, from a fascinating collection of intaglios and memorial and mourning rings (Charles I seemed a popular subject) to the less valuable but often equally elaborate pilgrim badges. Although the rest of the objects come from England and Wales, the famous Lewis Chessmen are included, partly, I suspect because they featured in the first Harry Potter film. These dour little figures, carved from walrus ivory or whale's teeth in the 12th century, were found on the Isle of Lewis in Scotland in the 1820s. Far more numinous and ornate is the Iron Age Celtic Battersea Shield, dating from c.350-50 BC, and found in the Thames in 1857. A case of golden torcs from Snettisham in Norfolk is mildly exciting. I much preferred the slightly creepy silver-gilt Buntingford figurine, supposedly of a saint or other biblical character, and a Delftware dish depicting Charles II hiding in an oak tree. Historically mind-boggling was the hand-axe also found in Norfolk, and now tentatively dated to between 500,000 and 700,000 years ago. If correctly dated, this would suggest that Britain had been inhabited much longer than previously thought. But perhaps here we enter the realm of conjecture.

When I discovered that Buried Treasure is the first archaeology exhibition at the BM in almost 20 years, it was difficult to know whether to laugh or cry or simply be grateful. Is there no way that archaeological exhibition design standards can be improved and presentation made more adult? Why does archaeology voluntarily given itself such a bad name? This exhibition is gruesome. Even the jargon is hideous.

I'm rather glad my father dissuaded me from acquiring a metal detector all those years ago. I might have ended up wearing an anorak anxiously in pursuit of the next 'findspot', determined to beat my fellow 'metal detectorists' to the pot of gold at the end of the neolithic rainbow. Not that it's the gold that glitters – only the 'findspot'. If you take the art out of artefacts, you are left with the facts, and I have a sneaking suspicion that's the way archaeologists like it best. Luckily, however hard people try to disguise it, the romance and beauty remains yet in the objects themselves. Only the context repels.

EL GRECO

The National Gallery
14 February 2004

Something extraordinary and rare is happening in London: we have an incomparable El Greco exhibition in our midst. It doesn't really matter that it's being staged in the rebarbative dungeon-like rooms of the National Gallery's Sainsbury wing basement, for even those inconsiderate walls are alive with the strange music of El Greco's vision. For a few months the dungeon becomes a sacred crypt, filled with the fluttering spirits of El Greco's agonies, ecstasies and visitations, with a wild chant that cannot be stilled. Against such strong magic we are powerless: along with El Greco's saints and sinners our gaze drifts inevitably heavenwards.

The artist John Craxton has spent more than 50 years in close study of El Greco, and has lived much in Crete, the island from which El Greco himself hailed. He believes that the artist's upbringing in Crete was crucial to his development as a painter, that he was very much a Cretan painter, rather than a Greek Byzantine one.

Crete under the Venetians, whose colony it then was, was a culturally liberated land when the young Domenikos Theotokopoulos (1541-1614) began to train as an icon painter. In the first room of the exhibition is a recently discovered icon of 'The Dormition of the Virgin', from the Monastery of Ermoupolis on the island of Syros. In muted gold and red it greets the visitor with only a shadowy premonition of what will be El Greco's mature style, for it conforms to the accepted template for this subject and presents few opportunities for experiment. Together with the much-damaged panel of 'St Luke Painting the Virgin and Child', with its dim echoes of an emerging Italian influence, the artist's early years are adumbrated. But in the same room hangs 'The Entombment of Christ', dating to the late 1560s, in which the expressiveness of the faces clearly shows El Greco's growing powers of characterisation.

In 1568 El Greco travelled to Venice, where he is said to have studied briefly under Titian. Certainly that master's influence, along with the colour sense and chiaroscuro of Tintoretto, may be increasingly discerned in El Greco's work. By 1570 he had moved on to Rome, where he spent several years drinking at the fount of classical art, but only absorbing what would be useful to his increasingly defined personal vision. (Interestingly, Michelangelo was a key inspiration.) In 1577 he settled in Toledo, the ecclesiastical capital of Spain, where he was to make a substantial reputation with his religious paintings and portraits. After his death his work was forgotten with shocking rapidity, until rediscovered and reappraised in the 19th century. Today his rough brushwork and radical distortions look surprisingly modern. (I have to keep reminding myself that he was a 16th-century painter, a near-contemporary of Nicholas Hilliard.) We are touched upon the raw by his directness.

In a recent letter John Craxton pointed out that it is El Greco's ability to dematerialise flesh that sets him apart from his contemporaries – a quality that was inherent in the Byzantine traditions of the artists among whom he was brought up in Crete. This is why his work seems so spiritual – it effectively renounces the physical world. His flickering attenuated figures writhe upwards like candle flames, aspirant in both senses. Look at the gleaming exophthalmic gaze of 'St Peter in Penitence' and 'St Mary Magdalen in Penitence' hung on either side of 'Christ Crucified' in Room 2 of the show. St Peter's lustrous eyes (the subject became something of a speciality for El Greco) are fixed on the possibility of forgiveness, looking inward rather than at the world about him, and even the dramatically lit sky behind his head cannot distract him.

El Greco's art is one of action and reaction, of twist and surge and complex dynamics. A typical palette soon emerged, of green golds, opalescent blues, lime-green and whited magenta. He returned to the same subjects again and again, and although it may seem a dry art-historical occupation to compare different versions of the same scene, much can be learnt from this about El Greco's approach to his art. There are four variants of 'The Purification of the Temple' on view, for instance, each with a slightly different emphasis given to the vertiginous swirl of this extraordinary centrifugal composition. Compare the peripheral figures – the man lifting a chest at bottom left in the two later versions, for example. Why does he appear more convincing in the National Gallery's own version ? Is it the play of light across his back and arms, or the stricter definition of a cooler palette? We need to look at El Greco with close attention, and this is a good way of focusing the mind.

Certain paintings stand out. The magisterial portrait of St Jerome in the third gallery, with the brushwork of his robe taking on some of the same quality as that of his beard – a textural kinship which brings a memorable unity to the image. Opposite hangs 'The Agony in the Garden', all pupate rock forms and flowing drapes. The hanging is most effective in its juxtapositions: an emphatic installation for an emphatic artist. St Francis and St Dominic lean towards each other in prayer. In Room 4 of the exhibition, the central space is dominated by huge virtuoso canvases such as 'The Virgin of the Immaculate Conception' with its poignant background landscape and foreground flowers, and the amazing disjunctions of scale in 'The Opening of the Fifth Seal'. Here, in a vast outpouring which is both emotional and spiritual, is the concentrated genius of El Greco. Through broken, fluttery brushstrokes, the focus is gathered and dispersed over the whole surface of the picture. Traditional single-point perspective is abandoned, and the entire picture surface is activated through intricate rhythms and echoes.

The fifth and sixth galleries contain their share of wonders, including the magnificent landscape of Toledo and a strange wild 'Laocoon'. The last room is filled with portraits of gentlemen in ruffs, a sardonic bespectacled Cardinal and a romantically disdainful Trinitarian friar. Compared with the religious paintings, the portraits are considered and controlled, though painted with a dashingly effective freedom of gesture. The depth of feeling in 'Portrait of a Man', from the Metropolitan Museum of Art in New York, is almost excruciating in its humanity.

Some who have travelled the world and visited its museums are apt to belittle El Greco simply because they have seen too many copies, 'school of' or not so good variations on a theme. But this show is different. It is an exceptional privilege to have an El Greco exhibition of such quality in London. Such a thing is a once-in-a-lifetime event. No one, literally no one, should hesitate before being wrapped in the beautiful luminous ambience of his work. It is unique.

GILLIAN AYRES

The Royal West of England Academy, Bristol
20 March 2004

The RWA must be congratulated for staging this scintillating exhibition of recent work by Gillian Ayres. Ayres is one our finest abstract painters, a colourist of rare lyricism and wit. Her superbly composed paintings have a spontaneous joy and uninhibited verve to them which makes the heart dance. The RWA's beautiful, naturally lit galleries are the perfect setting for Ayres's dramatic canvases. their scale is just right. As the light changes on a day of wind and rain and sun, such as it was when I visited, the paintings progress through a sequence of moods, and show themselves in all their colours. Seldom is such a rich and satisfying visual experience to be found in galleries showing contemporary art.

Gillian Ayres was born in Barnes in 1930, in those pre-war days when, only a few minutes from metropolitan Hammersmith, Barnes was still properly rural. That countrified upbringing was important, for she derives much of her inspiration as an artist from the seasonal cycles of nature, re-interpreting the rhythms and narratives of the natural world, without ever attempting to describe them. She has lived in Barnes for much of her life, although in 1981 a decisive move was made to wilder parts – first to Wales and then to the West Country. She now lives on the borders of Devon and Cornwall, within easy reach of the sea. (Her West Country connections, together with a salient spell of teaching, 1959-65, at Corsham Court, the then home of Bath Academy of Art, combined to make her election as an Honorary Academician of the RWA something of an inevitability.) Her paintings from the 1980s and 1990s, and now from the new century, constitute a wonderful outpouring, a distinctive late style of such unforced vigour and joyous celebration as to render the word 'optimistic' completely redundant.

Where did this life-enhancing vision spring from? Ayres has always been a fiercely independent spirit, schooled at St Paul's in Hammersmith, where her best friend was Shirley Williams, before leaving for Camberwell School of Art at the early age of 16. This was not unheard of: a fellow junior student was Euan Uglow, whose career followed a more predictable Camberwell trajectory, on to the Slade, and a lifelong inquiry into appearances which resulted in a 'realism' of the most radical order. Ayres could not have been more different. She felt hemmed in by the teaching at Camberwell, and walked out of the school in 1950, a month before the final examination. It had no relevance for her, so she left, and embarked upon the course of self-discovery which has led to the creation of some of the most successful and admired abstract paintings to be made in Britain since the war.

The story of Ayres's subsequent development towards abstraction is cogently told by Mel Gooding in his 2001 monograph on the artist, published by Lund Humphries. Gooding has been the driving force behind the RWA's exhibition, making the selection of some 40 works, and writing a catalogue note. As you enter the main exhibition space, Ayres's substantial paintings glow from the walls like beacons, with a gorgeous dark jewel-like tondo touched with gold, 'Riverine' from 1994, dominating the end wall. Among the most beguiling of the paintings in this airy double gallery are 'The Colour that was Here', 'Picos' and 'A Hazy Shade of Winter'. Ayres's idiosyncratic titles come after the paintings are finished, and are poetic and non-descriptive in character, often adding another level to one's enjoyment of a picture. (Not many artists could title a canvas 'Sucked Up Sunslips' and get away with it.) Further on there's a room of the impressive hand-coloured Carborundum prints that Ayres has recently taken to making with the assistance of master printer Jack Shirreff, and delicious small oils like psalms are interspersed among the larger works. (Both paintings and prints are for sale, with prices ranging up to the £50,000 mark.) Of the smaller pictures, 'West Float 1', 'Performance', 'Foss' and 'Rose Fair', all done in the last year or two, are particularly eloquent. Of the larger – and some are very large indeed – the ravishing triptych 'Bred of Summer's Heat' and 'Where are We Going?' swiftly become firm favourites. The colours are luscious, the materiality of the paint unhesitatingly emphasised in texture and impasto. This is pure painting, squarely addressing the question 'What can be done in painting that cannot be done in any other medium?'

A characteristic of Ayres's style is the bold use of black and white, sometimes to mark off and delineate areas of the canvas, at others to stand for passages of light or dark. When the white is employed in linear fashion, the effect is often similar to cloisonné – the identifying of discrete cells within the large whole, a form of emphasis which never becomes too regulated. Indeed Ayres's sense of composition is undeniably organic, a natural order which must be delivered through the senses and instincts rather than imposed by the brain. It is amazing that she manages to make a coherent image out of such disparate and (apparently) wildly conflicting ingredients. It is similarly a cause for wonder that her colours stay so fresh, that she doesn't muddy them at all, especially when you consider how she layers on the paint, yet still wants to preserve the evidence of the initial colour stained on to the canvas. Her layering is thus eminently visible: salmon pink over green, with white hazed in over the top. The brushstrokes are often strongly gestured, the paint mounting up in thickness, but the freshness remains.

As Mel Gooding has pointed out, Ayres offers us a different kind of truth to nature than realism proposes. There is a congruence of intent and meaning – Ayres's paintings speak of the underlying patterns of nature expressed through her individual vocabulary of forms – the rounded triangles and ovals, the mouths and zigzags, the leaf, petal and fruit shapes. She paints about the abstract properties of the visible world, its energies and manifestations. The artist works from inner necessity, creating from deep-seated impulse and guided by an ideal of the truth. 'We all want truth, that is, reality,' Ayres says. 'Art gets there in the form of poetic or artistic truths, which are products of the creative imagination ... You are always trying to find something you haven't seen before, an experience that is true to oneself.'

The distinguished art historian and long-time supporter of Ayres's work, Norbert Lynton, remarked at the exhibition's opening that 'writing about joy is very difficult'. The best thing I can say to you is, take the time to visit Bristol: the Ayres show is a feast not only for the eyes but also for the spirit.

RAOUL DE KEYSER: Edge of the Real

Whitechapel Art Gallery
1 May 2004

Why did Raoul de Keyser (born 1930) give up his first career as an art writer and sports columnist to become an artist? What supreme folly possessed him? But perhaps it's not too late to revert. Surely some newspaper magnate could be persuaded to give him a sinecure on a provincial weekly so that he could retire from a profession that he evidently entered by mistake. It's the only honourable solution, since for the past 40 years de Keyser has been producing pictures of such limited interest that even he must be bored to death with them. It would be an act of charity to release him from so burdensome a position.

Thankfully, his work is not particularly well known in the UK. This is the first major survey of his painting career in this country, and comprises 75 works. On the day I visited, attendance was sporadic at the Whitechapel – not helped perhaps by the fine spring weather and the fact that the top-lit galleries were, in places, blindingly bright with sunlight, making it difficult to focus on anything on the white walls. Visitors seemed glum and inattentive. The most fun was had by two elderly ladies carrying folding chairs which they carefully placed in front of the pictures. Comfortably seated, they speculated widely as to the subjects depicted. In these scarcely adumbrated canvases they saw whales at sea, ghosts, lions or possibly a map, trees or maybe creeping deforestation. Their interpretations were far more imaginative than anything else in the gallery.

For an essential negativity radiates from de Keyser's pictures – a denial of everything that makes painting so special: colour, composition, drawing, variation of touch and surface, all organised into a whole which tells us something new about the perceptual world. There is no hidden structure to this work, no inner necessity, no apparent reason to be. De Keyser's work is so marginal as to be off the page and out of the picture. There is very little to look at in his paintings, but he is neither properly a Minimalist nor a Pop artist, though his name is spuriously linked with both movements. Occasionally, he makes a good-ish beginning, as in the apricot-pink ground of 'Tors' [Torso], but nothing more is built upon it. The work is stalled.

Yet according to a brood of international museum directors writing in the catalogue, de Keyser is hard at work interrogating the very nature of painting. How to account for the high standing of his work? Perhaps because it reproduces well, and can even look quite impressive when only a detail is shown. But to visit a whole show of his paintings is to be confronted with a body of work that is admittedly modest in scale but utterly nugatory in meaning and relevance. It's a good thing this exhibition is free – I can't imagine anyone happily paying to see it.

To accompany the de Keyser exhibition and occupying two thirds of the upstairs gallery space is Edge of the Real – A Painting Show. Featuring 20 'established or emerging artists', it is intended to complement the Belgian 'master' and strike echoes from his work. (As easy to raise a resonance from cotton wool.) Thankfully, there is actually very little connection between these young-ish Brit artists and de Keyser, though the common theme is supposed to be images that 'hover between reality and abstraction'. Well, so does most art, so no bull's eye there.

With the spirits so lowered by the dreary pseudo-art colonising the rest of the Whitechapel, it is difficult to be enthusiastic about this oddly assorted bunch of artists, each represented by a single work – unless they cheat by doing multi-panel pieces. The highly talented George Shaw seems to have painted himself into a dim corner of the churchyard – perhaps it's time he went back and had another long look at the Pre-Raphaelites. David Thorpe contributes a rather mad and wispily intricate collage called 'Good People'. Andrew Grassie's work represents a triumph of technique over content, as he plugs away at his miniature photo-realist tempera paintings of sad interiors. Michael Raedecker shows off considerable stitchery skills but little else, while the elegant and fastidious drippings of Callum Innes look quite out of place in such sportive company. How else can one consider the hideous palette of Victoria Morton? The most effective piece is an inventive and immaculate collage entitled 'Core's Progress' by Ian Monroe. The Whitechapel used to put on such exciting and worthwhile shows – I hope it soon returns to form.

WALTER RICHARD SICKERT: The Human Canvas

Abbot Hall Art Gallery, Kendal, Cumbria
4 September 2004

Walter Richard Sickert (1860-1942) known as Walter up to 1924 and Richard thereafter, was an artist of genius – a superb draughtsman and printmaker, and a painter continually able to re-invent himself: his was a truly protean personality. Trained initially as an actor, Sickert was adept at disguising himself and presenting new sides of his character to the public view. He was an accomplished cook who loved to entertain, a wide-ranging conversationalist, a wit, and a prolific writer whose art criticism has a savour and tang all its own, however verbose and enjoyably periphrastic may be its expression. (This in sharp contrast to his art, which was a model of economy and exactitude.)

Sickert was born in Munich to a family of painters of Danish descent who moved to England in 1868. (He was later fond of saying that no one was more English than he.) He spent some three years working as an actor (1879-81), before determining to be an artist. In 1881 he studied briefly at the Slade, but found it more fruitful to apprentice himself to Whistler, for whom he worked as studio assistant for a couple of years. In 1883 he travelled to Paris with Whistler's 'Portrait of the Artist's Mother' en route for the Salon; he went also armed with a letter of introduction to Degas. Sickert had managed to hold his own against the redoubtable 'Jimmy', and he was now to do so again with the equally impressive and irritable Degas. He returned to England with his Whistlerianism distinctly modified by this new French connection.

In fact, Sickert was to be recognised perhaps above all else as the chief conduit of artistic influence between Paris and London. He is credited with introducing to England a moderate form of Impressionism, and was responsible for mounting – with his friend and colleague Philip Wilson Steer – the exhibition *London*

Impressionists at the Goupil Gallery in 1889. He was a dedicated francophile, living mostly in Dieppe between 1898 and 1905, and exhibiting alongside Bonnard, Vuillard and Matisse. In many ways he was an honorary Frenchman, though England remained his first love, and he was passionately dedicated to the great British graphic tradition of Cruikshank, Rowlandson and Hogarth. Revealingly, the third name in his artistic pantheon was the contemporary Punch cartoonist Charles Keene.

Keene is little remembered today, but his influence on Sickert was important in its way as the very different inspirations derived from Whistler and Degas. Sickert's father had been a draughtsman on a Bavarian comic paper so he understood perfectly the demands of such work, and the need for the highest skills of draughtsmanship and invention. For Sickert, drawing was the essential foundation for good painting, and his method of squaring up a composition from a preparatory study and transferring it to the canvas is sometimes visible in the finished painting. This is not to say that he was uninterested in the properties of paint – there have been few artists who exploited the physical potential of paint to quite such varied degree. He was fascinated by what paint could physically do, much as he was fascinated by what he called the 'gross material facts' of modern urban living.

Abbot Hall has mounted a small and intently focused survey of Sickert's career, consisting simply of 43 paintings, with no supporting drawings or prints. Nearly half of these works are borrowed from the Tate, through the Tate Partnership scheme, set up to benefit less-richly endowed provincial collections. (Appropriately, in another room in the museum is Degas's bronze 'Dancer Looking at the Sole of her Right Foot', also on loan from the Tate. Pity a Whistler and a Keene were not available, too.) The walls of the intimate galleries have been painted a deep blue-grey to provide a suitably darkened context in which to show Sickert's richly toned and coloured images. The exhibition opens strongly with 'The Red Shop' (c.1888) hanging near to the portrait of singer and dancer Minnie Cunningham, both pictures of simplified and eloquent design in flattened space, acknowledging the influence of Whistler yet moving on from it.

Sickert was expert at figures in interiors and because he relished the seamy underbelly of society, his gaze was often drawn to the extremes of human activity, and in particular to prostitution and murder. But it's a pity that so much attention is paid here to the so-called Camden Town murder. The nudes of this period are dark but shafted with light: vigorously brushed and almost clumsily hatched, the moulding of form is brusque but effective. There is a starkness about them, but also a peculiar and pervasive dinginess. There are seven here, and only one – 'The Rose Shoe' – is of lasting interest.

In the exhibition's third room we are greeted by the famous 'Ennui' – the epitome of suburban Sunday afternoon cafard. The mood lightens with a keen bit of hanging: 'L'Armoire à Glace', a compelling, electrically lit interior in recessive panels, next to the 'Brighton Pierrots', with 'The New Bedford', all vertical plush and shine, hanging alongside. What Sickert could do with surface pattern while still giving a sense of the sitter can be seen in his masterly 'Portrait of Victor Lecourt', while the late works of liberated colour based closely on photographs – such as the self-portraits as Lazarus and the Servant of Abraham, and the exquisite pink and green 'Variation on Peggy' – still pack a powerfully modern punch.

Yet this is somehow rather a safe and obvious selection. To do real justice to such an experimental artist the choice should have been more daring. Certainly more music-hall scenes (what about the high-stepping Plaza Tiller Girls from c.1938, and a couple of the earlier revolutionary theatre interiors?) and fewer 'murdered' nudes. Lesser known pictures, such as 'The Elephant Poster, Dieppe', 1910 (exhibited Browse & Darby, 1990) or 'Le Journal' (c.1906) which interestingly relates early to late work, or 'The Area Steps' (c.1928), would add another dimension to the complex

Sickert story. And then there's the glorious late red landscape of Bathampton, almost abstract in its colour combinations, which would have gone well with 'Variation on Peggy'. Some of these are admittedly in private collections, and may not be easily borrowed; others, such as the strange and splendid late painting 'The Raising of Lazarus', or 'Sir Thomas Beecham Conducting', reside abroad, and budgets simply won't stretch to such travel expenses. Such are the limitations imposed on the best exhibition organisers.

Other familiar images come to mind, such as 'The Bathers, Dieppe', 1902, from the Walker Art Gallery, Liverpool, or the late radical portraits of Hugh Walpole (Glasgow) and Gavin Henderson (The Farringdon Collection Trust). These, to my mind, would be infinitely preferable choices to the anguished self-portrait of c.1896, or the rebarbative, broken, blobby surfaces of the portraits of Jacques-Emile Blanche and Harold Gilman. That said, of course there are some lovely paintings on show – from the magnificent early rendition of the domes of St Mark's, Venice, and 'The Statue of Duquesne, Dieppe', to the light, airy vista of 'Belvedere, Bath' – which remind us how brilliant and unpredictable Sickert could be, and how much he has formed our perception of a whole period of European history.

WILLIAM ORPEN: Politics, Sex & Death

Imperial War Museum
5 February 2005

The first question to spring to mind concerning this most welcome and in-depth study of the Irish–British painter Sir William Orpen (1878-1931) is why the Imperial War Museum? Recently, there have been notable exhibitions of his contemporaries Augustus John and William Nicholson at the Tate and the Royal Academy respectively, but Orpen it seems does not merit a star 'art venue', his life's achievement (only a fraction of which was actually devoted to the subject of war) being relegated to a repository of machines of mass destruction. I'm sure the director-general and curatorial staff of the Imperial War Museum will forgive me for pointing out that their galleries are best known for their guns and tanks and planes (not to mention the gruelling Holocaust display), rather than for exhibitions of paintings. And yet the IWM does mount extremely good exhibitions of 20th-century artists – consider the Eric Ravilious show last year, and the Piper and Nash shows of earlier date. It just isn't known for it as the RA or Tate are. Does this weigh against Orpen?

It certainly demonstrates that he's still not taken particularly seriously by the art establishment, which has perhaps never really forgiven him for being so successful in his lifetime. As the press release reminds us, Orpen was 'probably the most famous painter in Britain' when he died. And yet there has never been an Orpen solo show in any of our national galleries. Why? True, he was not avant-garde in any noticeable way, pursuing instead a broadly realist course in the tradition of Velázquez and Manet (look at his handling of blacks in his portraits), yet he brought an original and inventive colourism to that mastery of tonality, and had his own distinctive vision of the world. He enjoyed great technical facility, but this is often held against him, and the dread word 'superficial' crops up too often when he is discussed. But look at any of the paintings that really engaged him — his best portraits, such as those of Lady Rocksavage and Count John McCormack, his mocking self-portraits, and nearly all the political and war work (the two categories overlap rather) – and the last adjective to come to mind is 'superficial'. In these pictures Orpen is deeply committed, and sends a complex series of signals to the viewer's heart and mind through the brilliant raiment of his paint.

The current exhibition design at the IWM is sensible and unobtrusive, allowing the work to be properly seen, unlike the any-angled Ravilious installation, which called attention to itself at the cost of the paintings. The first half of the show concentrates on Orpen's self-portraits and conversation pieces, his nudes and his allegories. There are even a number of dark genre paintings (such as 'The Valuers' and 'A Mere Fracture'), which both ape and subvert their Victorian models. Orpen is knowing but not obscure. 'The Knackers Yard' echoes Hogarth, Daumier and Pryde, while 'The English Nude' is a deliberate reworking of Rembrandt's 'Bathsheba at Her Bath'. Against these crepuscular subjects are set such lighthearted and light-filled studies as 'Park Lane Interior' and 'On the Beach, Howth'. The nudes are wonderfully frank for their time, possessing a conviction of satiated desire or early-morning melancholy which must constitute the very aim and meaning of figurative realism. Walking through this first gallery, one gains an impression of an artist who took his work, but not himself, seriously. Here is the extraordinary series of self-portraits in which Orpen sends himself up gloriously, acting any number of parts with a degree of self-awareness we find oddly modern. Here is an artist steeped in the Old Masters (Dutch Golden Age especially), who deals also in wit and irony, whose many acquaintances but few friends remarked on his peculiar mixture of jokes and bitterness, a small man who revelled in hard work and long hours and parodied himself as 'Ickle Orps'. A painter who readily mastered technique, and made of style a tool, not a motivation or identity – as was the case with the Vorticists, for instance. He depicts himself as sportsman, jockey, artist, rotter, soldier and socialite; or as Chardin, in a white dressing-gown with his head bound up, in his prize-winning costume for the Chelsea Arts Ball. In 'Self-Portrait with "Sowing New Seed" ', background details from one of his own allegories offer a fractured and plausible image of his innermost preoccupations, painted with all the stark assertiveness and contemporary sensibility of Kitaj. The second half of the exhibition, the military wing, is found by way of the immovable vastness of Sargent's great painting 'Gassed', reminding us that Orpen inherited Sargent's mantle of society portraitist. There are drawings on view here, including a beautifully sensitive black chalk study of Jack Knewstub, and an ink 'Self-Portrait on the Hills above Huddersfield', with Orpen debunking himself as lord of all he surveys. A stern portrait of Churchill appropriately heralds the war section, which consists of five galleries, mostly of scenes from the first world war and Orpen's stint as an official War Artist. This addition makes the exhibition a large one, and fully justifies its presence at the IWM. Orpen gave all the war pictures from his 1918 exhibition at Agnews (opened by Lord Beaverbrook and visited by 9,000 in its first month) to the IWM, which accounts for the number of works here.

Orpen was a master of the combined pencil and watercolour study (look at such searing images as two wounded RFC officers breakfasting and 'A Death among the Wounded in the Snow'), and his control of charcoal was exquisite (see the drawings of men just out of the trenches near Arras). But one of the finest war pictures is the oil 'German Wire, Thiepval', which works both as a documentary study and as an original painting in its own right. Quite different in mood, but equally inventive in colour, is 'View of Montmartre' (1919), done when he was in Paris for the Peace Conference.

A staunch supporter of the common soldier and against the 'frocks' (the frock-coated politicians and diplomats all set to make a hash of peace), Orpen had difficulty in coming to terms with his war experience. He had begun to drink hard and may have suffered some sort of breakdown. He may also have contracted syphilis, which would account for his rapid physical decline. His art went out of fashion, and only began to receive proper attention again in the 1980s. This exhibition should do something to rehabilitate his artistic reputation, but I fear it will not be enough. Despite the title – a mistaken and poor-taste attempt to sex up Orpen's image – this is a valuable show which deserves wide attention.

DAVID MILNE WATERCOLOURS: Painting Towards the Light

British Museum

10 September 2005

The Canadian painter David Milne (1882-1953) is not known in this country. His name is shamefully overlooked by the *Yale Dictionary of Art & Artists*, and there has never before been a show of his work here. The fact that there is one now is largely due to the vision and enthusiasm of Frances Carey, who acquired three watercolours by Milne while she was deputy keeper of Prints and Drawings at the BM. However, even when there is a really superb exhibition of his work in London, the public is not beating a path to its door. (Would it be different, one wonders, if the show had been mounted elsewhere – at the Royal Academy or the Tate, with their prestigious exhibition halls and effective publicity machines?) Quite frankly, people don't know what they're missing. Discovering Milne has enhanced the store of beauty in my mind, and opened for me another chapter in the history of watercolour – a chapter he occupies entirely on his own.

Milne was born in a log cabin in the wilds of Ontario, the tenth child of émigré Scots farmers. A clever child who excelled particularly at botany, he grew up to be a teacher, but wanted to be an artist and took a New York correspondence course in how to paint. In 1903 he went to New York to be an illustrator, enrolled in the Art Students League, and made a precarious living painting window signs for shops. He was inspired by Rockwell Kent and other older contemporaries such as Robert Henri, and tried his hand at pastels and etchings. From 1912, he concentrated on watercolour and oil (he showed two oils and three watercolours in the Armory Show), gradually developing his signature style of watercolour – a highly original treatment of the medium reliant on very little water and application with a hard bristle brush.

The exhibition begins with some of his early watercolours, which are more fluid in style than his mature work. A masterpiece of this period is 'New York Roofs' (c.1912), notable for the extensive areas of the support (in this case, illustration board) left blank. Milne was adept at letting the white of the paper work for him. He could draw a convincingly solid figure (see the roadsweeper in 'White Matrix') with a few coloured lines and an expressively contained shape. But he was equally skilled with black, in a typically anti-Impressionist way, and used it unsparingly. Although his early work is very French in spirit, the use of colour approaches the expressionist. 'Cobalt Trees', of probably the following year, is already daring in colour, while his understanding of the structure of trees shows signs of the mastery it would soon encompass. A couple of ink on Japanese paper drawings further demonstrate this structural, almost architectural, interest.

In December 1917, Milne enlisted in the Canadian army to fight rather than to paint for the cause. After some training in Toronto and rounding up deserters in Quebec, he embarked for Europe, only to be quarantined (against the Spanish flu that was devastating an already depleted populace) at Kimmel Park Camp in Wales. He was there when the Armistice was declared. On leave in London towards Christmas 1918, he discovered the Canadian War Records programme established by Lord Beaverbrook. Through the recommendation of P G Konody, the Observer's art critic and the Beaver's adviser, he became a war artist. (Konody also suggested a London dealer to Milne, but his advice was ignored, effectively depriving us of seeing Milne's work for nearly a century.) Kimmel Park Camp was his first subject, closely followed by other camps in Yorkshire, Hampshire and Sussex. Of his UK period, the High Street in Ripon is a fine, richly-coloured study (a little like the Camden Town painters), full of movement and his trademark use of black and white. In 1919 he visited France and Belgium, recording the aftermath of the war, the blasted countryside and bomb craters, the massed graves. The experience moved him deeply. These large watercolours are a remarkable, if bleak, achievement. Look at the expanse of 'Montreal Crater, Vimy Ridge', big enough in reality to accommodate a church, a couple of figures poised at its lip to add human scale. As he said, 'the man changes, and with that, the painting'.

Milne returned to North America and resumed life in the tiny village of Boston Corners in upstate New York. Here he painted some of his finest landscapes, such as 'Dark Shore Reflected, Bishop's Pond' (c.1920). Succinctly structured, fluently composed and ordered, the economy of means echoes the exactness of placing. Milne perfected a highly experimental technique of applying watercolour over his preliminary graphite drawing in dry, discrete touches of opaque pigment like gouache or tempera. Water was sometimes applied last, the reverse of normal watercolour method. It was enormously effective in the depiction of landscape, and particularly of reflections in water. The sparely brushed forms expertly laid out on textured paper have an astringency that is curiously sensual.

In a couple of flat cabinets are examples of his coloured drypoint etchings, so similar in appearance to the watercolours, but less radical. There are some nice ripple effects in red, blue and yellow, but the dry brushing of the watercolours is infinitely more exciting. Milne gave up watercolour for 12 years, from 1925 to 1937, and by the time he returned to it, something fundamental had changed. His late work, made with failing eyesight, has none of the intensity or passion of his early landscapes, and tended towards whimsical memory pieces. One here, 'Snow in Bethlehem', has a slightly tougher Chagall-like charm, but most of these figure subjects are soft-centred. The exception is a series of four wonderfully loose Turneresque watercolours of a storm over islands, made in 1951, in which he reverses black and white, playing with negative and positive, and painting the lightning dramatically black.

This exhibition, organised by the Art Gallery of Ontario with assistance from the Canadian High Commission, has been designed to raise Milne's profile abroad. An excellent hardback catalogue has been published to accompany the show (currently selling at the unbeatable price of £14.95), which sets him in perspective and context, and illustrates the work extremely well. The watercolours have been carefully selected (no charmingly faded examples here) and ring true in their pristine blacks, whites and reds. If I have one quibble, it is that the blues suffer, being shown against a backcloth of blue in the display cases. And the blues are one of the marvels (together with the greens and rusty browns) of Milne's style. I urge you to ascend to the fourth floor of the BM and visit this show. It's an eye-opener.

PORTRAYING THE SELF

22 October 2005

This is the season of the self-portrait. At the Royal Academy until 11 December are 150 self-portraits by Edvard Munch (reviewed in this column three weeks ago), the depth of his obsession bordering on sheer tedium. Just opening at the National Portrait Gallery is the first major museum study in this country of the self-portrait, from the Old Masters to now. A most distinguished collection of self-portraits by 20th-century British artists assembled by the writer Ruth Borchard, which has been touring this country and will visit America next year, has now found a permanent home in London. And an exhibition of 30 pictures by Cherry Pickles (born in Bridgend, South Wales, in 1950) opens at Piano Nobile Fine Paintings, 129 Portland Road, London W11, consisting entirely of self-portraits (until 29 October).

Munch almost gives self-portraiture a bad name. He had the visual equivalent of verbal diarrhoea (this is a man who left more than 20,000 works by his own hand to the City of Oslo), and he turned to self-depiction again and again for relief from his latest neurosis. Munch was incarcerated in the prison of self, but at least he painted the bars different colours and drew his nightmares on the cell walls. The range of media he employed, and his very considerable skills with paint and line, make this rampant self-obsession (just about) tolerable. A smaller show than the RA's would have done him greater service, but as a point of comparison with the NPG's survey it is valuable viewing: *Self Portrait: Renaissance to Contemporary* is a blockbuster with attitude – 55 painters glaring down at us mere mortals from the Olympian heights of their creativity (until 29 January 2006).

Leaving aside for a moment the (at times) bizarre selection of artists, it's a great pleasure and a privilege to have a 500-year span of Western self-portraiture to compare and contrast. From van Eyck to Chuck Close via such major modern masters as Courbet, van Gogh and Cézanne, this exhibition is packed with instruction and delight. It's always possible to quarrel with someone else's selection, but I do find it irritating when art is sold like CDs and the artists featured here are trumpeted as '55 of the world's greatest'. It's admirable that so many women are included, but to place Judith Leyster, Anna Dorothea Therbusch-Lisiewska or Sabine Lepsius among the world's greatest is simply ludicrous. Even the better-known women, like Suzanne Valadon and the ubiquitous Frida Kahlo, are out of their depth in such a categorisation. Interesting artists perhaps, but certainly not great. Neither are some of the male inclusions - for instance, Hans Thoma, John N. Robinson (the token black) or Francis Newton Souza.

Why (one may ask how) are such artists chosen over the dozens more eligible? Souza is an interesting case in point. Indian-born, he came to England in 1949, subsequently living in New York and India. His particular brand of spiky and distorted figuration has its admirers, but its appeal has remained fairly restricted until now. In the new hang at Tate Britain, Souza is designated an 'important artist' and accorded a whole room, and the NPG, ever ready to follow the Tate's lead, has included him in this show. A shame that Souza didn't live to see his promotion: for one of his political interests it would have been highly amusing. His work is much more at home in the informal Borchard Collection (it's actually Borchard's Souza which has been loaned to the NPG), and will eventually find its place alongside the likes of Cecil Collins, Anthony Eyton, Anne Redpath, William Gear and Anthony Green in a new Arts Centre in north London.

Scheduled to open in the autumn of 2008, King's Place in King's Cross will be a landmark multipurpose building by architects Dixon Jones, which will include a 450-seat auditorium and an art gallery, as well as offices. The Borchard Collection will be on permanent display there, and the Centre will develop an emphasis on self-portraiture, with plans for a yearly award. This kind of encouragement can only be a shot in the arm for self-portraiture in this country. In the meantime, further details about the Borchard Collection can be found in Philip Vann's rewarding study of British self-portraits in the 20th century, *Face to Face* (Sansom & Company, £30). What makes an artist's self-image more compelling than a photograph of him or her? A new book of art-world photos by the veteran Jorge Lewinski raises this question. *Portrait of the Artist* (Royal Academy Publications, £24.95) gathers together some 120 black-and-white shots, dating from the Sixties to the Nineties, of such luminaries as Eileen Agar, Roger Hilton, Carl Andre, Alan Davie, Euan Uglow and Richard Wilson. Like all books of artist photos (the classic of the genre is *Private View* by Snowdon, with texts by Bryan Robertson and John Russell, published in 1965), it's a fascinating document, and often revealing. Two photos in particular sum up its strengths: Patrick Heron poised like a dancer in mid-conversation, marking time with a pencil, and Peter Logan looking like Nijinsky doing 'Singing In The Rain'. Yet no single image, or the whole book collectively, challenges the most meagre self-portrait, for in that we have evidence of the artist's hand and mind (sometimes even the heart) at work. And the result is often a complex and many-layered thing, a mixture of honest self-appraisal and calculated presentation. The photo book is an excellent addition to the library but can never be a substitute for the art.

Cherry Pickles, however, is the real thing. She has been painting away quietly in West Wales and Greece for the past 25 years, occasionally showing work and building up a reputation among other artists and informed observers. Her work is hardly familiar to the general public, but, as this exhibition demonstrates, it deserves to be more widely known and appreciated. (I must declare an interest at this point: I wrote the essay in the catalogue which accompanies the show.) Pickles is a figurative painter, taught by such masters of the craft as Uglow, Myles Murphy and Patrick Symons, who has worked long and hard to realise her own vision of the world. Although she paints extensively in other genres, landscape in particular, the self-portrait has proved to be her most successful vehicle to date. But these are self-portraits with a difference. Pickles paints her image distorted in old mirrors, often to the extent of being virtually unrecognisable. Her interest lies in how images are interrupted or imperfectly transmitted, how the edges of things appear in a car's rear-view mirror, or how a wine-glass obscures the features.

Pickles travels to Greece three or four times a year, staying in Delphi, Mykonos or Lesbos, in annexes administered by Athens Art School. There she has painted some of her most telling self-portraits, in a conscious if temporary exile from hearth, home and family. She deliberately uproots herself, and confronts a self unprotected by the cocoon of everyday life. It's an extreme thing to do, but it perhaps helps to account for the originality and inventiveness of her work. The more I think about it, the more remarkable it becomes. This exhibition offers a powerful group of images: intense and memorable.

MORANDI'S LEGACY: Influences on British Art

Estorick Collection, 39a Canonbury Square, N1
29 April 2006

The pre-eminent Italian still-life painter Giorgio Morandi (1890-1964) is frequently called an artists' artist, which is usually taken to indicate that his extreme formality or painterliness (depending on who is arguing the case) appeals more to those in the know than to the man in the street. Morandi undoubtedly does have a deep and lasting appeal to artists, as this exhibition reminds us, but his profoundly unassuming and contemplative pictures also speak directly to a wider public, if the context is congenial. Morandi's work is quiet, concentrating on groups of jars and bottles or odd corners of landscape, and in the bustle and cacophony of a mixed exhibition they can be overlooked. However, this is a mixed exhibition with a difference: it is devoted not just to Morandi's own work, but also to his influence on later generations of British artists – specifically to those working today, though five of the 12 artists featured here are now dead. The 'Still Life with Bottles', 1942, by Giorgio Morandi, on loan to the National Museum of Wales show nevertheless proposes a living tradition, a follow-through of interests and shared visual concerns which is heartening to find in this age of studied diversity and mindless repetition.

Curated by Paul Coldwell, artist and director of the postgraduate programme at Camberwell Art School, the exhibition intersperses a fine selection of Morandi's paintings, drawings and etchings with examples of work by late-20th-century British artists. (Were no earlier painters influenced by Morandi? What, for instance, did his near-contemporary William Nicholson think of him?) Nowadays 'influence' is a dirty word among progressive academics – who perhaps don't care to accept that their own ideas owe anything to anyone else – and Coldwell duly prefers to suggest connections and set up 'conversations' between Morandi and his chosen dozen.

The trouble with this approach is that absolutely any artist might have been chosen, whatever their real relationship to Morandi. Some will say that this is in fact the case — the inclusion of Rachel Whiteread proving the point. Certainly Professor Coldwell might have insisted on a closer relationship between the artists, to the exhibition's profit, but this would doubtless have interfered with the intensely personal nature of his own intellectual journey round Morandi. (This is further adumbrated in the handsome catalogue, £12.95 in paperback and fully illustrated.)

The show is a small one, confined to the two downstairs rooms at the Estorick. It starts on a high note, with a lambent Ben Nicholson of floating rectangles and near-squares, borrowed from Kettle's Yard, set against a blocky Morandi landscape. One of Coldwell's conversations is certainly set up between Morandi's brushy treatment and the sanded swirls in the Nicholson, which oddly enough doesn't really occur with the other, more complex Nicholson still-life hung to the right. Why? Perhaps because it strives too hard for its effects. Next to it are two poignant landscape drawings by Morandi, eloquent for what has been left out of them, juxtaposed with the amorphous slather and harry of an early romantic Christopher Le Brun painting. Tenuous connections continue with Paul Winstanley's soft-edged TV lounge hung next to another fine Morandi. It's good to find Vic Willing's early still-life from 1957 in such mixed company, though the catalogue reproduction is much crisper and more intense in colour than its actual rather worn splendour.

One of the comparisons in this show that really makes sense is the next grouping, of David Hockney with Morandi. Some people tend to disparage Hockney's etched illustrations for Grimms' Fairy Tales, probably because they are better known than much of his other work. Actually, in this case, the drawings stand the test of familiarity. Morandi was also a masterful etcher, whose prints became popular before his paintings even though he taught himself the craft from old manuals on the subject, and to see his etchings next to Hockney's is revealing of both artists. Morandi's fabulous etching 'Savena Landscape' is inventive in the same way as Hockney's 'Sexton Disguised as a Ghost'; in both the production of surprising shapes and forms is what primarily beguiles the eye, and leads on to recognition and pleasure.

Forget the exhibitions subtitles, such as 'The Personal Archive' and 'Lost and Found'; they're taken from the catalogue and offer only a distraction to looking. In the second room is yet another superb Morandi painting, a 1956 still-life borrowed from a private collection (the generosity of owners who've lent to this show is much appreciated), succinct and succulent in blocks of pale colour – beige, green, grey, pink, brown and blue. The forms abut, yet seem also to draw away from one another, as if with a shiver of recognition (desire or distaste?). The large grey William Scott still-life next to it is distressingly over-inflated by comparison, vapid and meagre in its use of shapes. An unhappy conjunction. The specificity of Euan Uglow's still-life comes as quite a contrast. In it you can read the labelling on the tin, and the pattern is clear on his Delft jar, unlike Morandi's preference for dusty or disguised surface. (He would often coat a bottle with paint, which had the effect of making it less specific. But it also made it opaque, therefore easier to see and to depict.) Uglow thought Morandi's paintings beautiful and was much drawn to the non-fussiness of the shapes. The encounter of these two artists is a fruitful one.

Much is made of the cool muted light in Morandi's paintings, the opposite of what is perceived as being typically Mediterranean. It is suggested that Morandi appeals to the British through this coolness of palette and through his passion for understatement. But it must be the formal variety of the Italian master which speaks to sculptor Tony Cragg, here represented by a sensual curvy bronze vessel, though one of his sand-blasted glass pieces would have been more appropriate. The show draws to an end with a Patrick Caulfield still-life and a tremendous minimal Morandi of 1955. Upstairs is another room of Morandi's drawings and etchings from the Estorick's permanent collection. And at the top of the building, in a further room. are three glorious early oils by Zoran Music (born 1909), always worth a look.

Professor Coldwell thinks that Morandi had no affection for his bottles and jars. I find this hard to believe – the evidence of the paintings is against it. Morandi is tender, as well as rigorous and austere. The work is not emotionally cold even if it is cool in colour. Nor is it dingy and light-deprived, but luminous. It is also more complex than it first appears. His still-life elements have been likened to personages, actors upon a stage. (This seems to be the justification for including a DVD of a 35-minute 1980 performance called 'Homage to Morandi' by a trio of young men styling themselves 'Theatre of Mistakes'.) A still-life of profiled pots and bottles is sometimes like the silhouette of a walled town with towers, the buildings huddling defensively together as they have for centuries in Morandi's native Bologna. Still-life as cast of characters, still-life as environment: an imaginative reinterpretation of deliberately limited resources. Morandi, like so many great artists, was a radical in conservative guise. The saving grace of this exhibition is that there is so much of his work to see and savour.

Painting the Cosmos: Landscapes by G F WATTS

Watts Gallery, Compton, Surrey
26 August 2006

That eminent Victorian George Frederick Watts - Strachey thought of including him in his seminal study but was sadly deflected - is at last undergoing something of a revival. In his lifetime one of the most famous of contemporary painters (though his works never sold for quite the vast sums realized by Millais or Burne-Jones),

Watts has been sadly neglected. His ambition was to be a history painter, and he spent much of his long life and considerable energies on allegorical pictures which today find little favour. His portraits, which he often used as a means of subsidizing his less popular High Art compositions, are recognized as supreme examples of the art, and were given a comprehensive showing at the National Portrait Gallery in 2004. His second wife built a museum to his work, near Guildford in the leafy Surrey village of Compton, and this is now urgently in need of restoration. Part of the scheme to raise awareness of its plight is a splendid display of Watts' landscape paintings, a little-known aspect of his oeuvre. Previously shown in June at the supportive St James dealership of Nevill Keating, this exhibition is the first devoted to his landscapes to be mounted anywhere in the world.

Watts (1817-1904) was the son of an impoverished Hereford piano-maker, and was largely self-taught. In 1843 he won a prize to decorate with history paintings the new Houses of Parliament, and travelled to Italy on the prize-money. He studied fresco there and absorbed the classical approach to landscape painting which was to influence all his subsequent explorations in that genre. No Parliamentary commission emerged from Watts' proposals though he won first prize in a second competition. He became known instead as a portrait painter until his allegories were shown in the early 1880s, when they began to exert a tenacious hold on the popular imagination. Watts Fever reached its height towards the end of his life and during the First World War, when men and women flocked to a gallery in the Tate hung with his paintings to seek solace in time of need. It became a sort of secular chapel like the Rothko room is today. Reproductions of hugely famous images such as 'Hope' (known as 'Patience on a Monument' to its detractors), depicting a blindfold girl with but one string left to her lyre, were hung in households throughout the land, and brought comfort to millions. Obvious in its symbolism perhaps, but no less effective for that. Variously known as 'England's Michelangelo' or the 'Kensington Titian', Watts was as full of ambition as he was of lofty ideals. He said he found painting 'very like torture', but never ceased to apply himself to it, even though he took up sculpture when he was 50. He painted landscapes throughout his career, but to begin with as a predominantly private indulgence. Landscape for him was not a matter of the higher naturalism, but rather an imaginative response to the spirit of place. Constable, for instance, was of limited interest to him. Watts didn't want to paint what he saw so much as 'the impression left on the mind'. Yet in his finished pictures he often remained remarkably faithful to his initial sketches. Comparison of the three early watercolour studies of the Carrara mountains, made around 1845 on his first visit to Italy, with subsequent oils on the subject, reinforce this belief. (The same mountain ridge reappears in the allegorical 'Chaos'.) There's also a very beautiful watercolour of a stand of cedar trees, shown here near a slightly earlier oil Watts made of a single cedar in the garden of Little Holland House, where he often stayed. The watercolours are a revelation of delicacy and skill.

Watts did not publicly exhibit a landscape until 1868, but the first examples in this delightful show date to 1845, and depict Petraia and Fiesole respectively. Neither is a particularly dramatic prospect, though the latter offers a variety of natural detail and a rich creamy sky. Nearby is a very strange little painting of the Greek island of Cos, with the upper half given over to a sensitive landscape profile, but the lower containing a frieze of vaporous and sexless figures, no doubt for Watts adding some unspecified allegorical meaning, but for us making it more difficult to take the picture seriously.

Generally, however, Watts kept figures out of his landscapes, and landscape pretty much out of his figure paintings. The resulting pure landscapes were most often painted, and re-painted, in the studio. (A late picture, such as the Tate's impressive 'Study of Clouds', was worked on over 10 years.) The exception here is 'Helwan', an oil on paper sketch carried out in 1887 when Watts was on his second honeymoon in Egypt. It is disappointing: a flattish, uninflected scene with a couple of pyramids like pimples on the horizon. Far more arresting is 'A Sea Ghost' of the same period, a subtle grey penumbral study of a ship appearing through fog, like the wreck of the Mary Deare. In this painting, as in the radiant 'After the Deluge; the Forty-First Day', Watts is edging towards Turnerian or Whistlerian abstraction. The post-Flood picture is a great allegorical image, but also a radical essay in painting light, alive with non-descriptive surface marks worthy of an abstract. Here is the mystical side of Watts. As the poet Arthur Symons noted: 'his landscape is that of one for whom the finger of God is continually creating the earth over again'.

The Watts Gallery houses the master's studio collection in a listed Grade 2* Arts and Crafts style building. Entering through the lead-faced doors decorated with stylised leaves and flowers, either right into the main galleries, or left down into the sculpture wing, the visitor is struck by the singular atmosphere. It is welcoming but conspiratorial, intimate yet uplifting. The green walls and gold ceilings are an oddly appropriate setting for Watts' art. There's a beautiful portrait of the artist as a romantic young man, and the famous 'Wounded Heron', a moving and exquisitely painted early work, done for typically humanitarian reasons. (Watts was also moved by the suffering of the starving Irish, and painted several avant-garde social conscience pictures of considerable power.) There are other portraits – particularly fine is the recently acquired Ionides family group – and the masterly 'Paolo and Francesca' (1872-5). Elsewhere a version of 'Mammon', a hideous bestial figure, crushes the life out of hopeful youth. This place is unique: there's nothing like it anywhere else in the country. (Ring 01483 810235 for opening times.)

On 15 September, you may help to save and renovate the Watts Gallery, by phoning in to the BBC2 programme Restoration Village and voting for Compton. Watts, who was instrumental in founding both the Whitechapel Art Gallery and the National Portrait Gallery, and gave up much of his life to public-spirited work, in turn deserves our support now.

WATERCOLOURS AND DRAWINGS FROM THE COLLECTION OF QUEEN ELIZABETH THE QUEEN MOTHER
The Queen's Gallery, Buckingham Palace
2 September 2006

The best-known exchange between artist and royalty must be King George VI's celebrated remark to John Piper, who had been painting the castle and surrounding parkland at Windsor: 'You seem to have had very bad luck with your weather'. It was the early 1940s, and Piper had invested his watercolours with a brooding quality he no doubt thought appropriate to the mood of the times, and which also echoed his own essentially Romantic vision. The project was a commission from Queen Elizabeth, and extended to 26 views, a rare feat of modern topography that also turned out to be good art. But even the Queen thought Piper's lowering skies a little overbearing, and reportedly suggested he might 'try a spring day'. Usually, however, her passion for collecting art was confined to the purchase of existing works of art, rather than commissions, which was in many ways more supportive of the artists, being a direct encouragement of their efforts.

As Kenneth Clark, Surveyor of the King's Pictures (1934-44) and a friend and advisor of the Queen, wrote to her in 1938: 'Under Your Majesty's patronage British painters will have a new confidence, because you will make them feel that they are not working for a small clique but for the centre of the national life'. From childhood onwards, Queen Elizabeth displayed an interest in art which blossomed into real enthusiasm as she grew older. Her most intense period of collecting inevitably took place in the years of King George VI's reign, 1937 to 1952, when personal pleasure in the activity was mingled with royal duty. But the fact that her acquisition of art was by no means confined to these years attests to her very real love for painting and drawing.

Although not a devoted follower of the avant-garde, Queen Elizabeth was progressive rather than conservative in her taste. A number of the best artists working in Britain around the mid-point of the 20th century are featured in her collection, with substantial painters from an earlier generation – William Nicholson and Sickert, for example – also represented. The charming exhibition in the Queen's Gallery commences with portraits: Lady Elizabeth Bowes-Lyon, as she was in 1907, depicted by the miniaturist Mabel Hankey, and a fine charcoal profile drawing by Sargent, dating to just before her marriage to the Duke of York in 1923. Sir Muirhead Bone's vivid black crayon drawing of the end of Coronation week contrasts effectively with Claude Muncaster's more sedate but gaily-coloured scene of Piccadilly on the Coronation route.

There are several historical acquisitions of consequence made by Queen Elizabeth, including a Gainsborough chalk drawing 'A figure in a landscape' (rather more effective if you block out the figure), a beautiful Wright of Derby watercolour of an Italian house atop a splendid rampart of wall, and a couple of John Varley watercolours, of which the view of Snowdon is the finer. There's also a superb Paul Sandby: 'Windsor Castle and part of the town' (c1765), a marvel of clarity and light. A cabinet of drawings contains Augustus John's masterly but tender study 'Dorelia, standing' (c1907-10), a sweet Berthe Morisot study of a seated girl and Max Beerbohm's amusing caricature of Edward VII. The works hanging in this gallery indicate an eclectic taste: from the Japanese-style woodcuts of Elizabeth Keith to the robust Celtic traceries and flickering colour of David Jones' window picture, 'The outward walls' (1953). The Norfolk artist Edward Seago (1910-64) was a frequent guest at Sandringham, and he presented Queen Elizabeth with a picture each year on her birthday and again at Christmas. Seago could be an effective landscape painter, so it is disappointing to find such lesser examples of his work as the watercolours here. But then we should not necessarily expect an artist to give away as presents examples of his best endeavours. Much better things are to be seen by the Australian artist Norma Bull, who worked in England as an unofficial war artist, living in this country between 1937 and 1947, and exhibiting her work at Australia House in 1947, where Queen Elizabeth purchased her pictures. Particularly poignant is her pen and watercolour study 'The Chelsea Royal Hospital Infirmary, as destroyed by enemy action' (1941) with a red-coated Chelsea Pensioner pensively surveying the damage. 'Rocket bomb exploding in the air over London' (1945), with its cartoonish cloud, or puff of smoke, is an altogether more light-hearted witness of the times.

Half-a-dozen of the famous Piper watercolours are on show, demonstrating his genius for depicting architecture, and four intimate watercolour sketches by another close friend of the Royal Family, Sir Hugh Casson. Queen Elizabeth was fortunate in her friends and advisors: besides Clark and Casson, there were the collector Sir Jasper Ridley and the writer Sir Osbert Sitwell. Another cabinet, containing personal letters from artists (including a fine decorated epistle from Rex Whistler, who died so young), demonstrates the affection in which she was held. She seems too to have evinced an endearing fondness for rogues, those arch-bohemians the art world throws up from time to time, and who often become popular public figures. (I'm thinking particularly here of Augustus John and John Bratby. Bratby not only painted the Queen Mother's portrait but presented her with one of his crayon drawings of Venice.) Among the other exhibits, in this modestly-sized exhibition of just over 70 items, are three splendid charcoal and ink figure drawings by David Wilkie, and a rich landscape watercolour by David Young Cameron. Coming right up to date, there is the exceptionally competent watercolour 'Desks at Royal Lodge' by Hugh Buchanan, commissioned by the Royal Household in honour of Queen Elizabeth's 100th birthday.

This exhibition tells a heart-warming story, significantly characterized by affection and enthusiasm. (A lavish catalogue, competitively priced at £7.95, recounts the history of the collection in more detail.) Today the situation seems very different. Certainly royal patronage has changed in its various emphases and incarnations, but there doesn't seem to be a collector of the stature of Queen Elizabeth the Queen Mother among the present generations. Perhaps another will emerge. It would be nice to think so. In the meantime, we have a further exhibition (or perhaps several) to look forward to – the oil paintings in the Queen Mother's Collection. Including distinguished pictures by Paul Nash, Matthew Smith and Augustus John, to name but three, it will offer a more complete view of the scope of this enjoyable collection, and a greater impression of its identity.

DAVID HOCKNEY: Portraits

National Portrait Gallery

DAVID HOCKNEY: A Year in Yorkshire

Annely Juda Fine Art, 23 Dering Street, W1

21 October 2006

It's difficult to believe that the golden boy of British art – as David Hockney remained for so many years – now has more than half-a-century of work behind him, or that he will celebrate his 70th birthday next summer. His technical versatility and immense skilfulness have seen him through many different guises along the short path from faux-naif to sophisticate, including print-maker, photographer and set-designer, inspired draughtsman and impassioned theorist, but it is as a painter that he will surely be judged, when the verdict of posterity eventually arrives. And as a painter, there is a curious emptiness at the heart of his endeavour. In spite of all the tricks and the supreme dexterity, there is a lack of feeling, of human understanding to his art. Painters deal in surfaces, but they can also plumb the depths. Hockney however does not.

He is a superb draughtsman, and there are many examples of his exceptional ability in the substantial new exhibition at the NPG. Featuring over 150 exhibits, including paintings, drawings, prints, photo-works and sketchbooks, it offers a colourful introduction to his art and will no doubt prove spectacularly popular. Hockney has the common touch, and it is partly because his work is generally pleasing and relatively undemanding (his theories about optics are far more complex than his art), that it appeals across the board. His technical gifts and native wit have carried him a long way, but it is evident from his intellectual restlessness and addiction to ideas that his artistic practice has long ceased to satisfy him. (How many years has he devoted to a study of Renaissance optical gadgets? The latest expanded edition of his apparently controversial book *Secret Knowledge: Rediscovering the Lost Techniques of the Old Masters* is just published by Thames & Hudson at £24.95 in paperback.) Has the taste for scholarship deepened his art? No, it seems merely to have served as a distraction.

The show opens with a c1954 oil on board self-portrait, Hockney in quizzical, almost supercilious mood above the Bradford rooftops, and continues with a bright collage and then a lithograph, three very different ways of depicting, an early warning of the diversity to come. Opposite is the marvellous sequence of 16 etchings from 'A Rake's Progress', Hockney standing to good effect on Hogarth's shoulders and peering at life in the early Sixties in London and New York. Sharply-observed but visually inventive, these images are as fresh today as ever. The large 'Portrait Surrounded by Artistic Devices' (1965) develops Hockney's graphic imagination in paint before the American portraits create a new academicism, tough, resilient and not without originality. These super-real, quasi-symbolic double portraits – 'Henry Geldzahler and Christopher Scott' (1969) being particularly powerful – set high standards for realistic depiction. 'Mr and Mrs Clark and Percy' (1970-1) has long been a national favourite, and it stands up well, with its piquant mixture of coolness and sentimentality. Far more direct and intriguing are the black ink line drawings, of Henry and Gregory and Peter, brilliant summaries of three-dimensional form, which move without hesitation into more formal portraits of Priestley, Auden, Kitaj and Richard Hamilton.

The crayon studies which come next are altogether gentler: sweeter in colour and temper, though no less acute. Look, for instance, at the drawings of Warhol and Man Ray, or 'Celia in a Black Slip Reclining'. Besides his self-portraits, Hockney has always given most care and attention to the depiction of his parents: from the quiet but intense 1955 portrait of his father to the many paintings and drawings of his mother. Like his hero Picasso, Hockney scours past art for inspiration, which gives art historians something to write about, but he doesn't seem to add to it or make it his own in the ways that Picasso did. You may think that comparing any artist working today with Picasso is unfair, and it's not something I would readily attempt, but Hockney actively courts such comparison. Look at 'Artist and Model' (1973-4) in which he etches himself sitting opposite the older artist. Or the cubisty multi-canvas portraits and photo-works he began to make at this time. Some of these are affecting, such as the composite Polaroid of Patrick Procktor or the pretty profile of Gregory, or the wittily fragmented painting of restaurateur Peter Langan; even the tapir-like head of Christopher Isherwood. But Hockney gets less interesting when obsessed by an idea which tends to overshadow the art. Henceforth his career appears to be peppered with lessons from some advanced art school: today we'll do reverse perspective or study the camera lucida. The art suffers as a consequence. As the exhibition moves into the Eighties, the work becomes seriously compromised. All the phenomenal skill, the knowledge of line, the ready facility with colour and texture seem to be jettisoned. From now on, it's as if Hockney wants to be a master of the slapdash, of Seriously Bad Painting. The Wolfson Wing of the NPG plays host to the more recent work. The visitor is greeted by a striking image of the transvestite Divine, a transitional portrait from 1979 which has many of Hockney's original qualities of design and colour, as well as intimations of the new brutishness. The late portraits, whether in oil or watercolour, flaunt their insensitivity, their outrageous banality. The viewer can only gasp at the crassness of it all, the deliberate crudity. Is this work intended as a satire on a society gone mad with self-indulgence and self-importance? It looks like it. Only some of the drawings recall the early spirit, the generosity and celebration.

At Annely Juda is a virtual sell-out exhibition of 25 of Hockney's latest landscape paintings, done in Yorkshire over the past year. Much has been made of these plein-air oils, and Hockney's return to England from the fleshpots of California. They're jolly enough in an essentially decorative way, but entirely devoid of any profound resonance, any meaningful connection with the spirit of place. They don't look like the English landscape and they don't feel like it. But they could be an exile's dream of home: superficial, sentimental and necessarily unreal. Over-heated colour and slack drawing is no substitute for close observation and real understanding. I find it impossible even to begin to warm to this hasty, caricatural, synthetic vision: Yorkshire is traduced. I wish I'd had time to visit the Spencer Gore exhibition at Letchworth Museum and Art Gallery (until 28 October) to tell you about an artist who used pattern and bright colour in the landscape to really astonishing effect. But perhaps you'd best judge for yourselves.

PETER DOIG
WALTER SICKERT
EDWARD BURRA

Tate Britain

KEN KIFF

Marlborough Fine Art

23 February 2008

Peter Doig has aroused much passion in recent months for the prices his paintings have started to fetch in the world's salerooms. For many, he is not only the acceptable face of contemporary British painting, but a buoyant export and bright international star. Even those who dislike painting and prefer less demanding forms of art such as installation and photography are prepared to make an exception for Doig, perhaps because he is easy on the eye. Ten years ago he enjoyed a fairly prestigious show at the Whitechapel, now he's given the main galleries at the Tate's Millbank branch. The Whitechapel show left me unconvinced of his virtues though I remember liking one or two of the smaller pictures. Now we have the chance to see what all the fuss is about. Is Doig the brand really worth the millions it can now summon?

Eight museum rooms of paintings (including some drawings) by a single artist can be enough to sink a reputation. Doig, who looks quite strong in mixed shows of contemporary work, begins to evaporate here. He makes work which reflects upon his peripatetic life: born in Edinburgh in 1959, he grew up in Trinidad and Canada, came to London to study at Wimbledon and Central St Martins, went back to Canada in 1986 to work as a scene painter in the film industry, and returned to England for postgraduate study in 1989. He won the John Moores Prize in 1993 and was nominated for the Turner Prizer in 1994. In 2002, he moved back to Trinidad where he now lives and works, though he teaches in Dusseldorf. Like so many younger artists he is constantly on the move, as if chasing some elusive grail. Photographs are the compositional starting point of his paintings. Doig is apparently obsessed with memory, yet says nothing of value about it. He likes blurry photos that fudge the facts but are strong on atmosphere. He says 'the photograph is really just an extension of memory'; actually it is a very particular distortion of memory. He also calls it 'a way of remembering shapes'. For Doig, it seems more a source of self-indulgent nostalgia. It's revealing that early on he thought he might earn a living as a theatre designer: his work, mostly large-scale, is reminiscent of flats and backcloths, and is probably as ephemeral. It has a superficial charm and sweetness of palette that rapidly wears thin.

Some of the paintings made in the early-to-mid 1990s have a more lasting presence, when the paint-handling works both with and against the rather banal imagery. When in the later Nineties he changed from thicker paint to thin washes, the complexity of the surface lost its unexpectedness, its variety of incident. If you're going to rely on photographs for visual information then the weight of the painting has to be borne elsewhere – in the drawing, colour, design (pattern). Doig can be seductive with colour and adept at pattern, but the content is too light to anchor his work. The most recent paintings are among the flimsiest. It's quite evident that Peter Doig's international appeal is built upon clever marketing of work that demands very little of its viewers. The exhibition will tour to ARC/Musée d'Art Moderne de la Ville de Paris (26 May – 14 September) and Schirn Kunsthalle Frankfurt (8 October 2008 – 11 January 2009).

I have nothing against artists who use photography per se, and I've long been an admirer of the photo-based work of Walter Sickert. But then he was never led by the camera, and was far too wily and inventive an artist to be constrained by the limited information a photograph can provide. There are a number of very fine Sickerts in another show at Tate Britain at this very moment, *The Camden Town Group* (soon to be reviewed in this column), though none of his radical late works. Another artist who drew inspiration from photography, particularly the German Expressionist kind, was Edward Burra (1905-76). Room 18 at Tate Britain is currently hung with seven of Burra's paintings on the theme of New York's Harlem, its street life and jazz.

Burra is a major figure of 20th century British art, a maverick of the first water, whose paintings of the seamier side of human behaviour have a strength and originality lacking in most contemporary painters. There hasn't been a proper Burra show for more than 20 years, and now all we have is one low-key room of archive material and a handful of small paintings. It's not nearly enough to form an assessment of Burra's peculiar subjects and remarkable skills, but at least it's a taste of a very particular artist. My worry is that by mounting a display like this, the Tate will feel it has done its duty to Burra, and there won't be another show of his work for decades. Much is often said about the scarcity of good English artists, yet the 20th century was particularly rich in them, and we hardly get a chance to see their work shown publicly – that's left to the more enterprising commercial galleries.

For an artist who really used paint creatively and who was a marvellous colourist into the bargain, visit the Ken Kiff show at Marlborough Fine Art, 6 Albemarle Street, W1 (until 1 March). A whole group of previously unseen paintings and works on paper comes as a timely reminder (some seven years after his death) that in him we have a major artist, insufficiently appreciated. I am a longstanding Kiff supporter – I knew him well, wrote the main monograph on his work and contributed an essay to the catalogue of the current exhibition – but I urge you to make up your own mind about his art. Go and see it: there is a gentleness and serenity to his imagery even though it probes the darker recesses of the unconscious. The draughtsmanship is exact and unfaltering, the colour compelling and joyous, the stuff of paint worked in ways which add meaning and fluency to the archetypal subject matter.

Kiff dared to embrace fairytale as well as myth, the mundane and the heroic, and distilled from their convergence an original vision of startling relevance. Just the sort of artist who deserves a Tate retrospective. Can we expect one? We can hope.

UNPOPULAR CULTURE

De La Warr Pavilion, Bexhill-on-Sea
7 June 2008

This is not a review, for I haven't yet seen the exhibition under discussion, it's an expression of mixed incredulity and interest. The exhibition is called *Unpopular Culture*, and is an artist's selection from the Arts Council Collection. On the Press Release is a photo of its selector, the potter and personality Grayson Perry, dressed familiarly in women's clothing. The show of some 70 paintings, sculptures and photos, is apparently by unfashionable 20th century British artists. The available press photos are by the lesser-known exhibitors – David Hepher, Meg Rutherford and Jack Smith – but the selection also includes such well-known and well-loved names as Henry Moore, Edward Burra, John Piper, L S Lowry and Paul Nash. Unpopular culture? Who says so?

A friend of mine went to the launch of the exhibition which took place at that Modernist architectural masterpiece, the De La Warr Pavilion at Bexhill-on-Sea. (The building was designed in 1935 by Erich Mendelsohn and Serge Chermayeff, refurbished and re-opened in 2005, and sits on the Marina among the ranks of the well-retired like an abandoned liner.) My friend is an admirer of Grayson Perry and was impressed by the selection of works, but even he was incensed that so many great British artists were designated 'unpopular'. He thought it might be a publicity stunt of some sort by the savvy Mr Perry, who is after all a media celebrity, and has his finger on the pulse of the nation's press and would never knowingly underestimate its ignorance. To hard-pressed journalists, the combined might of 20th century British art would be a mere nothing compared to Mr Perry batting his eyelashes and showing his legs to the cameras. And judging by the column inches generated by the event, the show has already been a success. I make it a policy to avoid reading the crasser art journalists in the broadsheets (it's not good for the blood pressure), but a colleague rather gleefully drew my attention to one Sunday review of *Unpopular Culture*. This particular critic seemed positively to exult in his ignorance of many of the artists in the show, lamenting the dreary loser nature of the black-and-white past as against the colourful success story of today. I wish it were so: poor deluded scribbler. A society gets the art it deserves and our quick-fix depraved sensationalism is spot on. As Philip Larkin wrote in 'Going, Going', his magnificent lament for vanishing England: 'greeds / And garbage are too thick-strewn / To be swept up now, or invent / Excuses that make them all needs'.

But I couldn't believe that the whole thing was simply a publicity exercise on behalf of Perry Enterprises, so I turned to the catalogue for further enlightenment. This is a handsome hardback volume of essays, pictures and poems, priced at £17.99 (special exhibition price £12.99). It contains a spirited essay by Mr Perry himself, an experienced and competent writer, and an intelligent commentary by the poet Blake Morrison. Mr Perry admits to choosing the exhibition's title and claims that the art he has selected, roughly covering the period 1940-80, and the artists who made it, were not the subject of daily stories in the press or gossip columns, and thus could be accurately termed unpopular rather than popular. He then mentions the exception: John Bratby, who was a grand master at supplying the papers with stories and spicy titbits from his personal life, in order to fuel his reputation and sell his art.

Bratby was in fact the first modern British artist to be a successful media manipulator, closely followed by that somewhat more photogenic limelight-junkie David Hockney, but Mr Perry is disenchanted with the 1960s and rules out any Pop artists from his selection. As he writes: 'This is partly due to a suspicion that the swinging Sixties, in all its groovy glory, was really only enjoyed by a minority, and partly because I'm a bit tired of the hackneyed nostalgia for a psychedelic, World Cup-winning, Mini-driving, miniskirt-wearing, Beatles-loving supposed golden age'.

Mr Perry was born in 1960, and his selection breathes the more austere air of post-war shortages and rationing, evincing an aesthetic longing for the decade before his birth. Trawling the catalogues of the Arts Council Collection, he was drawn to 'works that could be characterized as subtle, sensitive, lyrical and quiet'. Three separate categories of art particularly appealed to him: figurative painting, bronze sculpture and documentary photography. He writes: 'I may be reactionary or nostalgic, but for me these artworks conjure up an age before our experience of ourselves was muffled completely by the commercial and sophisticated intermediaries of television, advertising and digital communications'.

There is much to applaud and agree with here, but in the days of yore which Mr Perry celebrates, there were far fewer art galleries to mount exhibitions, and those that did take place were invariably reviewed in the daily press. There may not have been less appetite for salacious gossip, but there was far less of it printed in serious newspapers, and arts editors saw it as their duty to an intelligent readership to inform them of what was going on in the art world. Culture was not unpopular. Today, critics are constrained by myopic editors into reviewing only the same big museum shows as all the other papers, with an unseemly and childish race to be first into print, as if reviews were news rather than comment; or they are encouraged to chronicle the latest guff from the currently fashionable.

The coverage that this magazine, a weekly, gives to the arts is far wider than many daily newspapers. I wish more arts editors would take the initiative to cover a greater range of exhibition than just the obvious. What has happened to subtlety? Has it been so marginalized that it's now unrecognisable? Not on the showing of Mr Perry's selection, which, because of Mr Perry has (thankfully) attracted rather more attention than it would have otherwise done. I trust his interest in the artists he's selected is sincere. He has remarked that: 'in an art world inured to shock one of the last sins available to the artist is to be slightly conservative'. I hope this doesn't mean that his selection was actuated solely by the desire to shock, though shock can be salutary. However, if this show does manage to inform a new audience that there was worthwhile and enjoyable painting and sculpture being made in England before art was so utterly dominated by the fashionable, then it will have performed a considerable cultural service.

There are many pleasures: Paul Nash, Lowry and William Roberts offering different takes on seaside excursions. Excellent documentary photographs by the likes of Bert Hardy and Tony Ray-Jones record what Grayson Perry calls 'a lost world of close-knit communities'. I particularly look forward to seeing the Burras and Paolozzis, the very different versions of Hammersmith by Victor Pasmore and Ruskin Spear, Alan Reynolds' oil 'The Village – Winter' (1952) and Leonard Rosoman's 'Gardens on Different Levels' (1955).

For Mr Perry, Nash, Pasmore, Piper and Rosoman 'know how to make a virtue of grey as only a Briton can. I find, in these pictures, an attractive humility and elegance, qualities that might be described today as not being media friendly, but which I wish to celebrate'. I salute Mr Perry for using his own celebrity to bring to a wider audience some of the remarkable talents of 20th century British art, and in doing so his provocative exhibition title must be deemed a highly successful strategy. The show is at Bexhill until 6 July, then tours to the Harris Museum and Art Gallery, Preston (19 July – 14 September), DLI Museum and Art Gallery, Durham (15 November 2008 – 4 January 2009), Southampton City Art Gallery

(17 January - 15 March), Aberystwyth Arts Centre (21 March - 10 May), Scarborough Art Gallery (16 May - 5 July), Longside Gallery, Wakefield (18 July – 25 October), Victoria Art Gallery, Bath (7 November 2009 – 3 January 2010). Plenty of choice, so no excuse to miss it.

ANCIENT LANDSCAPES - PASTORAL VISIONS: SAMUEL PALMER TO THE RURALISTS

Victoria Art Gallery, Bath
20 September 2008

Bath is a nearly always a joy to visit, though in recent years it has become a focal point for the disaffected youth (and middle-aged) of the area, and I've known people say they feel safer at night walking around London. But the architecture remains beautiful and evocative, the Roman baths are still a wonder and you can have a sumptuous tea at the Pump Room. There are good book shops and currently at the Victoria Art Gallery, down by Pulteney Bridge, is the second part of an exhibition devoted to the Romantic strain in English art.

Don't be mislead by the title: although in its entirety this is a wide-ranging exhibition, it was organized by Southampton Art Gallery (and thus draws heavily on that remarkable permanent collection) and was originally intended for a much larger museum. In Bath, restrictions of space mean that the show has had to be cut in half – but like an earthworm, both halves have continued to flourish. Part 1 dealt with the historical context, the Samuel Palmers, the Graham Sutherlands and the Paul Nashs, and Part 2 comes up to date with the Brotherhood of Ruralists. This is particularly fitting as the Ruralists lived (mostly) in the West Country and foregathered from time to time in Bath. But I'm not so certain about this notion of coming up to date. Although there are recent works here by the

Ruralists, there is nothing by other Romantics who might be equally at home in such exalted company. I can think of a number of artists whose paintings embody a romantic landscape vision of the poetic and the particular: Jeffery Camp, George Rowlett and Julian Perry, to name but three. Is then this selection rather a predictable one? I shall attempt to answer that later.

As viewers who now visit the Victoria Art Gallery may have missed Part 1 of the exhibition, let me give you an idea of the ground it covered. The over-arching theme is the effect of Samuel Palmer's etchings on 20th century British art (Sutherland called Palmer the English van Gogh), but to state it so baldly is not particularly helpful. Palmer did not spring fully-armed from the head of Zeus, but was hugely under the influence of that arch visionary, William Blake. So the show in fact begins with Blake's marvellous illustrations to Thornton's *Pastorals of Virgil* (generously given to Southampton as part of the David Brown Bequest). Palmer described them revealingly as: 'visions of little dells, and nooks and corners of Paradise; models of the exquisite pitch of intense poetry'. He could have been writing about his own work that was to have such an influence on F L Griggs, and through him, on the early etchings of Graham Sutherland.

Sutherland gets a good showing in Part 1, not just his prints, but also a trio of oils on the theme of lanes and woodland pathways. Paul Nash, one of the greatest of British 20th century landscape painters, is represented by delightful early works such as 'Under the Hill' (1912) and by major paintings such as 'Landscape of the Megaliths' (1934), 'November Moon' (1942) and 'Eclipse of the Sunflower' (1945). Please note the presence of such lesser lights as Paul Drury, Joseph Webb and Edgar Holloway, and comparative unknowns like Graham Robertson, John Lefevre and James Sellars. Good to see S R Badmin and John Elwyn of the company. The range is impressive, though I could have done with more than a single image by the brothers Spencer, Stanley and Gilbert, and the solitary Hitchens. Perhaps the idea needed to be focused better? A catch-all survey can give a confused flavour of a period or tendency, while a more discriminating selection can be paradoxically more informative.

However, Part 1 proved very popular in Bath, with nearly 16,000 visitors, many of them returning more than once. It reinforces my belief that the Romantic pastoral strain is the most original and most deeply-felt of our landscape manifestations in England. It's not just reactionary nostalgia, but the identification of a powerful source of inspiration in the national psyche. If you still want to see Part 1, you could go to the next and last venue in the exhibition's tour, Falmouth Art Gallery, where it will run from 20 September until 1 November. But Falmouth has even less space than Bath, so it will be showing a reduced version of the original show. Perhaps better to buy the catalogue (a substantial paperback priced at £19.95), though it is somewhat text-heavy and indigestible, and marred by misprints. The illustrations are also rather small. But I suspect it will be a useful source-book for many who do not have ready access to original sources.

Meanwhile Part 2 presents Ruralist treasures. The Brotherhood was born at a dinner party on David Inshaw's birthday in 1975, and was about escaping the modern urban world for something more expansive and Victorian. Peter Blake, the most famous Ruralist and in some respects its flag-waver, described their aims as: 'the continuation of a certain kind of English painting; we admire Samuel Palmer, Stanley Spencer, Thomas Hardy, Elgar, cricket, English landscape, the Pre-Raphaelite… Our aims are to paint about love, beauty, joy, sentiment and magic. We still believe in painting with oil on canvas, putting the picture in a frame and, hopefully, that someone will like it, buy it and hang it on their wall to enjoy'.

That's a useful definition of the Romantic current in English art – the ability to recognize and convey the magic of a place. Although

Peter Nahum, in an afterword to the catalogue, makes a strong argument for Graham Ovenden being the giant of late 20th century English landscape painting, rightful successor to Paul Nash, I would disagree. For my money, David Inshaw is the artist who emerges as the strongest and most inventive of the Ruralists. He is a landscape painter of real evocative power – look at his depictions of the strangeness that is Silbury – whose best work seems to unite the qualities of Nash and Stanley Spencer. It's his pictures that stand out in this exhibition.

GERHARD RICHTER: 4900 COLOURS
Serpentine Gallery
LUCIAN FREUD: EARLY WORKS, 1940-58
Hazlitt Holland-Hibbert, 38 Bury Street, SW1
18 October 2008

At the Serpentine is an exhibition of little squares of colour, randomly arranged in grids. There are 49 paintings on show, each one composed of four panels consisting of 25 squares each. They are painted in enamel on something synthetic called Aludibond, on boards or plates attached directly to the wall. The colour combinations are selected by chance through a specially developed computer programme, and the initial idea for the work was sparked by the industrial colour charts produced by paint manufacturers. Gerhard Richter (born 1932) has been making paintings based on colour charts since 1966, and after a lot of trying, he has finally sold the idea to a credulous world.

It seems that Richter himself has a high estimation of these pictures. He is quoted in the publicity material as claiming: 'They are the only paintings which tell no story. Even abstract paintings are like photos of a non-existent reality, of an unknown jungle. Here there is no illusion. They say nothing and evoke no association.

There are simply there, pure visual subjects.' What arrogant tosh. It's the sort of comment clever artists think they can get away with nowadays because nobody knows any better in this sorry culture of ignorance. Richter pontificates as if he'd just invented geometric abstraction, when it's all been done before over the last 100 years, time and time again. Yet people in the art world who should know better treat him as if he were some kind of guru. Admittedly he has done some vaguely interesting work with blurring and distorting in his more figurative paintings (oh yes, this great master turns his hand to all sorts and types of art), but his chief distinction at the moment lies in being over-rated. On the press release he's loudly trumpeted as 'one of the world's greatest living artists', so of course there's a lavish hard-backed catalogue to accompany the show. But I can't find any justification in its pages for thinking so highly of Richter. The idea behind these boring pictures is an intellectual conceit exploited more effectively in literature many years ago by such innovative writers as Raymond Queneau in his *One Hundred Million Million Poems* (1961). And the visualization is equally unoriginal. As the painter John Hoyland has pointed out, '4900 Colours' looks like something by the Swiss Elementarist Richard Lohse (1902-88), just less inventive and a lot less interesting. Unlike Richter, Lohse is not particularly well-known in this country, though the commercial gallery Annely Juda shows his work from time to time.

If you still like Richter enough and want to support the Serpentine, you can buy one of a specially made edition of 80 paintings – though if each is unique why are they numbered in an edition like a multiple? They measure just less than eight inches square, and cost £12,000. Then you could take your own coloured board home with you, though I fail to see what excitement or uplift it could confer, other than a specious trophy value. The Serpentine work is very similar to a design Richter made for a stained glass window in Cologne Cathedral, unveiled last year. I can see it working quite well as a window, but in a gallery it's a complete waste of space.

Phrases like 'aleatory iteration' and 'monotonous polychromy' crowd the essays of the catalogue, rather like the shrieking of the parakeets in Kensington Gardens as they pursue each other through trees just beginning their seasonal colour change. I have to say I found more intellectual and emotional stimulation and far greater aesthetic satisfaction in looking at the autumn trees than at Mr Richter's colour charts.

For a complete contrast, I urge a visit to the exhibition of early works by Lucian Freud (1922-2011). Here is indisputable evidence of an original poetic sensibility coming to grips with the problems of making a visual image with paint. One of the earliest paintings here, of a box of apples, was made when Freud was 17 and it betrays the influence of his teacher Cedric Morris in the vigorous paint-handling and modelling of the subject. But the real delight of the exhibition is to see Freud working on a small scale with fine brushes, condensing his emotional and retinal responses into paintings of a wonderful tautness. These highly-detailed mesmeric renditions have an almost late medieval Flemish intensity. They are strange and compelling and rather beautiful.

Most of the sitters are not identified, as if their names are unimportant. (This too is reminiscent of the late medieval/Renaissance habit of painting a person, rather than Sir Somebody Something, captured for a moment in paint on their journey from the cradle to the grave.) Half-titles, such as 'Head of a Poet' or 'A Woman Painter' seem designed to pique the viewer's curiosity without satisfying it. I began to find this a bit annoying. I cannot accept that knowing who the subject is stops one looking closely at the paintwork or the clarity of line. Freud himself is quoted as saying 'if you don't know them, it can only be like a travel book', which can be taken either to refer to himself or to the viewer. Whichever way, it is surely a diminishment of the enjoyment: if you're travelling round a country (or a face), it helps to know what you're looking at. And given the remarkable nature of Freud's gallery of friends and connections, it seems something of an affectation not to name them. Just to confuse the issue, some *are* identified - Stephen Spender and Gerald Wilde, for instance. One a considerable public figure (whatever you think of his poetry), the other a little-known monocular abstract expressionist who once lived in a cave. High society and low life?

Catherine Lampert in her useful catalogue (£20 in paperback) discovers in one painting 'a hint of a life of privilege brought to a precipice; the canvas showing through the thinly applied paint lends a very subtle measure of recoil'. An interesting notion, but does this apply to any painting in which the canvas shows through the paint? I think not. So perhaps the recoil is in Freud himself. The fierce scrutiny to which he subjects his sitters has always seemed to me to border on distaste. However, identities and lineage are evidently important, as Lampert spends half-a-dozen pages explaining who these sitters are. So we may go round the show and find David Gascoyne in the thick-lipped 'Head of a Poet' (c1945) or John Craxton in the fresh-faced though sunburnt 'Portrait of a Man' (1946) or Henrietta Moraes voluptuous in a blanket.

I used to think the virtuoso technique of black and white conte on Ingres paper employed in the drawing of Christian Berard was remarkable, but seeing it here in the company of so many oil paintings of greater originality, it begins to look mechanical. Freud's unusual gift of interlocking the naïve and the sophisticated, the untutored and the knowing, gives these pictures an edge rarely encountered in modern British art. By their disquiet shall we know them.

DAMIEN HIRST: THE BLUE PAINTING

The Wallace Collection

JOHN WALKER: INCOMING TIDE

Offer Waterman & Co, 11 Langton Street, SW10

ANTHONY EYTON

Browse & Darby, 19 Cork Street, W1

HUMPHREY OCEAN

Sidney Cooper Gallery, St. Peter's Street, Canterbury

7 November 2009

Weeks ago, when the review schedules were first plotted, I had thought to include here a feature on Damien Hirst. Although I find his work unremittingly thin, I thought I would give it another chance. After all, he is showing new paintings he'd made himself rather than instructed a studio to produce. But the results are so feeble and insignificant that detailed execration (however enjoyable) is more than they're worth. Hirst's product thrives on publicity, and his new show has generated so many hundreds of column inches that he must deem it another successful ploy, however vituperative the critical response. The real loser is the Wallace Collection, demeaned by Hirst's strategic incursion. At least the visitor may rinse the eyes with some of the Wallace's masterpieces after the vacuous tawdriness of the Hirst room, but in both senses it's a poor show.

What makes this unholy alliance between art and mammon all the more distressing is the amount of really good painting around at the moment. John Walker (born Birmingham 1939) is one of those artists who have slipped off the critical radar in recent years, simply because we haven't been shown his work in this country. His reputation, as both painter and teacher, stood very high here in the 1970s and 80s, although at that time his star was also rising fast in America and Australia. Since 1992 he has lived and taught in Boston, with a bolt-hole in Maine. In 2006 he began his Seal Point series based on the landscape of the Maine coast, which he has painted fruitfully in both large and small formats. At Offer Waterman is a selection of his small paintings (from the 200 or so he has completed) and very fine they look too.

Walker is best-known in this country for his large and powerful abstracts, full of gestural marks and intimations of primitive ritual. The painter Stephen Chambers (born 1960) recalls that when he was a student at St Martin's (1979-82), 'John Walker was the biggest beast in the playground', and many of the tutors were his 'total disciples'. Walker's influence was for a while all-pervasive. The innovative gallerist Nigel Greenwood represented him, and even after Walker moved to Australia in 1979, there was a major show of his work at the Hayward (1985). But the silence since then on the Walker front has been pretty deafening for those who remembered to listen. So this new exhibition is a major event.

How good then to see Walker's latest work breaking new ground and moving so effortlessly between abstraction and figuration. In a sense he has returned to his roots in the landscape, though the subject of these small upright panels (each measures 7¼" x 5½") is just as much the way paint can be tellingly manipulated. Walker found a set of Beano or Bingo cards in a studio he was renting on the Maine coast, and started to paint on them. In some he allows sections of the grid of numbers or the lettering to show through the paint, in others he applies the paint more deeply to the unprimed card. The surfaces of these paintings are liquid and luscious. Walker explores the paradox of how he can suggest lots of detail without being at all specific. The flatness of the card is at once contradicted by his ability to conjure great expanses of space. The vertical format means that the forms are stacked up, and the fact that Maine faces east means there are no dramatic sunsets depicted. But otherwise these little paintings are marvels of compression, running the gamut of painterly effects. After such an appetizer, what we need now is a museum show of Walker's work since 1985. Is it a critical or editorial failing that there is so little coverage in the national press of exhibitions mounted by commercial galleries? This column is determined to buck that trend. At Browse & Darby (19 Cork Street, W1, until 20 November) is a really splendid exhibition of paintings of Australia by the veteran realist, Anthony Eyton (born 1923). Last year he travelled out to the Antipodes on a kind of pilgrimage to Uluru (better known as Ayers Rock). He made a series of gorgeous pastels on site, and has subsequently been working on large oil paintings of various aspects of the subject back in his south London studio. The results are some of the finest paintings of a long and distinguished career. Although Eyton stays close to the shifting appearance of his motif, the freedom of his paint-handling is inventive and beguiling. His depictions of Ayers Rock are rich in colour (occasionally almost savage in the preponderance of burnt orange or bright terracotta) and full of incident. The sacred quality of the place is brought home to us in no uncertain terms.

Meanwhile, out of town is an exhibition I have yet to see, of Humphrey Ocean's paintings (at the Sidney Cooper Gallery, St Peter's Street, Canterbury, until 7 November). This public gallery was once the art school where Ocean (born 1951) was a student in the early 1970s. The deceptively simple paintings he terms Perfectly Ordinary (the exhibition's title) constitute a vision of everyday life as seen through a car windscreen, or posed (in the case of his portraits) in the blankness of the studio. 'The quirks and behaviours of England are my natural territory', he says. Ocean is the Philip Larkin of the visual cadre.

PETER LANYON

Tate St Ives

16 October 2010

In the first retrospective of his work for nearly 40 years, Peter Lanyon (1918-64) is given the kind of recognition long his due.

A major figure in the St Ives group, his work holds its own on an international stage even though it remains rooted in his native Cornwall. He was an inventive and innovative painter who conjured up the sensation of being in certain places and experiencing particular weather conditions. This was not an art bound to the earth's surface, and it began by delving beneath it, with the Cornish miners, and increasingly rising above it – quite literally, into the air in a glider. Lanyon took up gliding in 1959, and he died aged only forty-six, following a gliding accident. The question on everyone's lips – what might he have done had he lived? – is answered in part by the unsettling work in the last room of this exhibition.

Lanyon believed that the artist occupied an important and responsible position in society, 'at the centre of the new and emerging myths of our time'. He wasn't interested in the self-indulgent artist, obsessed with autobiographical musings. For him the artist was 'not just a recorder of impulses but also a responsible person, responsible to man. That means to man's aspirations as well as his aberrations'. In pursuit of his investigation into man's condition in relation to his surroundings, Lanyon moved rapidly through a stylistic evolution which encompassed cubist-inflected subterranean imagery and his own interpretations of tachism and abstract expressionism. Although often compared to de Kooning, his work has a potent individuality that makes it hard to categorize.

For a change, all the galleries at Tate St Ives have been commandeered for Lanyon, so he shares the space with no one else. The work is arranged chronologically and has been well and intelligently selected. Lanyon's sculptures have been given equal prominence with his paintings throughout, and there are a couple of his finest in the first gallery – 'White Track' and 'Box Construction No 1', both dating from 1939-40. This was when he was first finding his feet as an artist, and much under the influence of Ben Nicholson, Naum Gabo and Adrian Stokes. His early paintings are reminiscent of Barbara Hepworth or Gabo sculptures, enclosed pregnant forms or images of underground chambers. The big painting in the first gallery is 'Porthleven', done for the Festival of Britain in 1951, but some of the smaller works, such as 'Portreath' and 'Carthew', have a greater poignancy, however pale and abraded.

Downstairs, in what is un-poetically called Lower Gallery 2 and is actually a beautiful semi-circular viewing gallery for Porthmeor beach, the work gets more gestural and more abstract, in fact more like Lanyon's contemporaries William Scott and Roger Hilton. Lanyon did not consider his paintings to be truly abstract, and their content remains closely linked to the Cornish landscape and to the human figure. Look at the lively brushing of 'Farm Backs' and 'Inshore Fishing', both 1952, or the more heated palette and richer textures of 'Primavera' and 'Saracinesco' of the following year. Here too is 'Europa', a massive reclining nude, for which he made three sculptures, the two survivors positioned near the painting.

Go upstairs again for the suite of three galleries which show Lanyon moving swiftly through a number of different painterly incarnations before ending his career far too soon. Blue starts to penetrate the mind here. It will become the most salient colour of Lanyon's mature palette, a key perhaps to intensities of mood, but surely more to do with the increasingly airborne nature of his vision. The abstracted landscape of 'St Ives Bay' and 'Wheal Owles' gives way accordingly to the more elemental vision of 'High Wind' and the dynamic vortex of 'Rosewall' (1960). By now Lanyon had begun gliding, and the impact is evident in such paintings as 'Thermal' and 'Soaring Flight'. Red also begins to assume a greater importance in the paintings – as edging or accent or outline. Lanyon's assemblages have now become shards of coloured glass and off-cuts of wood, studio detritus thrown together to provide clues for paintings, and it's possible to see their forms transfigured in a painting such as 'Antigone' (1962). By the last room, red is counterpointing the blue, in my least favourite painting 'Saltillo', and in 'Glide Path', with its diagonals of black rubber tubing.

'Clevedon Bandstand' (1964) looks oddly like a washing machine, with its white oval superimposed on an upside-down black pedestal form, and 'Lomnica (Marica)' brings ribbons of lilac to the red and green controversy. This last gallery looks very fresh and compelling, as Lanyon worked at full throttle: inventive, uncompromising and very much pushing the boundaries of his art.

These paintings are difficult to assimilate and take time to cast their spell. Lanyon's later work combines a thinner application of paint with a greater build-up of surface in the form of collaged objects which complicate the structure of these semi-relief works. The colours become increasingly synthetic, and the arctic blues I personally find so hard to take are joined by pale violet and harsh green. The white priming often shows through or beside the paint. The visitor may well benefit from lingering in the last two galleries, or returning to them having completed the circuit of the exhibition. The longer you look, the more coherent and convincing – and utterly strange – these paintings appear. Originality pulses out of them.

The exhibition is curated by the Tate's Chris Stephens, who has made a particular study of Lanyon for more than 20 years. He has opted to focus on the technical aspects of the artist's work, rather than responding to what Lanyon himself felt was important – his subject matter, and its relationship to his beloved Cornwall. Stephens has chosen this route in order to locate Lanyon more securely within the context of international modernism, a context that attaches greater importance to the formal or abstract aspects of art, rather than to what are perceived as such provincial and old-fashioned matters as landscape and spirit of place. Yet without that umbilical relationship to a particular landscape, Lanyon's art would never have existed, and to assess it in purely formal terms is to diminish it.

Stephens contends that Lanyon's constructions 'were some of the most original works of art of their time'. The only precedents he finds for them are among the work of Picasso and Schwitters, yet surely they are only a development of the collage and relief technique prevalent among such contemporaries as Eileen Agar and Margaret Mellis. Lanyon, who was in the RAF during the war, recorded that 'a mentality common to many of the air force fitters and riggers was a kind of beachcombing, to see what was interesting or valuable and good salvage ... This finding something to make into something else was a fundamental part of my existence'. It was an attitude easily adapted to his art. Lanyon saw his constructions as essential to the development of particular paintings, as preparatory studies. It is his paintings which command our attention: they are the peak of his very considerable achievement and the crown of this magnificent exhibition.

WORKING THE LAND PART II: HARRY BECKER

Gainsborough's House, Sudbury, Suffolk
13 November 2010

Harry Becker (1865-1928) is one of those artists too often dismissed as being of regional interest only, who feature but rarely in the art chronicles of the period. He is most widely known for his illustrations to Adrian Bell's celebrated Suffolk trilogy – *Corduroy, Silver Ley* and *The Cherry Tree* – and it is worth noting that Becker's pictures were matched to Bell's prose after the artist's death, though they seem to be made for each other in their near-perfect setting. As Bell wrote of him: 'He painted the whole struggle of man in the getting of bread – with earth and weather'. Becker's fresh and feisty realism, which borders on Impressionism (in its British manifestation, at any rate), is a superb tribute to the East Anglian landscape and the people who worked it.

For this reason, Gainsborough's House has made Becker the subject of Part II of a themed exhibition, following a show of the photographs of Justin Partyka (born 1972) who portrays the plight of the modern agrarian community. Becker's ploughmen, harvesters, sowers and gleaners are in the long tradition of Breughel, Millet and van Gogh, but depicted with a fluidity and lightness of touch that reconnects him to the work of Gainsborough and Constable. Becker initially discovered his theme of manual labour (one to be later so thoroughly explored by Josef Herman) at Antwerp, where he studied at the Royal Academy. His freedom of expression was encouraged by working with Carolus-Duran in Paris, who recommended open-air painting and among whose other pupils was Sargent, and developed out of an increasing passion for working from life. Becker drew sheep in Kent and cattle in Holland, and enjoyed some success exhibiting in London.

For a number of years around the turn of the century he apparently exhibited nothing, before finding a new lease of life and inspiration in Suffolk. For 15 years he toiled with the workers on the land, sharing their long hours. Witnesses recall Becker shining with sweat, not from the heat of action but from the emotion – the empathy – generated by what he saw. His deeply felt response accounts for the authenticity of his act of witness, the compelling truth of his work. He worked fast to salvage the spontaneity of his emotions and developed a wonderfully economic style of expression. He drew like the wind, with an urgency that had no time for the scenic or the pretty. He depicted life on the land as he saw it, and the energy crackles off the drawings, prints and small paintings gathered at Gainsborough's House.

I had not realised how good a printmaker Becker was. His powerful drawings transfer easily to lithographs, but the revelation is in the etchings. Look, for instance, at his 1914 etching of haymakers with a hay wagon. One of Becker's greatest subjects is the labouring body in movement or at rest, and the way in which he manages to convey its sense of solidity which is both separate and individual yet also an embodiment of the landscape. The intimate relationship between figure and landscape is natural to Becker, so deep and instinctive is his understanding of the realities of rural life. Look at his various studies of men with scythes. He is equally good at horses, and one of the loveliest things here is two horses yoked together, drawn in red chalk. A couple of straight landscapes show how well Becker knew his adopted patch, and how lyrically he celebrated it. Adrian Bell said, 'He put the blaze of God on things.' High time he was better known.

MODERN BRITISH SCULPTURE

Royal Academy
29 January 2011

There has already been a certain amount of controversy over this exhibition: not just the predictably ruffled feathers of Royal Academicians omitted from the selection, but the kind of ill feeling amongst the Academy's organizational staff which gives a museum a bad name. This is a great pity, as the exhibition is a remarkable one – out of twelve rooms, eight contain some of the best-displayed Mod Brit sculpture I've seen for a long time, in interesting and revealing juxtapositions. After that the exhibition trails off alarmingly, implying that the state of contemporary British sculpture is a parlous one. This is simply not true, so this fizzling-out is a serious misrepresentation. How did it arise? Well, the exhibition was selected by the art historian Penelope Curtis (newly-appointed director of Tate Britain) in collaboration with the sculptor Keith Wilson. They have set out to make a personal and provocative choice in order to stimulate debate and raise the questions of what constitutes sculpture and what constitutes British, let alone what we mean by that knotty term 'modern'. The result of this bold initiative is a series of galleries filled with art, closely juxtaposed or widely spaced, which makes us look again at old favourites and anew at less familiar names. There are around 120 exhibits, including sculpture from Native American, Indian and African cultures, which supply the effective counterpoint and illumination for works of British make. The intrusion of what might be called 'influential foreigners' is one of the things that makes this exhibition so exciting – at least in its early stages.

The first gallery, the octagon, contains (just) a vast model of Lutyens' 'Cenotaph', surrounded by photographic banners of Epstein's 'Cycle of Life' sculptures, made for the British Medical Association in The Strand, and later shamefully defaced and bowdlerized. At once we are invited to consider public sculpture and the monument and their role in the community – a particularly important issue in this era of the 4th Plinth and too much hideous fifth-rate junk masquerading as sculpture in public places. The second gallery is equally crowded with exhibits, but it contains so many brilliantly inspired pairings and groupings that I found myself almost continually smiling with surprise and pleasure.

Impossible to name all the lovely and eye-opening exhibits, so I shall content myself with a brief list. Good to see Maurice Lambert here, with a wonderfully camp Narcissus, also called 'The Seed', c1932. Opposite, a tremendous John Skeaping seated figure carved in marble makes me yearn once again for a proper solo exhibition of this artist, but experts tell me there simply isn't enough top-quality work. Henry Moore at his most abstract, with the rabbit-eared elmwood 'Family' of 1935, is next to Leon Underwood's beautiful Gauguinesque 'Totem to the Artist'. Underwood, who taught Moore and was a brave and innovative sculptor in his own right, is desperately neglected these days. Hereabouts are Barbara Hepworth's slim African blackwood 'Torso' and Eric Kennington's lavishly sensual 'Earth Child', also Charles Wheeler's elongated but oddly compelling 'Mother and Child'.

Interspersed are objects from British Columbia, Mexico, the Congo, Mesopotamia. The disadvantage of emphasising links with so-called primitive art, and thus skewing the selection, is that a formidable modernist such as F E McWilliam is represented by 'African Figure', one of his earliest wood-carvings, and not by something stronger and more typical. But generally, the comparisons and juxtapositions pay off admirably. Neo-Assyrian reliefs only add to the greatness of Charles Sargeant Jagger, while helping to cast light on the sources of his own magisterial relief, 'Belgian Peasants Assisting the British Wounded'. Frank Dobson's succinct 'Seated Torso' carved in 1923 from Ham Hill stone may reveal the influence of Picasso and Chinese art (the sculptor visited Paris in 1922), but a lot more research needs to be done on Dobson, another cruelly neglected early modernist.

Room 3 is refreshingly empty, containing only two sculptures: a 1924 marble snake by Moore and Epstein's magnificent alabaster 'Adam', which puts the entire 2009 RA show of Epstein, Gaudier and Gill in the shade. This single piece deserves as much detailed attention as you feel able to give it: not for its sexual power, but for the supreme potency of its forms released from the stone by Epstein's uncanny skill in carving. Room 4 contains a startling but immensely effective juxtaposition: Alfred Gilbert's intricate bronze 'Jubilee Memorial to Queen Victoria' with Phillip King's strangely tented 'Genghis Khan', a winged conical abstract in purple plastic. (A survey of King's sculpture through 50 years is at Flowers, 82 Kingsland Road, E2, until 19 February.) Charles Wheeler's 'Adam' looks on in open-mouthed disbelief, while Lord Leighton plays with his snake in the far corner. This is a room to shake up your preconceptions. Room 5 moves the argument into ceramics, presenting Chinese ware against William Staite Murray, and bringing in sculptures by Paule Vezelay and Hepworth, and a couple of relief paintings by Ben Nicholson. (One, a tiny incised card relief, from Kettle's Yard, is exquisite.) In Room 6, a mere two sculptures play out the dialogue between figuration and abstraction through the persons of Moore and Hepworth. An environmental construction takes up the whole of Room 7, re-created from a 1957 installation in the Hatton Gallery, Newcastle, by Victor Pasmore and Richard Hamilton, in which coloured acrylic panels are suspended from nylon thread and articulate the space. It looks marvellous: infinitely fresher than so much contemporary installation art. Room 8 features a single painted steel and aluminium sculpture by Anthony Caro, 'Early One Morning' (1962), which also looks splendid. And there the exhibition should have ended.

The remainder is so thin and scrappy as to be embarrassing. One good Barry Flanagan and a Tony Cragg stack in the big gallery 9 cannot redeem or enliven these hectic conceptual wastes. Even Carl André's once infamous bricks fail to make this room sparkle. Enter Damien Hirst in Gallery 10, in the dubious company of Jeff Koons (presumably Hirst's 'influential foreigner', or equivalent of African sculpture). Bill Woodrow lights up a corner of Gallery 11, and Gallery 12 ends the show on a note of humour with veteran prankster Gustav Metzger going for Page 3 girls, and Sarah Lucas offering a 'Portable Smoking Area'.

But the sense of let-down is palpable in the lack of significant sculpture in the last four rooms. Although it's a great relief not to have to look at the overrated institutional art of Kapoor and Gormley, we are also deprived of beautiful and inventive work by the likes of Nigel Hall and Michael Sandle, Bryan Kneale and David Nash, Eilis O'Connell and Ivor Abrahams, not to mention substantial artists of an earlier generation such as Kenneth Armitage and Lynn Chadwick. The curators propose an alternative tradition: it's one that disappears like so much hot air, leaving only the Cheshire cat's smile.

THE POETRY OF DRAWING

Birmingham Museum & Art Gallery
19 February 2011

Drawings are often valued as an artist's first thoughts, the most direct and intimate expression of his or her response to a subject. Looking at a drawing, you feel you can see the artist's mind at work – in a much more spontaneous way than in a painting made from preparatory studies. Yet in the rather ridiculous established hierarchy of art, drawings are ranked much lower than paintings, perhaps because they are generally considered to be working tools, less durable than oil on canvas, and frequently not preserved with the same care as 'finished' pictures. Our age, which is fascinated by process, gives more attention to drawings but still does not esteem them as highly as it might. As a result, there are plenty of opportunities for collectors, if top-quality paintings are beyond their reach.

Perhaps not, though, in the Pre-Raphaelite market-place. The great and sustained popularity of the Pre-Raphaelite Brotherhood has ensured that prices remain high, and many of the finest examples of PRB drawing are already in museum collections, as can be seen from this excellent exhibition. Birmingham has long held the premier collection of PRB works on paper in the world, so it is the perfect place to stage this show.

If you have time and energy after doing justice to *The Poetry of Drawing*, wander upstairs for more PRB treats such as 'The Death of Chatterton', paintings by Arthur Hughes and Millais' famous 'Blind Girl'. There is even a room of well-chosen 20th century British artists to bring us up to date, with fine examples of Paul Nash, Bomberg, Ben Nicholson and John Armstrong, and a couple of cracking Sickerts. Not to mention the Anglo-Saxon gold and silver from the Staffordshire Hoard. The PRB show starts with a section called 'Challenging Academic Drawing', which highlights the kind of academic studies from the antique a student was expected to turn out. Here too are drawings from the life, hefty nude figures among whose solidly-drawn forms Rossetti's frail girl in 'Study for Ecce Ancilla Domini!' on pale blue paper looks positively wispy. Rossetti is often considered to be a weak draughtsman, but he comes out rather well in this exhibition, clearly a master of a different kind of evocative mark-making, particularly effective with pen and ink or pastel. Here too are some early Ford Madox Brown drawings and watercolours, made for his unsuccessful entry to a mural competition for the Palace of Westminster, the subject 'Chaucer at the court of Edward III'; the pencil compositional study being the finest.

The PRB was founded in 1848 by Rossetti, Holman Hunt and Millais, and it must not be forgotten how radical their art appeared, how revolutionary. They saw the dead hand of the Academy everywhere, and wanted to supplant false academicism with honest naturalism and moral edification. And they were certainly industrious in their efforts. Look at the crisp observational drawing of Millais, the obsessive detail of Hunt or the atmospheric ink and wash of Rossetti. Familiar figures emerge from PRB mythology – Lizzie Siddal, initially discovered and persuaded to sit by Walter Deverell, before Hunt and Rossetti got hold of her. Millais used her most famously as the model for his great painting of Ophelia floating downriver – the pen and ink compositional study for this is here, with a pencil head. Also a couple of Siddal's own pictures: technically inept but wonderfully moody.

Ruskin was a great supporter of PRB beliefs, and was particularly drawn himself to the close observation of nature, as witnessed by his own drawings, such as the exquisite study of ivy against a swirling ground like a waterfall. William Henry Hunt is typically represented by a birds' nest, surrounded by apple blossom and primroses. The botanical school really get going here, with a couple of fervent works by Frederick Sandys, again of ivy. John Brett's 1862 watercolour of a gentian is a highpoint of this kind of nature study. I like his sister Rosa's intense landscapes (though not her sentimental bunnies). From nature back to people with a series of portraits of the leading protagonists: I especially enjoyed Rossetti's well-inked caricatures of his friends, complete with speech bubbles. 'Slosh!' says Millais, in shorthand for Sir Sloshua Reynolds, meaning bad art or bad ideas, and Hunt answers 'Of course!'

The coloured chalk portraits of Fanny Cornforth show what Rossetti could do when he put his mind to highly-worked drawing, while his sketch of himself sitting for Lizzie Siddal, and his caricature of his sister in a tantrum smashing things, are further evidence of his mordant wit and innate poetry. Then there's a whole section on stained glass and another on applied art. I had prepared for the stained glass by dropping in at the impressive cathedral (1715) in "High Town", where there are four beautiful windows by Birmingham-born Burne-Jones. Back in the exhibition there were both studies and glass panels on show. And still the show goes on, through minor figures like Simeon Solomon and Frederic George Stephens, to major paintings such as 'The Last of England' and 'The Finding of the Saviour'. An extraordinary array of work.

Trips out of London have the unfortunate habit of making one dissatisfied with galleries in the metropolis. There seems to be so much more space in provincial museums, the staff are courteous and friendly, and there are none of those irritable crowds of the elbowing leisured classes fighting for their 20 seconds in front of a masterpiece. In the Gas Hall of Birmingham Museum & Art Gallery, this large exhibition has been laid out with an almost prodigal spaciousness, which makes it a joy to visit. In fact, the Birmingham experience was much more like one of those treasured memories of visiting a grand palazzo abroad, where it is considered properly respectful as well as a mark of the highest civilization to have space around your illustrious exhibits. As a consequence, the viewers who were there when I visited took their time over examining these intricate drawings, seemed seriously interested in what they were looking at, and were unflustered by a press of people wanting to stand in their place. The audience contained a nice mix of young and old and the atmosphere was relaxed but intent. The whole trip for me was a real pleasure. The exhibition, which travels to The Art Gallery of New South Wales, Sydney (17 June – 4 September), is accompanied by a book entitled *Pre-Raphaelite Drawing* by Colin Cruise (T&H, £29.95 hb, £19.95 pb). It's a clearly written and lavishly illustrated account, but no substitute for the first-hand experience of seeing these remarkable drawings. Book your travel to Birmingham now.

WATERCOLOUR

Tate Britain
26 February 2011

Another vast exhibition at Tate Britain, but one which will no doubt prove popular with the public. Watercolour is a national pastime, and the English tend to wax proprietorial about it. As a painting medium it appeals greatly to amateurs because it's nearly always possible to do something passable in watercolour which couldn't be achieved in oil paint without more knowledge, application and experience. Passable yes, but not distinguished: it takes a very great deal of skill to achieve the more than ordinary in watercolour, and herein lies its seduction and challenge. The stakes are raised by the existence of a tradition of great watercolour painting in this country, which prospered with particular insistence in the period 1750 to 1850.

It is often said that the English are adept at watercolour because of the climate – the mild, wet and changeable weather that gives rise to so many wonderful skies and cloud effects. Water calls to water, so to speak. Now along comes this exhibition to 'reassess the commonly held belief that the medium first flourished during a "golden age" of British watercolour', to "challenge the notion that watercolour is singularly British" and to 'overturn such assumptions' as watercolour being a medium for traditional representational painting, for depicting landscape, the sea and picturesque buildings. In other words, another example of that curatorial insistence on moving the goal posts in order to invent an argument and something new to write about. Luckily, as with most art world politics, much of this can be safely ignored, and the average exhibition-goer can enjoy a varied and at times provocative collection of pictures.

The show, which is partly thematically arranged and partly chronological, opens with some marvellous early examples of watercolour in the work of manuscript illuminators and miniature painters. But already we see the 'opening up' of the argument to include the medium of tempera (as used in the two earliest manuscripts borrowed from the British Library), which is not strictly speaking watercolour, since its essential quality is its binding, or tempering, with gum or egg. What a treat it would be to see a whole exhibition devoted to tempera, from medieval times to the present, not forgetting the English tempera revival of the first half of the 20th century. One feels rather short-changed to have tempera shoved in with watercolour. Never mind, there are some truly splendid things here, including one of Van Dyck's studies of a coastal town (perhaps Rye?) – a pity not to have a couple of these very early examples of watercolour landscape – two Wenceslaus Hollar topographical scenes and the haunting Nicholas Hilliard portrait of George Clifford, Earl of Cumberland.

Among the maps and miniatures there are also a pair of memorable Inigo Jones pen and ink costume designs for one or other of the masques he was always running up, evocatively tinted with watercolour, and an exquisitely detailed pollard oak at Chichester by John Dunstall, dating from c1660. Then we move into nature studies, with botanical and geological illustration to the fore, Sarah Stone's 'Shells and Coral' from the 18th century' comparing very well with John Fullwood's 20th century stones. For some reason Edward Lear has been sidelined here, with a drawing of a Whiptail Wallaby, when what we really wanted to see were one or two of his remarkable landscapes. Entering the second large room of the Linbury galleries, the visitor is greeted by a superb Edward Burra landscape of Northumberland from 1972, and chronology gives way to mix and match, which can of course be equally instructive. To the left is a solitary Eric Ravilious painting (why only one example of this quintessential 20th century practitioner of watercolour?), and beyond is a powerful monochrome ink and wash John Piper of glaciated rocks in Snowdonia, nicely sandwiched between Cotman's 'On the Downs' (c1835) and Alfred William Hunt's November rainbow of 1866. A flat cabinet hereabouts shows off sketchbooks by Turner and Piper. Turner's famous 'Blue Rigi' is in this room, as are Girtin's equally celebrated 'White House at Chelsea' (1800), a Francis Towne which doesn't really do justice to his originality, and an R P Bonington of Verona of some distinction. Next to the Burra there's an intriguingly textured painting of Kentish hop gardens by an artist unfamiliar to me, Cecil Lawson (1851-1882), and beyond that a cracking Charles Rennie Mackintosh village landscape (c1927).

Don't miss the madly-detailed Richard Dadd view of Rhodes, hatched and stippled with tiny eye-boggling dabs, and the more lenitive panorama of an Egyptian oasis in World War 2 by Edward Bawden. Holman Hunt is here, always worth looking at, and another big Burra, of a Mexican church, one of his crankier interiors. The next section, dealing with 'The Exhibition Watercolour', is rather forced and finished and generally lacking in spontaneity. Nevertheless, there's a brightly-washed 1920s 'Nativity' by Dorothy Webster Hawksley, Arthur Melville's softly atmospheric 'Blue Night, Venice' and the vividly intense 'Streatley Mill' by George

Price Boyce. A 'How to do it' section follows, in which technique is explained under the watchful gaze of such masterpieces as Turner's 'Scarlet Sunset' and Whistler's 'Beach Scene'. Good to see a large work by Rebecca Salter here, one of our best contemporary practitioners, who is currently enjoying a large survey exhibition at the Yale Center for British Art in Connecticut. The next theme to be addressed is war, and Burra is given prominence here once again – almost as if the Tate wants to steal the thunder of Pallant House's forthcoming Burra retrospective (22 October 2011 – 19 February 2012). Luckily there are a lot of other war artists to choose from, and inevitably Paul Nash and Graham Sutherland feature, with rather a good Sargent, in which the harvest goes on regardless of the crashed aeroplane in the background. As the show moves towards its end, the mood turns introspective. Under the heading 'Inner Vision' are great things by Blake and Paul Nash, rather obvious choices by that underrated master David Jones, perhaps too much Burne-Jones. Good to see a fine Chris Le Brun ziggurat hung between Samuel Palmer's 'Hilly Scene' masterpiece and Rossetti, and I can just about see the point of including Beardsley, but the dreadful Simeon Solomon? And Victor Hugo is fun, but totally out of place.

The contemporary section of unbelievably feeble Tracey Emins and equally insignificant squiggles by Bethan Huws is thankfully enlivened by a series of witty David Austens and an intriguing grid study by Lucy Skaer. In the last room the definition of watercolour is stretched to breaking point with a large acrylic on canvas action painting by Sandra Blow. I admire Blow's work, but it is completely out of context here. Much more appropriate are the two lively and irreverent Roger Hilton gouaches (honouring his centenary) and the sequence of Alexander Cozens blot studies from the 18th century. On the opposite wall is a fabulous group of Turners – 10 watercolours, mostly beginnings of things featuring sea and sky, culminating in the radically minimal 'Boat at Sea'. Better to draw a veil over the contemporary offerings at the far end of the gallery, though these are somewhat redeemed by Callum Innes' delicately beautiful layered washes.

In sum, it's an odd selection, but though that can be more stimulating than a predictable one, there are one or two glaring omissions I cannot overlook. Constable, Linnell and Wilson Steer are incredibly absent. Among the moderns where are Frances Hodgkins, John Nash, Josef Herman, Elizabeth Blackadder, Norman Adams and Henry Moore? I would have included examples of the masterly figurative-to-abstract compositions of Alan Reynolds from the 1950s and early 60s. Reynolds is criminally undervalued in the unbalanced art world of today, though next week I hope to write about him at some length. As for *Watercolour* at the Tate – it's a show to enjoy selectively. Whether it's worth a hefty £12 admission fee when nearly half of the exhibits come from the Tate's own collection (and thus should be free), remains open to debate.

IDA BARBARIGO AND ZORAN MUSIC

Estorick Collection
14 May 2011

At the Estorick Collection, a modest North London townhouse, there is until 12 June a most engaging exhibition devoted to two artists, husband and wife, whose work is not particularly well-known in this country, though both are recognized and celebrated internationally. Ida Barbarigo (born Venice 1925) first met Zoran Music (1909-2005) at an exhibition of his paintings in Trieste in the spring of 1944. Their burgeoning friendship was interrupted when Music was arrested by the Nazis, who first accused him of spying and then wanted to recruit him. He refused and was deported to Dachau.

Zoran's horrific experience at Dachau scarred his mind and his creative imagination, and was only to surface years afterwards in his work. As he said much later: 'Even now the eyes of the dying are still with me'. In 1945 he was able to return to Venice (where Ida was living), but it was not until 1971 that he began the great series of images collectively entitled 'We are not the last' about his concentration camp experiences. He always said that without Dachau he would have been an illustrative painter: internment made him go to the heart of things.

Ida, meanwhile, had been pursuing her own artistic trajectory. From a very early age, she was haunted by a sense of destiny – that she would grow up to be another Leonardo or Christopher Columbus. After toying with the idea of becoming a musician (she learnt classical guitar), or an architect (she made very precise drawings for an architect uncle), Barbarigo decided to capitalize on her innate talent for drawing and painting. She studied at the Accademia with her adored father, who was professor of painting there, but the academic training was more than a little tedious. Her father dealt intelligently with her need to rebel. 'If you don't feel like working, don't bother', he would say. 'Go and have a coffee on the Zattere'. Ida felt liberated: 'I loved the whole feeling of freedom and light and movement you get the moment you were outside in Venice'. And it was here no doubt that she felt the first stirrings of one of her most fruitful subjects – abandoned cafe tables and chairs which symbolize their fleeting occupants.

On a recent trip to Venice I had arranged to meet and interview Ida, but unfortunately she was unwell, and I had to make do with a guided tour of her magnificent apartment overlooking the Grand Canal, conducted by her friend and interpreter, the Venetian writer Giovanna Dal Bon. The rooms are filled with beautiful things: three massive plain glass chandeliers depend from the ceiling of the main chamber, there are lots of paintings and drawings, a room of etchings, and a flight of plump, slightly chipped plaster *putti* across one of the walls, made by various members of Ida's family, Venetian artists for more than 500 years.

Her father, Guido Cadorin, was a distinguished modernist painter, and I note a striking depiction of the lagoon, a portrait of his mother (shown in the 1911 Biennale), and ceramics designed by him as well as textiles for Fortuny. (Guido, multi-talented, also designed mosaics, and a feeling of these can sometimes be discerned in Ida's work.) Ida's mother, Livia, was a painter too and Guido's favourite pupil, and there's a display of her small poetic tempera paintings of trees in one of the rooms off the central studio/living space.

A mini-retrospective of Ida's paintings was laid out on an avenue of easels, including several important pictures that will be lent to the Estorick's exhibition. Among the newer works at the studio end of the apartment were a number of paintings featuring the 'Terrestrials', impish figures like clay models which represent the barbarian hordes of modern life. These are perhaps Ida's demons – naughty but full of electricity, dancing and scuffling in fruitful ambiguity. (They could be tourists invading Venice.) In this room stand four of the celebrated cafe chairs from the Zattere, in red metal, wooden slatted. 'She used the chairs as a virus inside Venice', says Giovanna Dal Bon. Perhaps they played a similar role to the Terrestrials – a subversive agent, a way of commenting on the weight of Venice's past while allowing a contemporary element to intrude, like yeast, and bring the city to life again.

The critic and curator Michael Peppiatt, who knew Zoran and Ida well and has written perceptively about their art, recalls that 'whenever you went out with them, it was like being with the king and queen of Venice'. Peppiatt relished their grand hospitality and in particular their spectacular New Year parties. He describes Ida as 'a bohemian aristocrat'. A beautiful woman, with more than a passing resemblance to the Italian film star Monica Vitti, she has enjoyed the admiring attention of many men in her life, including Francois Mitterand, in whose Presidential cavalcade Ida and Zoran would sometimes travel. (Music and Barbarigo used to live for half the year in Paris, though always returning to Venice.) Peppiatt also notes Barbarigo's wicked humour, seen especially in the way she depicts sunbathers on the Lido as corpses washed up by the sea.

The relationship between Ida and Zoran was a very special one, an alliance based upon respect and distance. Although they married in 1949, as artists and human beings they pursued parallel paths, living separately and maintaining separate studios – until the last years of Zoran's life, when Ida cared for him in her home – and meeting by arrangement for drinks and dinner. (Zoran would telephone to request the pleasure of Ida's company.) Dal Bon describes Music's dreamy and contemplative nature, his abiding sense of doubt, like a permanent trance, whereas Babarigo's attitude is 'one of natural ecstasy, out in the open, drawing on sudden enchantments, illuminations, details that "miraculously" move her and beg to be followed.' Their different temperaments have resulted in very different kinds of painting, which are displayed together at the Estorick for the first time since a joint show in November 1946 in Trieste, when Ida was still known as Cadorina. (She adopted the pseudonym Barbarigo around 1950.) The Estorick exhibition, entitled *Double Portrait*, after Giovanna Dal Bon's fascinating book about the couple (paperback £35), tells the story of their life together, rather than comparing their work.

The exhibition is arranged in the two ground floor galleries, with groups of evocative black and white photographs of the artists hung in the corridor between. There are flat cabinets of photos and documentary material, revealing the fundamentally intertwined and supportive temper of their existence. In gallery 1 are early portraits of each other, from the 1940s, and two later and more exploratory ones: Ida's of Zoran from 1967, Zoran's of Ida from 1988, both deeply moving. Here too is an early painting of chairs (1954) by Ida, in pronounced linear arrangements, striped like tram-tracks, and one of Zoran's beautiful landscapes with horses. In gallery 2 there is a polyptych of Ida's 'Terrestrials' and a big painting by Zoran from 1989 of him and Ida in the studio. A later chairs picture, 'Chairs Apart' (1974), inspired by St Mark's Square, shows Ida moving her linear investigations further towards form and mass, object and shadow, lyrically expressed. Her portraits, like the 1967 one of Zoran and the lovely painting 'To Go to the Seaside' (1966) are deliquescent, the paint very much on the move, dripping and melting with reflections. If Zoran's art was a progression towards silence, Ida's is a dialogue which never grows less. Both deserve to be better-known.

RAVILIOUS IN ESSEX

Fry Art Gallery, Castle Street, Saffron Walden, Essex
23 June 2011

The Fry Art Gallery is housed in a Victorian Gentleman's Gallery of two main rooms, built in 1856 for the Quaker banker Francis Gibson. It was first intended to accommodate his own collection, but was always open to the public, and in 1985 it was taken over by the Fry Art Gallery Society, a charity set up to create the North West Essex Collection, of work by artists of the locality. The primary focus is on the remarkable group of painters and printmakers who settled in nearby Great Bardfield from the 1930s to the 1970s, and which included Edward Bawden and Eric Ravilious, John Aldridge, Michael Rothenstein and Kenneth Rowntree. The Fry's permanent collection is now a considerable resource, and in addition the gallery mounts regular temporary displays to broaden its appeal. The current show is devoted to the last decade in the tragically short life of Eric Ravilious (1903-42), dealing with the years when he actually lived in Essex.

Ravilious was a brilliant draughtsman who used watercolour to tint and animate his compositions. (Interestingly, his works were referred to as watercolour drawings.) But his mastery of watercolour should not be played down: at art school he discovered the previously rather overlooked 18th century topographical watercolourist, Francis Towne, and later he studied the very different but inspiring techniques of Cotman and Samuel Palmer. At the Royal College, Rav (as he was affectionately known) was directly influenced by the teaching of Paul Nash, himself a master of watercolour and the ways it might be used in a modern context. In fact, although Ravilious was no radical modernist, he managed to achieve a sort of sublime timelessness in his cool and classical use of the medium; a style the lucidity of which is instantly recognizable.

In 1932, Ravilious and his wife Tirzah moved to Great Bardfield to share Brick House with their friends Edward and Charlotte Bawden. Ravilious and Bawden worked well together, and had recently collaborated on some well-received murals for Morley College in London. A mutual friend, the wood-engraver Douglas Percy Bliss, described their relationship: 'Eric admired Edward's dour creativeness, his sheer professionalism, and Edward believed in the elegance and fastidious taste with which Eric was endowed. They worked together in perfect amity'. Nevertheless, there was inevitably some degree of friction between the two couples, and in September 1934 Eric and Tirzah moved to their own home at Bank House in Castle Hedingham, before their final move in 1941 to Ironbridge Farm, near Shalford. Meanwhile, the contemporary taste for country life, mirrored by a kind of 1930s diaspora of writers and artists leaving the cities to live in villages, helped to create a market for Ravilious' distinctive watercolours, which began to sell well.

In the smaller of the two galleries at the Fry is a superb display of 18 Ravilious watercolours, prefaced by a piquant ink portrait of him by his friend and colleague Thomas Hennell, another artist to die in the Second World War. One of the key paintings here is 'Prospect from an Attic', a vista of backyards, roofs and trees, painted from the roof of Brick House when it was being repaired. It has a little of the magic realism of John Nash's early work, but a crisp linearity that is all Ravilious' own. Another memorable subject is 'Village Street', actually Falcon Square in Castle Hedingham, across which a man and a woman cycle on a wet day. 'Late August Beach' depicts a group of 19th century bathing machines at Aldeburgh, wheeled huts drawn up among the boats and a prominent anchor. There are a number of unfamiliar images borrowed from private collections (such as the hallucinatory 'Tree Trunk and Wheelbarrow' or the pale but beautifully structured 'Ironbridge at Ewenbridge') and cabinets of books illustrated by Ravilious, from the celebrated *High Street*, to *Twelfth Night* and the *Cornhill Magazine*.

The main gallery is full of treasures, including the recent Fry acquisition, 'Caravans' by Ravilious, from 1936, and a wall of his 1941 submarine lithographs. There are also good things by Kenneth Rowntree, Keith Vaughan and Michael Ayrton, as well as lesser-known but demonstrably interesting artists such as Sheila Robinson. Display drawers house a number of fascinating preparatory drawings as well as some of Edwin Smith's evocative photographs. The other major presence here is Bawden, with a room off the entrance hall given over to him (though it includes a wall cabinet of Wedgwood china decorated by Ravilious), and several of his splendid large linocuts and wallpaper designs on prominent view. The gallery is open, admission free, Tuesday, Friday and Sunday afternoons, and all day Saturday (11am – 5 pm), and offers a wide range of publications and some original art for sale.

The exhibition also launches a new book on Ravilious, the third in a series of monographs on the artist published by The Mainstone Press, with the general title of *Ravilious in Pictures*. The previous books focused on *Sussex and the Downs* (2009) and *The War Paintings* (2010), the new one being *A Country Life*, and dealing with Ravilious in Essex and Suffolk. These slim, elegantly designed, landscape format hardbacks are extremely good value at £25. Each contains an introduction by James Russell, and then detailed commentary on the 20 full-page colour plates. Russell writes clearly

and entertainingly, displaying an extensive knowledge of Ravilious'
life and the wider social and historical context in which he worked.

Russell suggests that what attracted Ravilious to Essex was
'perhaps less the landscape than the continuing survival in that
isolated region of human enterprise on an intimate scale.... the
villages of rural Essex remained essentially local, pedestrian and
old-fashioned'. Thus Ravilious was able to find enough subjects for
his watercolours that interested him. Brought up over an antique
shop, like another gifted 20th century English watercolourist,
John Ward, Ravilious developed an eye for relics of the past, for
the forgotten and generally un-regarded, and for antiquated
machinery in particular. (Among the book's illustrations are
poignant depictions of an abandoned Talbot-Darracq motorcar, a
steam-powered tractor and the wooden skeleton of a No 29 bus.)
Ravilious' careful scrutiny of his subject is matched by the close
attention that Russell pays the artist's pictures, and the enthusiasm
with which he explains them. Both book and exhibition are highly
recommended.

GRAHAM SUTHERLAND: AN UNFINISHED WORLD
Modern Art Oxford, 30 Pembroke Street, Oxford
21 January 2012

For as long as I've been interested in Modern British art, I've been
fascinated and intrigued by the work of Graham Sutherland (1903-
80). One of the first Cork Street exhibitions I went to as a schoolboy
was of paintings, gouaches, watercolours and graphics by Sutherland
from the collection of Douglas Cooper, held at the Redfern Gallery
in the autumn of 1976. I was enormously impressed, particularly
by the golden-eyed toad rampant, the thorny sentinel figures, a
1944 Welsh landscape and a gouache of bomb-damaged buildings
from 1942. (My recall is not always quite so accurate: in fact, I have

the fold-out card from the exhibition before me as I write.) Only much later did I learn that the reason that the great collector and art historian Douglas Cooper was selling his Sutherlands was because he had fallen out with the artist – not an unusual occurrence for such a touchy and irascible man – and wished publicly to withdraw his favour, having long been a committed Sutherland supporter.

Sutherland's reputation at that time stood very high, and his prices reflected his widespread popularity. His work was admired and collected on the continent, the Italians being especially avid in their pursuit of his graphics, of which there was a correspondingly wide variety. Sutherland lived mostly abroad, and had acquired the status of an honorary European, despite the many powerful landscapes he had made in this country, very much in the English romantic tradition, before the end of the Second World War. It was said by some that he had lost his inspiration by moving to the south of France, and severed an involvement with the spirit of place which had been forged in Pembrokeshire in the 1930s. Actually, Sutherland had already started to go back to Pembrokeshire, and to reconnect with the sources of his vision. He made his first trip back to Wales in 1967, and returned regularly until his death. This new stimulus is evident in the late work, though he never quite re-acquired the sustained and effortless lyricism of his early Welsh period.

After his death, as so often used to happen in the art world, Sutherland's reputation collapsed. Many felt he had been overrated and oversold. He was out of fashion for 20 years, during which time his work was hardly shown in public galleries and good examples of it could be bought relatively cheaply. The last decade has seen a steep rise in his fortunes, though he has not yet returned to his former eminence. Today British 20th century art in general is being reassessed, and the big fish such as Moore, Piper and Sutherland are subject to renewed study. Sutherland's early work is more easily acclaimed, to the detriment of his later career, as was evident from the major Sutherland show in 2005 at Dulwich Picture Gallery, which only ventured up to 1950. More research needs to be done on the whole of his achievement, and the public deserves to see a carefully selected museum retrospective of his later work before judgement can be made. The current, and hugely enjoyable, show at Oxford follows prevailing opinion by sticking to the early work, with a mere trio of later examples (one from 1969, two from the 1970s) to whet the appetite.

The exhibition is curated by George Shaw (born 1966), a Turner Prize nominee who principally paints the Tile Hill housing estate in Coventry, where he grew up. Coventry, of course, is where Sutherland's great tapestry adorns the modern cathedral, a piece of popular and well-received modern public art which helped to establish Sutherland's reputation in his lifetime. In a rather idiosyncratic and oddly Blakean catalogue essay ('the insistent worm Sutherland burrows invisibly and deeply into the mythology of my own imagination'), Shaw dismisses Sutherland's tapestry as 'wonderfully irrelevant'. As an art student he was much more impressed by the mass of studies for it in the Herbert Art Gallery opposite the cathedral.

Shaw evidently has his own take on the older artist. He writes that Sutherland was 'not interested in things, certainly not in things as they are, but perhaps in what they once were and will be, of what they could be... His suns, hills, valleys, roads, roots and skies are not our first encounter with the world around us: it is a second-hand deliverance, used up, tattered, passed on – the marks of its previous owners all too apparent. There is nothing new and nothing finished in Sutherland's world'. And then he writes specifically of the works on paper (of which this exhibition is exclusively composed): 'I see in them the very indecisive and urgent journeying that marks my own daily thoughts and actions both in the studio and the world beyond'. In other words, this is what you might call a highly personal interpretation.

The theory behind the exhibition is clear from the title, and is confirmed in the other catalogue essays – that nothing in Sutherland's world is finished. Has it not occurred to anyone involved in this show that drawings and studies tend, by their very nature, to be unfinished? They are working drawings, evidence of the process by which a finished painting is arrived at. Or else – a much smaller proportion – they are drawings made for exhibition and brought to a pitch of resolution so that they can be displayed and sold as works of art in their own right. Our society prizes drawings in a way which would have surprised the artists of previous centuries, who saw them only as a means to an end and rarely worthy of preservation. Sutherland however was the product of a fragmented modernist culture, an artist trying to make sense of a landscape literally and metaphorically devastated by world war. His work can be said to deal in fragments, but his vision, his world, is no more unfinished than any other artist's.

If you can ignore the show's intellectual pretensions (hardly Sutherland's fault), this is a fine selection of 85 mostly small works in the huge white barn-like upstairs space of the museum, and three smaller rooms off. The best drawings are in the big room: swarms of dabs or cup-shaped brush-marks, scrawls and extended stabs of pen-line, brushy areas of soft colour, poignant but somehow dingy – green-blue, ochres, fawns, grey-blue, dim yellow. This is the landscape explored through the mind, allowing all sorts of levels and degrees of interpretation from the stagy to the neurotic. The sun sets between hills, yet the space conjured up is at once compelling and unconvincing, the overlays of watercolour wash blurring forms and outlines into a subfusc vibrancy. Dark traceries of ink huddle round colour accents in crayon or pastel, like flashes of light or tongues of flame. Here is richness, here is energy – in one of most rewarding exhibitions I've seen in months.

ROSE WYLIE: BIG BOYS SIT IN THE FRONT
Jerwood Gallery, Rock-a-Nore Road, Hastings
HENRI HAYDEN
Browse & Darby, 19 Cork Street, W1
FFIONA LEWIS
Redfern Gallery, 20 Cork Street, W1
31 March 2012

As exhibitions in London's public galleries become increasingly mobbed and unpleasant, it is heartening to report that the drive to take art to the provinces continues apace. New museums seem to be opening all over the country, from Wakefield to Margate, and although one may entertain doubts about their sustainability, their enhancement of our current cultural budget is very welcome. The latest public art gallery to open on the south coast is in Hastings, a once rather grand town that has in recent years been down on its luck. It takes more than an hour and a half to get there from London by train, and there isn't a fast road, and these factors have contributed to keeping the town just outside the easy commuting belt. The consequent availability of inexpensive housing has long encouraged artists to live there, and there is a lively artistic community in the town.

Despite plummeting educational standards, I hope that everyone has heard of the Battle of Hastings, though not everyone will know that the principal engagement of the Norman Conquest actually occurred eight miles to the north of the town. However, Hastings has always taken the credit and its historical standing as one of the Cinque Ports was reinforced when it became a highly fashionable watering place in the mid-18th century, and later a popular seaside resort. An important fishing port, though the industry was hampered by the lack of a natural harbour and the failure of all attempts to construct an artificial one, Hastings still possesses the largest beach-based fishing fleet in England.

I first got to know Hastings more than 20 years ago through visiting John Bratby, who had bought himself an extraordinary pile called The Cupola and Tower of Winds, on the edge of the town. Hastings then was rather seedy. During the last decade there have been brave attempts to regenerate the local economy, with the building of the University Centre and the Sussex Coast College, and now the Jerwood Foundation has contributed largely to the cultural amenities by commissioning a new building to be their visual arts centre. This will be a venue for temporary exhibitions as well as the base for the Jerwood permanent collection.

The £4million building, designed by HAT Projects and clad with grey-black ceramic tiles hand-glazed in Kent, makes a striking statement at the edge of the fishing beach. The tiles work well with the tall black weatherboard net huts, such a feature of the area. Inside the gallery is a large ground-floor space for temporary exhibitions, with a succession of seven smaller rooms (down and up) where the permanent collection will be hung in rotation. These spaces have been sympathetically laid out, with top-lighting as well as windows through which to view the world outside. The domestic scale of the rooms mirrors the domestic size of the paintings in the permanent collection – the quality of which is one of the chief surprises of this venture.

I knew the Jerwood Foundation had collected some paintings, but I must confess I had no idea of the extent and variety of their holdings. About one third of the collection is currently on view, and it ranges from Frank Brangwyn's combination of still-life and landscape, 'From my Window at Ditchling', c1925, the first painting bought for the collection, to Maggi Hambling's powerful yet poignant portrait of her elderly neighbour, 'Frances Rose' (1973). The focus is on Modern British and the artists who won the Jerwood Painting Prize, but the character of the works is frequently unexpected. Obvious examples of an artist's style have often been eschewed in favour of an unusual image which packs a slightly different punch. Thus, downstairs is a marvellously minimal William Gear abstract landscape, simply a slightly angled thin red line dividing areas of subtly modulated brown and black. Upstairs is a splendid and atypical landscape by Mark Gertler, of an Irish yew at Garsington.

Among the other glories are a lovely Shropshire landscape by Ivon Hitchens, a hard-edged wartime still-life by John Craxton and good things by Augustus John, Frank Dobson, L S Lowry, Bratby, Alan Reynolds and Robert Medley. The temporary exhibition space is devoted to paintings by Rose Wylie (born 1934), bold figurative images of uncompromising directness. Wylie confronts head-on our society's lemming-like tendency to banality, and makes witty comments on our obsessions with style, time, image and self-image. Her practice is based firmly in the probity of drawing and her wry observations of human behaviour. This linear language is then translated to large loosely-painted canvases, in a style which takes the term 'short-hand' to new levels, mixing the narratives of film and cartoon with vigorously expressive paint-handling. Wylie points out her admiration for the Bayeux Tapestry, and the empty canvas backgrounds to the action (so like her own), and this Norman connection makes it even more appropriate that she should have the inaugural exhibition at this impressive new gallery.

Back in London, let me draw your attention to two exhibitions that I have already written about, inasmuch as I've contributed essays to their accompanying catalogues. Both are in West End commercial galleries, where some of the most interesting shows come and go with scarcely any coverage in the nation's press. Only a favoured few galleries (such as White Cube and Gagosian) tend to receive regular reviews, for the simple reason that they show artists who are currently fashionable. Yet a few years ago there was good coverage of what went on in London's large community of private galleries – because it was recognized that they presented a wide variety of high quality art, and it was thought that the art-going public would be interested in knowing what was available. The official view today is very narrow, severely limited by fashion and vested interest. There needs to be more written about the sheer diversity of art on offer in the capital – not the same old handful of exhibitions reviewed by all the critics.

At Browse & Darby (19 Cork Street, W1, until 5 April) is a delightful exhibition of oil paintings, gouaches and lithographs by the French artist Henri Hayden (1883-1970), once well-known here, but now generally unfamiliar. His work was shown a lot in London in the 1960s, he's well-represented in the Tate, and it's clear that some of our contemporary artists were aware of him, (Mary Fedden, Rose Hilton, Craigie Aitchison.) Hayden was a Polish refugee who settled in Paris and worked his way through the influences of Renoir and Cubism to a brand of very pleasing lyrical landscape painting. His simplified forms and plangent colours were applied to still-life as much as landscape, and offer a beguilingly abstracted and poeticized approach to subject matter. Meanwhile at Redfern Gallery (20 Cork Street, W1, until 26 April) is a show of new work by Ffiona Lewis, entitled 'Figurine and Landscape'. Lewis (born 1964) has already built up a loyal audience for her distinctive landscape and still-life paintings, often attractively light-filled and celebratory. Her recent work builds on these firm foundations (her approach is decidedly structural – not surprising for a painter who trained as an architect) and tackles her subject with new authority. She has been spending a lot of time recently in Suffolk, which she sees as much softer and darker than the Atlantic coast of Devon and Cornwall where she grew up. Her landscapes have become correspondingly darker as she has explored the presence of black in her creeks and meres and tree-scapes. These powerful new works, with their complex echoes of both classical and romantic (from Claude to Paul Nash), are moving beyond the familiar Lewis territory of still-life and landscape towards a new ingredient: the human figure. As yet the figure appears mostly as sculpture or figurine, but I feel this is a new direction for Lewis rich in possibilities. All three shows are highly recommended.

DAMIEN HIRST
Tate Modern
ALIGHIERO BOETTI: GAME PLAN
Tate Modern
ARTURO DI STEFANO: LASTING
Purdy Hicks Gallery, 65 Hopton Street, SE1
12 May 2012

People go to exhibitions for different reasons, and although I was highly critical of David Hockney's recent show at the Royal Academy, I accept that a great many people visited it and came out smiling and uplifted. They tended to be individuals who don't usually go to exhibitions or look at real painting, and it may thus be said that they had very little idea of what they were actually looking at, or indeed should be looking for in an exhibition of painting, but if the experience made them happy, where's the harm – you may ask – in that? Undoubtedly a great many went because it was the thing to do, and they felt better for being able to say that they'd been there and done that. There is much emotional reassurance to be derived from a group activity of this sort, and it should not be mocked, though it has precious little to do with art. As Anthony Burgess observed: 'Art is rare and sacred and hard work, and there ought to be a wall of fire around it'; though nowadays it is often confused with spectacle. Damien Hirst (born 1965) has benefited enormously from this lack of distinction.

An inspired curator and a self-promoter and salesman of genius, Hirst has regaled the art market and the media with a constant series of stories and stunts which have pushed his personal celebrity and his product ever higher. A conceptual artist, he's had some memorable ideas for installations which deal with life and death, explored principally through the preserved carcases of animals. Most of his other ideas are banal, but the marketing skills of the team he employs are so effective, and the media in general so willing to endorse the delusion that Hirst is a major artist, that his work has been hyped beyond belief. So much so that it is now the subject of a major retrospective at Tate Modern (not Tate Britain, of course, because Hirst is an international brand), and is even supposed to represent our cultural achievement for the Olympics. Strange then that the Tate show should be so unspectacular as to seem dull, when it's not actually looking tawdry.

The spot and spin paintings scarce merit a mention, the ashtrays and pills point a very simple comment on contemporary society, and only the sad, dopey butterflies, hatching out in the Tate and dying there before being de-winged so that their most decorative body-parts can be made into mock stained glass, seem to offer a parable for contemporary art. It's highly revealing that Hirst refers to his 'artworks', rather than paintings, installations or sculptures. 'Artwork' actually means the illustrations for something printed, and up to now has been most commonly used in advertising. Recently hi-jacked by the less literate members of the art world, it's assumed to mean 'work of art', but actually it hasn't lost its advertising gloss. Artwork is about marketing and so is Damien Hirst. The last room of his show makes this abundantly clear: a shop in which Hirst merchandise may be purchased, from elaborate silkscreen prints at over £30,000 to humble postcards, from butterfly-printed deckchairs to spin umbrellas, sterling silver pill cufflinks, butterfly bone china or skate boards.

By contrast, the exhibition of work in various media by the influential Italian artist Alighiero Boetti (1940-94) looks marvellous, though it too is marred by too much arid conceptual material. The show starts to get interesting with 100 embroidered panels entitled 'Order and Disorder'. The best of Boetti's work is related to fabric in some way – the biro drawings composed of parallel lines of different densities that look woven, a rather beautiful large cafe-au-lait embroidery on linen from 1979 called 'The Hour Tree', or the brightly decorative maps. The latter may document the political shifts during the Cold War, but their primary impetus and appeal is aesthetic. Like Hirst, Boetti only determined how a thing should look and then had it executed by assistants, and I still think art loses much of its resonance and meaning by such deputizing. However, in the last room of the exhibition a vast embroidered collage entitled 'Everything' certainly highlights the seductiveness of his methods.

Altogether more worthwhile is an exhibition of new paintings by Arturo Di Stefano round the corner from Tate Modern, at Purdy Hicks Gallery in Hopton Street. Di Stefano was born in Huddersfield in 1955, of Italian parentage, and lived in Italy as a child for a couple of years before returning to England which has been his home ever since. He studied at Goldsmiths and the Royal College and has established a solid reputation as a painter of predominantly urban subjects in the tradition of Sickert and Kitaj, but with a sophisticated Italian edge that looks back to the Renaissance as much as to the achievements of Modernism. Actually his work is much more subtle and complex than such a sketchy outline can convey, and the current exhibition of new paintings marks a high point in a very interesting career. The show is accompanied by a well-illustrated catalogue with a perceptive text by the poet Jamie McKendrick.

Di Stefano sometimes paints portraits, but more often he suggests the presence of people in his pictures by concentrating on aspects of the buildings they inhabit and the thresholds they cross. He paints doorways and arcades, corridors and staircases and balconies. These architectural features are usually deserted, uncluttered by demanding humanity, and sometimes they begin to dissolve at the edges, as in a dream. This is partly to do with Di Stefano's technique, which involves painting thinly and then taking a counterproof of a painting while it's still wet, thus transferring paint from the canvas to a sheet of paper and, in the process, gaining a new image. A beautiful oil-on-paper counterproof entitled 'Rose' greets the visitor to Purdy Hicks, a subtly sexualized drapery study of considerable presence, enhanced rather than diminished by its slightly worn and abraded appearance. In 'Cloisters, Ferrara (II)', the solid contours begin to smudge and waver, the columns to lose their substance and become semi-transparent, ghostly. Nothing is quite as straightforward as it seemed: appearances are threatening to fade, as if this corner of reality is a bit tatty, tarnished, used-up. Di Stefano's paint surfaces are wonderfully variegated, richly scumbled to give a distressed time-worn effect. Notice the disturbance of what you might assume to be the placid surface of 'Arcades, Bologna': another pattern of marks is superimposed on the record of appearances like smoke, or water run over glass. In 'Villa D'Este' the paint flares like flame in a draught, young and full of life in its depiction of this historic building. Downstairs a study of St Paul's offers a very different mood, more literally representational and Sickertian, contrasting with the lovely lucid abstractions of 'New England Nocturne'. And the exquisite 'Lantern' casts a tripled lambency before and beyond a gridded window. Magical.

PATRICK REYNTIENS

26 May 2012

The name of Patrick Reyntiens (born 1925) is indissolubly linked to the recent history of stained glass in this country. Reyntiens bridges the often troublesome gap between craft and art: not only is he a superb and innovative craftsman, but he is also a substantial artist. The second quality is not always recognized. Best-known as John Piper's associate, many assume that Piper was the artist behind their stained glass collaborations, with Reyntiens as technical expert. Actually, Reyntiens played a more creative role in their collaborations than is generally supposed. Certainly he is a painter and draughtsman of considerable originality, as can be seen in the new DVD, *From Coventry to Cochem: The Art of Patrick Reyntiens*. This well-made documentary runs for 71 minutes with a further 83 minutes of extras, including such delights as the 1967 film *Crown of Glass* about the making of the Piper/Reyntiens windows for Liverpool Metropolitan Cathedral.

Reyntiens, an engaging and charismatic subject ('I think my best invention's myself'), was born in Cadogan Square before his family moved to Brussels where his nanny read Dickens to him. Ampleforth and Edinburgh School of Art completed his education, and a strong religious faith sustains him. John Betjeman introduced him to Piper who needed help with his first stained glass commission, for Oundle School, beginning a 35 year collaboration, including the great triumph of the Baptistery window for Coventry Cathedral. But Piper's fame has overshadowed him: as Roy Strong says, Reyntiens should now be rediscovered as an artist in his own right.

THE ART OF MONARCHY
National Portrait Gallery
29 June 2012

Her Majesty the Queen has been a global celebrity for 60 years, and she carries her status with a naturalness and dignity that many of the more tearaway celebs would do well to emulate. She graduated from being a young and glamorous queen to a happy and fulfilled mother, but then had to settle for pausing in that most difficult of categories – middle age – for rather a long time, owing to the wondrous longevity of Queen Elizabeth, the Queen Mother. As the Queen now celebrates her Diamond Jubilee, in her own distinguished old age, it is revealing to consider how art and the mass media have helped to shape our changing perceptions of the monarch.

Notions of kingship have altered drastically since the legendary reign of the Queen's forebear, Henry VIII, whose image of massive power was so accurately captured in Holbein's four-square portrayal of him. Nowadays the personal ascendancy of the sovereign is much reduced, and the role survives in the somewhat emasculated form of a constitutional monarchy. The historian David Cannadine refers to this as 'a *feminised* monarchy', which can perhaps be best and most sympathetically embodied by a woman. The Queen has made a superb job of this, and her success may be in part attributed to her own comment: 'Let us not take ourselves too seriously'. Clearly, this applies to us too...

People want their monarchs to be different, special, but they also like them to come down to earth occasionally. (King George VI and his wife visiting the bombed East End, Edward VIII with his ability to chat easily to ordinary people.) But if they're down on our level all the time, there is no gratifying contrast when they do talk to us – no sense of benign visitation. And if the sovereign's presence becomes routine, or taken for granted, it loses its resonance and its magic: that way lies indifference if not downright contempt. So it's important that a degree of separation is maintained: monarchs cannot be seen to be entirely like us. It would make their job even more difficult.

These thoughts are occasioned by an exhibition at the National Portrait Gallery (until 21 October), entitled *The Queen: Art and Image*. The show has been touring the country for the last year, from Edinburgh to Belfast and Cardiff. Arriving at the NPG it has been housed in rather cramped quarters at the front of the museum, while the vast survey of Lucian Freud's unsympathetic portraits (mostly nudes) takes up the best galleries. Freud is everywhere, though thankfully his exhibition will have ended by the time you read this. He's even included in *The Queen: Art and Image*, with that dreadful portrait he painted in 2001. You know the one – Her Majesty looks as if she's just taken a pinch of snuff and is trying not to sneeze. Or perhaps sitting for Freud just got up her nose.

The exhibition begins with a technologically up-to-date lenticular print on a lightbox, a holographic portrait of the Queen by Chris Levine and Rob Munday entitled 'Equanimity'. I don't particularly like lenticulars, which seem to move as you walk past them and supposedly convey the three-dimensional reality of the subject. But undoubtedly there is a greater sense of presence in a lenticular than in an ordinary photograph, and I suspect that viewing this highly detailed (I cannot say lifelike) representation of the Queen is the nearest that many people will ever come to the real person. Which made the fact that a Japanese film crew was fooling around in front of it when I visited the show all the more unacceptable. This was disrespectful; but I suppose it was also publicity, and the NPG needs publicity (despite Freud) even if the Queen may have had enough of it.

I am old enough to remember the profound shock of the Aberfan disaster in 1966, when a colliery spoil tip slid down a mountainside and engulfed a school and 20 homes. 144 people died, most of them children. Prince Philip and the Prime Minister, Harold Wilson, at once visited the scene of this appalling tragedy, but it became evident that the public needed the Queen to be there too. She did indeed make a tour of the devastated area, nine days after the disaster, and her presence was much appreciated. But, in retrospect, the gap between the event and the Queen's response was seen to be significant. It was generally felt that the monarch now needed to be more in touch with the people, and more ready to respond to their needs. The royal mystique was widely perceived as causing too great a barrier between ruler and subjects.

After that, it became deliberate palace policy to present the Queen less formally, and to allow the human side of the figurehead more prominence. She became, in image at least, approachable. Thus she was photographed relaxed and laughing aboard the Royal Yacht or smiling at the rain from under an umbrella. Since then, the Queen has had to perform a high-wire act, being all things to all men. She has had to be (or seem to be) accessible and warmly human, and at the same time a living embodiment of exalted notions of lifelong duty and service, a bastion of stability and reassurance in a confused and rapidly changing society. (An informal but strong 1968 photograph by Cecil Beaton, of the Queen in an admiral's boat cloak against a depthless turquoise ground, sums up this dichotomy.) The Queen has become the most marvellous symbol of continuity – of the ability to survive whatever trials may be set before her, and this endurance has become closely identified with the continued existence of the nation as we know it.

The NPG's exhibition does not offer a reverential survey of royal portraiture, but rather a tasting of different responses to the person and role of the monarch. The sovereign may not be treated with reverence here, but the platitudes of contemporary art certainly are. Obligatory images by Andy Warhol and Gerhard Richter hang emptily beside reportage photographs. Gilbert & George get in on the act with a couple of postcard collages. The infamous Sex Pistols 'God Save the Queen' poster is here, and a large black and white cautionary photograph by Hiroshi Sugimoto of a wax mannequin purporting to be our regnant monarch. Hew Locke's 'Medusa' (2008) is a different kind of image of the Queen. Made out of cheap but brightly-coloured plastic jewellery, it's a tawdry assemblage of tat with yellow fog-lamp eyes. Locke grew up in British Guyana where the Queen's image was on the covers of school exercise books. His 'Medusa' looks like a giant obliterating doodle done in revenge for the unrelieved boredom of schooldays.

Altogether more enjoyable is Pietro Annigoni's famous 1954-5 portrait, 'Queen Elizabeth II, Queen Regent'. Commissioned by the Fishmongers' Company, it is rightly regarded as one of the greatest royal portraits of the 20th century, infinitely superior to Annigoni's NPG sequel of 1959. This thought-provoking display ends with a puissant portrait of the Queen, once again in her admiral's cloak, photographed in 2007 by Annie Leibovitz. The monarch is presented in solitary splendour, very handsome against a park-like setting of woods and water. Almost black and white, it is subtly tinted, giving colour to the Queen's face and to the gold clasp and buttons down her cloak. Magnificently understated, it is impressively dignified and regal. Just the image for the present occasion.

CARLO LABRUZZI: THE GRAND TOUR

Dickinson, 58 Jermyn Street, SW1

PAULA REGO: BALZAC AND OTHER STORIES

Marlborough Fine Art, 6 Albemarle Street, W1

PRUNELLA CLOUGH

Annely Juda, 23 Dering Street, W1

23 June 2012

It's a rare pleasure to find an unfamiliar artist of the 18th century whose work speaks to the contemporary mind as lucidly as Carlo Labruzzi (1748-1817). I had never heard of him before this show, being still in my playpen when the last Labruzzi exhibition excited the art world in 1960. Although celebrated in his day, he was largely forgotten in the 19th and for most of the 20th century, but it's clear from this excellent exhibition that he deserves a permanent place in the history books. Not much is known about him beyond the meagre biography that he was born in Rome the son of a weaver and finisher of velvet, and that his younger brother Pietro was also an artist and became court painter to the King of Poland.

Carlo Labruzzi was commercially successful and achieved not only the recognition of his contemporaries but the popularity of English visitors. (Lord Herbert remarked in 1799 that the three greatest foreign artists working in Rome were Hackert, Batoni and Labruzzi.) That extraordinary Welsh painter of Italian walls, Thomas Jones, knew him. English milords commissioned him to record the Italian sections of their Grand Tours. He painted a few portraits, but he was best known for his landscapes, either done *en plein air,* or made in the studio from notes on the spot. He was an assured draughtsman, and a watercolourist of distinction. As Sir Timothy Clifford, who has curated this exhibition for Dickinson, observes, we tend not to think of the Italians as masters of watercolour. (Being English, we think the English invented or at the very least commandeered watercolour.) The work of Labruzzi therefore comes as a delightful surprise.

The work in the current exhibition dates mostly from the late 1760s or early 1770s and has been taken from two albums of drawings and watercolours, mostly depicting the buildings and scenery in and around Rome, with several views of Naples and one of Venice. These sheets have never previously been framed or hung, being kept in the protected environment of the albums, and are consequently unfaded and remarkably fresh. I was allowed a preview of the exhibition in Dickinson's commodious Jermyn Street premises, and liked very much what I was shown. There are echoes of other artists to be discerned – Claude, Salvator Rosa, Canaletto – but Labruzzi has his own style and approach.

The delicacy of his touch is matched by a crispness of delineation, best seen in the pen work, and particularly in the sprigged foliage of the trees. He tended to begin in pencil, then apply a pale Indian ink wash, and finally add the colour; sometimes he used white heightening. One of the most beautiful of these watercolour topographical studies is 'A View of the River Tiber from the Monte Mario, Rome' (1779), while the subtleties of 'A View from the Palatine Hill, Rome, the Alban Hills in the distance' are panoramic and beguiling. Architecture is well served, particularly in the various versions of the Colosseum, but nowhere better perhaps than in 'The Temple of Minerva Medica', done in dark brown wash deliciously heightened with pale cream body colour, a courting couple in the foreground. For evocative delicacy of pencil work look at 'The Temples of Vesta and Fortuna Virilis, Rome', and for overgrown ruins (nature re-claiming man's encroachment) 'The Baths of Caracalla' is hard to beat. 'Trees in a Landscape, thought to be the gardens of the Villa Borghese' is very fine and shows what Labruzzi could do with straight landscape. All works are for sale in this enjoyable exhibition, ranging from under £1,500 up to £20,000, with a number of modestly priced works available: a real opportunity for the collector.

By way of potent contrast, try the current Paula Rego exhibition at Marlborough Fine Art, billed as a celebration of T G Rosenthal's new and expanded edition of his magisterial survey of Rego's complete graphic work. Originally published in 2003, this second edition contains chapters on five new print series and runs now to 386 pages, an increase of nearly a quarter. With well over 100 new colour illustrations, this sumptuous volume (£75 in hefty hardback) is indispensable for anyone seriously interested in Rego's work. A limited edition with a choice of two hand-coloured etchings is also available. The exhibition consists of a substantial amount of new graphic work – etchings and lithographs – plus some of the large pastels which Rego does so well, and which occupy a territory all of their own between drawing and painting.

There seems to be something of the deft inventiveness of Rego's late husband, Victor Willing (1928-88) in her new pastels, particularly discernible in 'The Psychiatrist' (2011) and 'In the Beehive' (2010). To my eye it's evident in the handling of materials and the shape-making, and also in the areas of vivid colour and simplification of form. This does not detract in the slightest from Rego's strength and originality of drawing, nor from her consummate abilities as a story-teller. These qualities come across superbly in her printmaking; her technical mastery of etching and aquatint especially has the incisive edge of the greatest satirists. Rego can be as horrific and bleak as Goya, and there is the same compassion at work too. Her disturbing images pull no punches: death pursues both monkey and maiden, as the *vagina dentata* grins at the skeleton. Human weakness and savagery have rarely been so thoroughly anatomized. And finally, last chance to see a splendidly various exhibition of Prunella Clough's work – paintings, prints, drawings, collages and objects – at Annely Juda, 23 Dering Street, W1, until 30 June. Unusually, there is no catalogue for this exhibition as it coincides with the publication of Frances Spalding's excellent monograph on Clough (reviewed in March), but it's a substantial show arranged over two floors. Clough (1919-99) was an artist of remarkable vision, who saw the world from a very individual angle, first of all painting beach detritus and the cabs of lorries, before moving on to the even less considered and recondite. She would paint a grass plot, a sweet wrapper or a twist of rope in a way that was both inventive and memorable, constantly experimenting with styles and means, printing, expunging and overlaying with imaginative freedom. Her palette varied from the dour to the garish via a very individual range of ice-cream colours, while her line sought out complications and meaning in unexpected places. From the hard-edged to the resolutely organic, her imagery tests the limits of recognition and resolution. A selling exhibition, works start at just £720.

DEREK HYATT: MEETINGS ON THE MOOR: THE BISHOP-DALE PAINTINGS

Art Space Gallery, 84 St Peter's Street, N1

FRANK DOBSON SCULPTOR 1886-1963

Fine Art Society, 148 New Bond Street, W1

30 June 2012

An important part of the critic's role is to search out artists, living or dead, whose work has disappeared from general view, and to attempt some kind of reassessment of their value. The trouble with most coverage of the visual arts today is that the same few artists are constantly written about because their work is currently fashionable. Editors seem not to encourage their critics to be wide-ranging. Meanwhile, museums and galleries are not readily inspired to put on exhibitions of less well-known painting and sculpture because they're primarily concerned with high visitor attendance and sales. As a result, the public is not best served – and neither are the artists. In an attempt to buck the trend, this review focuses on a painter and a sculptor who both deserve serious scrutiny.

Derek Hyatt was born in Ilkley in 1931, and has lived most of his painting life in Yorkshire where he still works. After an early training at Leeds and Norwich art schools, he came to London's Royal College of Art (1954-8), and soon began to exhibit his work professionally. He showed with Waddington's in the 1970s, and then briefly with Austin/Desmond, and although he's had 50 one-man shows since 1958, he hasn't exhibited in London for nearly 20 years, so his work is no longer familiar to the capital's gallery-going public. Inevitably he's better known and appreciated in the north of England, but it's about time his remarkable paintings were made more widely available. Art Space Gallery's new show is thus highly opportune.

Hyatt paints on board, rather than canvas, so he can keep altering the image, rubbing back and re-stating his intentions. He likes to quote the Italian historian Giambattista Vico's definition of imagination as 'the memory rearranged', and this is his own approach to painting the landscape that he loves. All is change, until the final image is discovered through the process of painting. As he says: 'Landscape itself is about substances changing in weather, lit by changing light'. Hyatt aims to convey to the viewer a sense of the reality of change against the solid backdrop of stone and moor. Painting for him is not a record of appearances but an investigation into the mysterious heart of things. His understanding of history and myth enriches his approach to landscape and endows his imagery with signs and portents, whether taken from the natural world and the cycle of the seasons, or from the impacted trace of man's own history etched into the rock. The group of small paintings (very affordably priced at around £1,500 each) which form the core of this magical exhibition lie at the very centre of Hyatt's endeavour over the last 30 years. Most have never before been exhibited, and together with some impressive larger paintings, they offer a substantial account of Hyatt's artistic preoccupations. The first thing to notice is the telling disposition of strong and exciting colour; the second is the frequent juxtaposition of linearity and transparency; the third is the sheer variety of mark and texture. The beautiful small paintings tend to be more direct and declarative, while the larger panels are often distilled into something altogether more allegorical and complex. Extraordinary formal invention makes its distinctive appeal through all these paintings, although some images need more decoding than others. Hyatt is a master of shape-music and colour-combination, also of metaphor and meaning, reserving a fluidity of style through which to generate his visions. With this exhibition he emerges as a major force in contemporary landscape painting: very highly recommended.

Every so often there's a brave attempt to revive the flagging fortunes of Frank Dobson, one of England's first modernist sculptors, who enjoyed considerable acclaim in the post-First

World War years, and then went out of fashion. His language was a contemporary classicism, with strong Jazz Age impulses and a marked sophistication of form. His preferred subject was the female nude which he rendered with appreciative attention and inventiveness. The last Dobson show of any magnitude was at the Courtauld in 1995, which sadly did little to put him back on the map. In recent years, he has been doing somewhat better in the auction rooms, and his sculptures, paintings and drawings have begun to feature again in mixed exhibitions in museums and commercial galleries. If ever there was an artist ripe for reassessment, it's Frank Dobson.

The present show at the Fine Art Society, in association with Gillian Jason who has for many years represented the Dobson Estate, offers a useful introduction to his work. (The handsome accompanying catalogue, with essays by Robert Upstone and Neville Jason, is also very welcome.) The earliest sculpture on show is a polished bronze from 1919, on loan from a private collection, entitled 'Dancers'. A dynamic almost Vorticist piece, it reminds us why Wyndham Lewis admired Dobson and wanted to claim him for the post-war avant-garde. Perhaps Dobson's most famous work of these years is the portrait head of Sir Osbert Sitwell (1922), also in polished bronze. Now in the Tate, it was originally owned by T E Lawrence, who described it as 'the finest portrait bust of modern times… as loud as the massed band of the Guards'. A new edition was cast in 1994, so examples of this masterly sculpture may still be purchased.

Portraiture was an important source of income for Dobson, and he was very good at it, as can be seen here from the plaster child's head of E Q Myers (who became E Q Nicholson when she married) and the 1923 bronze of the American author and friend of Hemingway, Robert McAlmon. A later but differently captivating portrait is the plaster of Admiral Sir William Milbourne-James KCB (1941), grandson of John Everett Millais to whom he sat as the model for 'Bubbles'; rather a contrasting facet of the admiral's personality.

Given Dobson's predilection, there are a number of nude female figures, in terracotta, plaster and bronze. In these, the rhythmic relation of simplified forms can be seen, as the sculptor reassembles the known parts of a body into a new harmony, with a newly realized emotional truth. Among my favourites are the grey terracotta 'Seated Torso (Study for Ham Hill Torso I)' of 1928, and the small bronze 'Bather' of 1943. Awareness of European sculptors such as Picasso and Maillol is evident in Dobson's work, but without compromising his originality. However, fate conspired against him, and in 1933 an accident to his left arm made carving virtually impossible. After that, almost all his work was modelled.

Although Dobson was eclipsed and superseded by Henry Moore, it's clear from stylistic analysis that both Moore and Barbara Hepworth were aware of Dobson's pioneering efforts, and in later years Moore remained a supporter of Dobson's achievement. Now that we have the chance to look at him afresh, Frank Dobson re-emerges as a sculptor of very real distinction, while the handful of his two-dimensional works here show him to have been a powerful and evocative draughtsman.

PICASSO PRINTS: THE VOLLARD SUITE

Room 90, British Museum

HENRY MOORE: LARGE LATE FORMS

Gagosian Gallery, 6-24 Britannia Street, WC1

14 July 2012

Another Picasso show, another Henry Moore? The experienced gallery-goer may wonder how a further exhibition of either master can be justified, but in fact both displays focus on very specific aspects of their creator's extensive careers, and offer new insights to even the most blasé viewer. I am all in favour of looking anew at great art, provided fashionable curatorial theories are kept within sensible bounds. Picasso (1881-1973) is so protean a figure that it is refreshing to have an exhibition which devotes itself to one particular body of work: in this case, the 100 etchings of the Vollard Suite. Henry Moore's monumental late sculptures are usually seen in a landscape setting: change their context and you stand to alter their meaning. Gagosian brings these works into an intensely urban, not to say industrial, space. Is the romance of the wild dispersed?

The British Museum has recently acquired a full set of the Vollard Suite – thanks to the generosity of Hamish Parker, a private and philanthropic individual – and is now the only public collection in the UK to own Picasso's extended masterpiece of etching. The hundred images were made between 1930 and 1937, the majority in 1933, and developed organically rather than in answer to a specific commission. Ambroise Vollard (1866-1939) was one of the great art dealers of his day, who became a millionaire through speculating on Cézanne's paintings, was unafraid to invest in avant-garde art and gave Picasso his first Paris show in 1901. He was also an innovative publisher of *livres d'artistes*, and it seems that the Vollard Suite may have been intended as some kind of book or portfolio with texts, a project cut short by Vollard's unexpected death in a car crash.

There is no particular narrative to the prints, nor did Picasso arrange them in any special order, nor title them. He was a great printmaker, producing almost 2,500 prints over his lifetime, from lithographs to linocuts, but etchings were at the heart of his print achievement. In the Vollard Suite, Picasso was free to let his invention play with line, and to range over a number of subjects that interested him at a fundamental and emotional level. While making these etchings Picasso was infatuated with his young muse and model Marie-Thérèse Walter, and her features reappear again and again. She was also the subject of sculptures by Picasso, who thought of himself at this point as more of a sculptor than a painter.

Vollard encouraged his sculpture, and the theme of 'The Sculptor's Studio', which forms so large a part of the Suite, is presumably a veiled tribute to the dealer. The linked themes of the artist and creation, and the artist and model, act as a kind of leitmotif throughout, investigating the joys and pitfalls of illusion as compared to reality. The images work on many levels, not least in dialogue with Picasso's favourite Old Masters: Rembrandt, the great master of etching, and Ingres, the draughtsman he perhaps admired most. There are so many exquisite and noteworthy images among the hundred, I have no room even to list them. Suffice it to say that the range of etched mark on offer here is predictably rich and varied, from unadorned but evocative outline to complex volumetric cross-hatching to the subtleties of aquatint. I am an admirer of the exhibitions mounted in the BM's Print Room by Stephen Coppel, and this one joins the list of his successes. The etchings are beautifully displayed and interspersed with highly relevant comparative images, such as an Ingres drawing, Rembrandt etching, Etruscan mirror-back or a Sicilian jug in the form of a Siren. Classical sculpture is also included, standing freely in the room. The mood changes from the relative tranquillity of 'The Sculptor's Studio' to the violence of 'The Battle of Love' to the uncontrollable irrationality of the Minotaur and the final pitiful impotence of the Blind Minotaur. All of human life? Pretty nearly.

Henry Moore (1898-1986) said that the sculpture that most moved him was static and strong and vital, 'giving out something of the energy and power of great mountains'. This declaration chimes with his belief that sculpture was 'an art of the open air', and a substantial proportion of his works (especially the largest of them) were intended to be exhibited in the landscape which had very often helped to inspire them. Gagosian's current exhibition breaks with tradition – and expectation – by bringing a significant grouping of the large late forms into a gallery setting, some of them for the first time. The results are intriguing, to say the least.

The star of the show is 'Large Two Forms' (1966), which dominates the main gallery space, crouched intently and powerfully like a complex knucklebone arch. This massive faded green bronze sculpture is firmly grounded yet twists and swerves through its forms like a rollercoaster, all profile and aperture and swooping follow-through. To walk in amongst it in a gallery is a marvellous experience of weight yet speed – here is truly something of the energy and power of mountains. The gallery walls contain it and frame it in a way that open landscape (even with trees) simply does not. This new setting throws the viewer back intimately onto the textured surfaces – bringing us face to face with the dynamic volume of the sculpture, its sensuality and surprise.

Next to it is a small dark green piece called 'Reclining Connected Forms' (1969), its surface rather too lacquered for my taste, and altogether formally less exciting. The large 'Three Piece Sculpture: Vertebrae' (1968) comes next, golden and polished, sitting on a thin cushion plinth, with lovely painterly surface markings in the patina, and a subtle sense of interval between its parts. In the far corner of the room is 'Two Piece Reclining Figure: Cut' (1979-81), another dramatic piece, arranged in an L, with a striking caesura in the horizontal element like two opposed flat irons. There are other works on view (and a single wall cabinet of small plasters, flints and bones), including a side room with two sculptures and another couple in the entrance hall. But these extras serve only to distract from the main thrust of this remarkable show. I wish it had been limited to the three giant pieces: 'Large Two Forms', 'Three Piece Sculpture: Vertebrae' and 'Two Piece Reclining Figure: Cut'. These look spectacular indoors, and make a visit to Britannia Street essential for any admirer of Moore or modern sculpture.

DIANA ON SHOW
METAMORPHOSIS: TITIAN 2012

National Gallery

21 July 2012

Metamorphosis is more than an exhibition, it is wider in its manifestations and implications. The Sainsbury Wing galleries are full of interesting works of art, but the Metamorphosis festival – for that is what it surely is – extends to the Royal Opera House and beyond, through dance and poetry. Unfortunately, there are only limited performances by the Royal Ballet, but these will be filmed and thus available for viewing, and the poetry is published in a handy illustrated paperback (price £8.99), with a learned but accessible introduction by the director of the National Gallery, Nicholas Penny. The theme of the festival is Titian, and we are celebrating the NG's recent acquisition (jointly with the National Galleries of Scotland) of 'Diana and Callisto', the third great Diana painting to join the national collection. 'The Death of Actaeon' was purchased by special appeal in 1972, and 'Diana and Actaeon' in 2009. All three are now on show together in the first room of this new exhibition, and very splendid they look too.

The idea behind the festival is to demonstrate Titian's continuing relevance, and all the work – in gallery, opera house and book – has been directly inspired by these three paintings. The curator responsible is Minna Moore Ede, and she must take the credit for initiating a remarkable series of artistic responses to the great art of the past. The achievement of Titian is timeless, but it's good to be reminded of this in such a positive and public way. This collaboration between the National Gallery and the Royal Opera House has resulted in three contemporary visual artists (Chris Ofili, Conrad Shawcross and Mark Wallinger) being commissioned to produce work which will then be translated into a trio of ballets by leading choreographers and composers. In addition, 14 poets (from Patience Agbabi to Hugo Williams, via Seamus Heaney) were also commissioned to write a poem in response to Titian. The range of work on offer is fresh and varied, but I will limit my remarks to the exhibition.

In the *Metamorphoses* of Ovid, the source of Titian's themes in these paintings, Actaeon is turned into a stag for chancing upon the goddess Diana bathing in her sylvan retreat, and subsequently torn to death by his own hounds. Callisto, once a favourite handmaiden of the goddess, is turned into a bear for the crime of falling pregnant. Both stories offer rich possibilities for interpretation, and they have certainly inspired the three chosen artists to new heights. Turn left out of the Titian room, once you have done feasting your eyes on this genius of Venetian painting, and you are in the Ofili room, a dimly-lit chamber of tropical delights, lush with colour and profuse organic growth. These paintings pursue the trail begun with the works in the last room of Ofili's 2010 Tate Britain retrospective, in which Sixties' psychedelia meets Art Nouveau, following the artist's relocation to Trinidad in 2005. The lurking mood mixes threat with seduction in a sprawl of falling, writhing forms.

The best paintings here mingle Ofili's pronounced decorative streak with unconventional imagery. In the painting 'Ovid-Destiny', the lower section is a crazy pavement of red, green, purple, yellow (some echo of Kitaj here), while two dark figures, like something out of the wayward imagination of Edward Burra, embrace on the extreme left. The luxuriant jungle settings of these six large and impressive paintings bring uncomfortably to mind flowers of evil portent. Also memorable is the yellow-dominated 'Ovid-Actaeon', with its looping fluid figures against a humid midnight ground, with sex the serpent rearing its dangerous head. From the lurid nightmares of Ofili's vision, it is something of a relief to turn to Mark Wallinger's darkened room, where the self-communing of art is a shade less personal.

Wallinger invites us to participate in something altogether

more insidious: a peep-show of a live girl at her ablutions. A small bathroom has been built in the blacked-out gallery, which we may walk round. There are various observation points at which the visitor may apply his or her eye for an illicit glimpse: first and classically, the keyhole of a locked door; then on the next wall round, a corner has been broken out of a frosted window, offering a clear, if partial, view; on the third wall, one may peer through the shutters of a long louvred window; finally, on the fourth wall, a pair of peepholes allow the spectator to look into the room through a two-way mirror. When Wallinger advertised for seven girls to fulfil this role of naked bathroom beauty, he stipulated that all must be actually called Diana, which is the title of his installation. The nature of art as voyeurism has never been so piquantly explored, despite Duchamp's late masterpiece 'Etant Donnés', and the knowing references to it here. The thoughtful visitor proceeds back though Ofili's jungle, perhaps pausing in a room of ballet costumes, before encountering Conrad Shawcross's robot, weaving about in its large glass case. Entitled 'Trophy', it consists of a mechanical aluminium limb holding a pencil of light which rears around a fixed pair of antlers (all that is left of Actaeon the stag), examining them. A little like a dentist's drill with a mind of its own, this computer-driven arm on its tripod is almost sinister, but not quite. The most intimidating moment is when it lurches into swift action and you can hear the surge of the motor.

Quite how effective this will be in giant form in the ballet devised around it, I cannot tell. There are two more rooms, one of filmed choreography, the other of set designs, which begin to suggest how the visual art moves and metamorphoses into ballet, through the inventive skill of composers and choreographers. I have always found displays of ballet costumes or designs singularly unenlightening, and models of sets only marginally more informative. For the full effect of the transformation, and the completion of this festival's wide scope, the visitor needed to see the ballets themselves, not available when I visited. A hint of the pleasure in store came through snippets of Mark-Anthony Turnage's beguiling music. At least the poetry book may be carried away to savour at leisure. I wish I could conclude this review neatly by quoting the Poet Laureate, Carol Ann Duffy, who observes in her poem on 'Diana and Callisto' that in the end 'it's all about paint', but only part of this exhibition (Titian and Ofili) fits that description. I am not usually an admirer of performance or installation art, but in this case Mark Wallinger's piece is brilliantly adapted to the theme and its meanings, while the swooping mechanical arm of Conrad Shawcross brings a futuristic sculptural reading to the sacred grove. I'm almost tempted to say that, for several centuries at least, Diana has never had it so good. The exhibition, by the way, is free.

HEATHERWICK STUDIO: DESIGNING THE EXTRAORDINARY
V&A
POSTERS WITH A PURPOSE
Christie's, 8 King Street, St James's, SW1
28 July 2012

Thomas Heatherwick (born 1970) is one of our most exciting and inventive designers, so it is somewhat unfortunate that he is much associated in the public mind with a project that failed, the memorably named 'B of the Bang'. This was a sculpture commissioned to commemorate the 2002 Commonwealth Games held in Manchester, and the idea was to create a sunburst of tubes and poles to symbolize an explosion of energy. It was a good idea and a formidable undertaking. Erected in 2005, it was plagued with technical problems and bits even fell off. It was taken down in 2009, and only the documentation remains. As I said, an unfortunate association, but also a salutary one, for it reminds us that the path of an innovative designer does not always run smooth, dependent as every visionary is on the skills of fabricators and engineers. Heatherwick himself comes from an engineering background, but his work is not limited to straight design and readily crosses the border with art. This is such a frequent occurrence today that it poses the question – do all designers secretly yearn to be artists? Certainly, you might expect an artist (rather than a designer) to be commissioned to make the 'B of the Bang' monument, if contemporary public sculpture were not in such a lamentable state. Heatherwick obviously came up with the best proposal, so it was just a question of implementing it. As the current, fascinating, exhibition shows, it is always easier to come up with seductive and impressive ideas than to realize them.

This does not mean that Heatherwick is a theoretical or research designer – his practice is firmly grounded in ways and means. He has a good sense of materials and explores their more extreme possibilities. Furthermore, he has a fertile imagination, and encourages those around him (since 1994 he has worked with a highly skilled team, hence the Heatherwick Studio appellation) to experiment and exceed themselves. This is what good design – or, for that matter, good art – is all about. Going beyond the possible, or at least beyond the expected, while staying rooted in the purpose for which it was created.

The exhibition, in the V&A's Porter Gallery, is piled high with objects and models, a stack of inspired thought, laid out and designed by the Heatherwick Studio itself. Thus models for the air vents in London's Paternoster Square, designed to cool an existing underground electricity substation, are placed well up in this tall room, and almost every available space is filled with virtuoso solutions for projects. The exhibits are interspersed with listening stations equipped with headphones, which offer rather long-winded explanations; these would benefit from editing. The famous rolling bridge, made in 2004 for Paddington Basin, so that boats can navigate the waterways – a kind of hedgehog version of

Tower Bridge – still looks poetic and impressive, even as a model. There's plenty of drama in Heatherwick's work: look at the Beach Café at Littlehampton, with its stacked French toast profile, or the wire and glass sculpture for the atrium of the Wellcome Trust, or the Seed Cathedral for the Shanghai World Expo (2010).The overlap with sculpture is a constant, evident in the affinity of some of Heatherwick's forms and materials with sculptors such as Eilis O'Connell (who has used woven metal) and Anish Kapoor and Richard Evans (who have both in the past made good use of a diminishing contour laminate approach). If our contemporary sculptors are jealous of Heatherwick Studio's success, then it's time they themselves tried a bit harder. The relationship between design work and architecture is intimate, never more so than when the Studio designs a power station (for Teesside) or the extraordinary-looking crumpled studios for artists in the woods of Aberystwyth. (Seeing these intriguing designs I wanted to be instantly transported there and question the occupants about their feelings for these unusual workspaces.)

Heatherwick Studio is very visible: among its recent realized designs are a new London bus (which I have yet to travel on), a spinning chair (several examples in the V&A foyer to roll around in) and an expandable zip bag. The freedom of ideas present in all this work is hugely beguiling, though rather brought down to earth by the hefty 600 page tome called *Making* (£38 in hardback) which accompanies the show. Heatherwick unites two qualities often absent from contemporary art: a sense of intellectual and emotional fun, and a desire to make not just strange but beautiful things. Long may his studio continue to surprise us.

I don't often preview auctions in this column because the turnover of sales is so brisk there's hardly time to forewarn the public of what's on offer, but over the summer Christie's are showing highlights from the London Transport Museum Sale, and the auction doesn't take place until October. Before you all start worrying that LT are selling off their crown jewels, the contents of this auction are posters drawn from duplicate stock held by the museum, and all proceeds will be used strictly for future acquisitions, as well as conservation and restoration of the existing collection. The sale is called 'Posters with a Purpose' and contains over 300 lots featuring the great names of English poster design in the 1920s and 30s, such as Edward McKnight Kauffer, Barnett Freedman, Edward Bawden, Paul Nash and Edward Wadsworth, as well as a host of lesser-known artists. Among the latter a powerful image from 1929 of open umbrellas, by Frederick Schneider Manner, bearing the legend 'No Wet, No Cold', echoes ironically through our English summer.

Frank Pick, the legendary manager of LT who initiated this colourful poster campaign, said it wasn't just about attracting passengers, but also about establishing goodwill and understanding between the public and the transport service. There is a glorious optimism to these images, a vision of London and its environs which looks on the positive side, to its real beauties and attractions. And there is idealism, hope for a better future, something we seem to have mislaid in our hectic consumerist lives. If you want to view the entire sale, this can be done online, or in person at Christie's South Kensington from 29 September until the auction on 4 October. Meanwhile, the highlights at King Street offer upbeat holiday viewing.

ROBERT HUGHES: A tribute

18 August 2012

With the death of the critic and historian Robert Hughes, a great beacon has gone out in the art world of the West. I take his absence personally, not because I knew the man (I only met him once), but because he was such an invigorating and perceptive guide to excellence. Of course I didn't agree with everything he said, but he wrote like an angel (possibly a fallen one) and he certainly made you think and even revise your opinions. Although I was aware that he'd been unwell for a long time, I was unprepared for his death at the age of 74, and feel robbed of the books he didn't write. What happened to the second volume of his memoirs, and what else might he have got around to writing?

Among the various tributes and obituaries I've read, the only one to come near the truth of the man was Adam Gopnik's in the New Yorker. Other commentators stressed Hughes's combative street-fighter stance, his memorable put-downs, his witty TV persona, his bikes and leather jackets. Only Gopnik talked about his 'enormous vulnerability'. I witnessed that when I interviewed him in 1996, and I don't think it was just because he had a hangover. (He probably didn't.) He was erudite, opinionated, funny and immensely sympathetic. I wanted to talk to him all day, because he didn't just hold forth but also listened, though I was mostly asking questions. It was this sensitivity, to people and places but especially to art, that made him the brilliant writer he was. I'll miss that, but at least we have the dozen or so books he did write. And the TV programmes.

One of Hughes's later crusades was for 'slow art', for 'art that holds time as a vase holds water; art that grows out of modes of perception and making, whose skill and doggedness make you think and feel; an art that isn't merely sensational or that doesn't get its message across in ten seconds, that isn't falsely ironic, that hooks into something deep-running in our natures. In a word, art that is the very opposite of mass media.' Those sentiments come from a speech given by Hughes at the Royal Academy's Annual Dinner in 2004, and deserve to be quoted on a regular basis.

Apart from the catalogues and books mentioned in the articles that make up this book, there is a vast body of literature on offer covering every aspect of the visual arts, which makes compiling a recommended list of reading an intimidating task. The following are writers who have the uncommon ability not only to write sense on a subject that too often elicits streams of breathy obfuscation, but to write well and passionately. They are masters of their trade and will lead you safely and enjoyably on your journey.

John Berger
Jeffery Camp
Andrew Causey
Kenneth Clark
Peter Fuller
E H Gombrich
Patrick Heron
Timothy Hyman
Robert Hughes
David Fraser Jenkins
Edward Lucie-Smith
Norbert Lynton
Michael Peppiatt
John Richardson
T G Rosenthal
John Russell
Brian Sewell (for a bracing blast of controversy)
David Sylvester
John Updike

Individual books I would commend include:

The Battle for Realism: Figurative Art in Britain during the Cold War 1945-60 (James Hyman. Paul Mellon Centre, 2001)
The British Landscape 1920-50 (Ian Jeffrey. Thames & Hudson, 1984)

British Romantic Artists (John Piper. Collins, 1942)

British Vision: observation and imagination in British Art 1750-1950 (ed Robert Hoozee. Mercatorfonds, 2007)

The Century of Change: British Painting since 1900 (Richard Shone. Phaidon, 1977)

Colours of War: War Art 1939-45 (Alan Ross. Jonathan Cape, 1983)

English Art & Modernism 1900-1939 (Charles Harrison. Yale University Press, 1981 and 1994)

English Watercolours (Laurence Binyon. A & C Black, 1933)

Eric Ravilious: memoir of an artist (Helen Binyon. Lutterworth Press, 1983)

The Genius of British Painting (ed David Piper. Weidenfeld & Nicolson, 1975)

John Ruskin: Selected Writings (ed Dinah Birch. Oxford University Press, 2004)

Modern English Painters vols i-iii (John Rothenstein. Macdonald & Co, 1952 and 1984)

A Partial Testament (Helen Lessore. Tate Gallery, 1986)

Recording Britain, 4 vols (Arnold Palmer, Oxford University Press, 1946-9. Updated V&A 2011)

School of Genius: A history of the Royal Academy of Arts (James Fenton. RA, 2006)

St Ives 1939-64: Twenty five years of paintings, sculpture and pottery (Tate Gallery, 1985)

Towards Another Picture: an anthology of artists' writings 1945-77 (ed Andrew Brighton and Lynda Morris. Midland Group Nottingham, 1977)

The War Artists: British Official War Art of the Twentieth Century (Merrion and Susie Harries. Michael Joseph in association with the IWM and the Tate Gallery, 1983)

Reference books in the form of Dictionaries of Artists run from useful paperbacks such as those published by Penguin or Yale to multi-volume specialist productions. Extremely good value are two series which have appeared over the last few years, and are still work in progress: the Public Catalogue Foundation's county surveys of oil paintings in public ownership, and the Public Sculpture of Britain (PMSA/Liverpool University Press). Both massive undertakings driven by individual commitment and enthusiasm.

The writings of artists themselves often cast the best light if not on their own work, then on their period and contemporaries. Head and shoulders above the rest are the irresistible Autobiography and Journals of Benjamin Robert Haydon (1786-1846), but Stanley Spencer, David Jones, Van Gogh, Wyndham Lewis, Constable, Michael Ayrton, Paul Nash, Keith Vaughan, Josef Herman, Sickert and Kitaj are members of that elite band who could handle words almost as well as paint. Memoirs of artists who are less distinguished writers are also worth looking at.

There is another genre of art books which is useful for non-artists to consider if they want to broaden their understanding, and this is the one which concentrates on the practical side of things. Not the ever popular 'How to ...' manuals, although some of these are mini-masterpieces, but ones like the Tate's *Paint & Painting* (1982), which looks at the history of the manufacture of pigments and colours and the influence this has had on artists' methods and practices over the years, and *The Impact of Modern Paints* (2000), similar but focusing on the second half of the 20th century, or the National Gallery's Technical Bulletins, which may not be everyone's idea of a light read but do explain some of the behind the scenes dilemmas and discoveries.

It would indeed be strange, in a book devoted to articles by Andrew Lambirth, not to mention the considerable body of other work by the man himself. A list of monographs appears at the front, but there are also many catalogue introductions and essays which by and large give the lie to George Orwell's wry comment on this somewhat overcrowded occupation: 'In certain kinds of writing, particularly in art criticism and literary criticism, it is normal to come across long passages which are almost completely lacking in meaning.'

A is a Critic

Pritchett, V S, 53
Public Catalogue Foundation, 104-7, 136-7
Purdy Hicks Gallery, 251

Queen's Gallery, 196
Queneau, Raymond, 214

Raedecker, Michael, 174
Raine, Kathleen, 148, 150
Rauschenberg, Robert, 130
Ravilious, Eric, 47, 106, 109, 136, 160, 179,
    234, 240-3
Read, Herbert, 64, 105, 128
Redfern Gallery, 63, 64, 243, 247
Redpath, Anne, 187
Rego, Paula, 12, 13, 39, 78, 162, 259, 261-2
Reynolds, Alan, 62-6, 209, 236, 249
Reyntiens, Patrick, 254-5
Richards, Albert, 106
Richards, Ceri, 81, 160
Richardson, John, 52-5, 86
Richardson, Michael, 22, 24, 88, 89
Richardson, Oya, 88, 89
Richmond, Miles, 70
Richter, Gerard, 213-15, 258
Ridley, Sir Jasper, 198
Robertson, Bryan, 36, 123, 187
Roberts, William, 209
Robinson, John N, 186
Robinson, Sheila, 242
Roebuck Collection, 105
Rose, Sarah, 70
Rosenberg, Isaac, 106
Rosenthal, T G, 261
Rosoman, Leonard, 209
Rossetti, Dante Gabriel, 230, 231
Roth, Dieter, 159
Rothenstein, Michael, 240
Rothenstein, Sir John, 108-11, 128
Rothko, Mark, 25, 36, 76, 151
Rothschild, Hannah, 97, 98
Rowlett, George, 11, 21-4, 87-9, 211
Rowntree, Kenneth, 240, 242
Royal Academy, 116, 178, 179, 185-6, 225, 278
Royal Academy Schools, 36
Royal Academy Summer Exhibition, 48,
    50, 100
Royal College of Art, 64, 96, 109, 161, 241,
    253, 263

Royal School of Needlework, 138
Royal West of England Academy, Bristol, 169
Rubens, Peter Paul, 73, 78
Ruralists, Brotherhood of, 33, 210-12
Ruskin, John, 120, 230
Russell, George, 116
Russell, James, 242-3
Ryder, Albert Pinkham, 145

St John Wilson, Colin, 81, 82
St Mary the Boltons, 78
St Mary's, Manchester, 78
St Martin's School of Art, 46, 218
Saatchi, Charles, 82, 83
Sainsbury family, 77
Sainsbury, Simon, 82
Saint Phalle, Niki de, 83
Salter, Rebecca, 235
Sandby, Paul, 197
Sandham Memorial Chapel, Burghclere,
    109, 122
Sandle, Michael, 228
Sandys, Frederick, 230
Sargent, John Singer, 180, 181, 197
Scott, William, 37, 191, 221
Seago, Edward, 197
Serpentine Gallery, 213
Shaw, George, 174, 245
Shawcross, Conrad, 270, 272-3
Shirreff, Jack, 171
Sickert, Walter Richard, 60, 82, 126, 141,
    175-8, 197, 204, 229, 253
Siddal, Lizzie, 230, 231
Sidney Cooper Gallery, Canterbury, 217
Sitwell, Sir Osbert, 198, 265
Skaer, Lucy, 235
Skeaping, John, 226
Slade School of Fine Art, 39, 49, 53, 67,
    104, 113
Smith, Edwin, 242
Smith, Matthew, 199
Smith, Tony, 92
Snowdon, Lord, 187
Solomon, Simeon, 231
Southampton Art Gallery, 210, 211
Soutine, Chaim, 35
Souza, Francis Newton, 186-7
Spalding, Frances, 160
Spencer, Gilbert, 136, 211

A is a Critic